GW01494083

CHINWAGGIN'

By the same author:

MARVIN GAYE
(1984)

MOTOWN: THE HISTORY
(1988)

MARVIN GAYE: I HEARD IT THROUGH THE GRAPEVINE
(1991)

EVERY CHART-TOPPER TELLS A STORY—SIXTIES
(1997)

EVERY CHART-TOPPER TELLS A STORY—SEVENTIES
(1998)

EVERY CHART-TOPPER TELLS A STORY—EIGHTIES
(1999)

DIANA ROSS: A LEGEND IN FOCUS
(2000)

STEVIE WONDER: RHYTHMS OF WONDER
(2003)

CHINWAGGIN'
THE CLASSIC SOUL INTERVIEWS

SHARON DAVIS

CHINWAGGIN'

First published 2006

ISBN 1-904408-08-7

© Sharon Davis, 2006

Published by BANK HOUSE BOOKS

All rights reserved. No part of this publication may be reproduced, stored in a retrieval system or transmitted, in any form or by any means, electronic, mechanical, photocopying, recording or otherwise, without the prior permission of the copyright owners.

Sharon Davis has asserted her moral right to be identified as the author of this book.

Designed and typeset in England by
BANK HOUSE BOOKS
PO Box 3
NEW ROMNEY
TN29 9WJ

CHINWAGGIN'

Chinwaggin' is dedicated to the memory of
our dearest Dusty

INTRODUCTION

I hadn't intended reprinting my *Blues & Soul* interviews but just lately there's been a lot of interest in them, mainly for research purposes for all manner of projects. So, I thought, 'why not?' and updated the cream of the crop. I have to admit it was quite an education for me searching through back copies of the magazine because each was a history lesson in music's time. Even more remarkably, I can actually remember when, where and how I secured most of the interviews. And, as if it were only yesterday, can almost see myself in the Praed Street offices, pleading with Bob Killbourn, my distinguished editor, for magazine space for some artist or other. I spearheaded several crusades during the eighties in particular—whether it be for equal rights for UK black artists, exposing fake groups, some gross error made by a record company or the rising cost of concert tickets—and poor Bob was forced to ride with them until I chanced upon another subject that needed my persuasive energy. Yes, being the only gal on the editorial team did have its compensations and, I can admit it now, I did get away with blue murder most of the time.

Believe it or not, some artists really preferred chatting to little ol' me. For instance, when interviews needed the feminine approach I was in my element, or when a girlie natter was on the cards, I was there. Hence, the ruthless editing pen was drawn for my interviews with Haywoode, Jaki Graham, Martha and Izora, in particular—because we talked for England! And interviews were conducted in all manner of places—in nightclubs where notes were scribbled on napkins and paper tissues; on coaches, where the din from travelling musicians and entourage obliterated the interviewee's voice on tape, or, in the case of one artist, walking along one of the busiest streets in London town.

However, by far the easiest and nicest interviews were held in the comfort and serenity of a hotel room or record company office—or, in the case of one interview included here, in a hotel bedroom. But, I have to say, the absolute worst were phoners: dreadful things. They were also dangerous because a dodgy transatlantic phone link could alter an interview's context just like that. Yes, BT really had a lot of answer for—and still do, I guess.

Before going any further, most of the interviews included here

CHINWAGGIN'

have been tidied up, and with others I've re-arranged quotes for continuity purposes. Also, instead of re-producing my interviews with Stevie Wonder and Marvin Gaye because they've been printed in full in my two books (*I Heard It Through The Grapevine* and *Rhythms Of W*onder), full interviews with Diana Ross, Lionel Richie, Smokey Robinson and The Temptations are included instead. Hope that's ok with you.

Do you know, I'd be lying if I said my life as a journalist was one big yawn. It was never that, but let me tell you now, it wasn't that glamorous either! There was plenty of hanging around involved; masses of disappointments when interviews were cancelled, or when they weren't even granted. Or collecting concert tickets that hadn't been left in the theatre box office. "Who's going to review the show?" you scream before heading for the nearest pub! And—my greatest hate of all—deadlines! Those wretched timetables carved in stone by editors. They always arrive too soon; there's no leeway, and I invariably missed them.

Naturally, there have been some embarrassing moments too, and one in particular immediately springs to mind. A phone link had been arranged between Valerie Simpson in Los Angeles and myself in my London flat. My very first chat with her as well, and to be honest I was chuffed to pieces. So much so that I couldn't help but boast to all who'd listen. Anyway, the allotted time arrived. No call. My heart sunk. Two hours later—nothing. Very reluctantly I admitted to those same people I had bragged to that the interview didn't happen after all. Did they gloat or what? Four hours later the bloody phone rang. An American voice asked "Is this Sharon Davis? This is Valerie Simpson calling." Totally convinced that one of my friends was now taking the piss, I retorted, not too kindly either. *"Oh yeah? And I'm Diana Ross!"* "I'm sorry I'm late in calling, but I got delayed this end. Is it ok to do the interview now...?" Once I had apologised profusely for my curt behaviour, we went on to have a blinding chat. Thankfully, I later had the chance to apologise to Valerie face to face.

Another uncomfortable moment I always mention concerned a lady I was half afraid of. She hadn't been nasty to me or anything like that, but I was a bit sceptical of her because of her image—of all things! How stupid can you get? Anyway, I waited four patient

INTRODUCTION

years to talk to Millie Jackson! Must have broken some sort of record with this. Then, lo and behold, I wasn't spared the blushes because when the phone interview was first arranged, she knew nothing about it, and was quite angry that I had dared to contact her. I felt a right f-f-fool. The second time some months later was also via the phone. My nerves jangled but I needn't have worried—the interview was s-s-sooooper! Suddenly, I wasn't half-afraid of her any more!

The other one I'd rather forget concerned Natalie Cole at The Mayfair Hotel, and my trudging across London in a downpour. She naturally looked a million dollars; I resembled a drowned something the cat had dragged in and steamed as the heat in Natalie's hotel suite dried out my clothes. How embarrassing was that?!

Actually, you may be interested to know that some artists I've pursued longer than four years. But first let me explain how the procedure works. Sometimes, publicity agents approached me or the magazine with offers of interviews, usually to promote an album, a tour and so on. Other occasions, I did the chasing, because I held a list in my subconscious of people I wanted to talk to. And, remarkable as it seems now, Diana Ross was top of that list! Sure, I'd been in her company several times—and indeed ended up working for her on specialised projects—but we'd never sat down to do an official interview. Eventually we did and it was simply amazing! On the other hand, Gladys Knight was rather reluctant to talk to me because she didn't want to answer my questions about Motown—"You don't want to know what I can tell you!"—yet I was fortunate to spend time in her and the Pips' company during their trips to the UK, thanks to DJ Graham Canter. That was a blast all of its own.

In 1979 I wrote articles on Dusty Springfield and Tina Turner. Twelve years later I interviewed Dusty in The Churchill Hotel, London! She was another in whose company I'd been, but, until 1991, not in a working capacity. That was just wonderful and I think I've still got the tape of that interview. Tina, I first spoke to in 1983—a mere four years wait—and mine was one of the first interviews to which she consented. Only drawback here: Tina was in Germany and I was in London. The dreaded phone link. After battling with three different German accents who were no help at

CHINWAGGIN'

all—Teeeeena?—I was connected to her room.

Two other ladies come to mind—Patti LaBelle and Nona Hendryx, both colourful in character and tongue, with fiery natures. Sensational people and undeniably talented. Patti (with her infectious laugh) had so many memorable experiences to relate that the interview spanned two magazines. While Nona, a little subdued at first, wove many a tale of note, so that I knew immediately a glorious interview would emerge. It's my belief that you need to experience life to be able to tell a story that other people want to read, and quite often, to do that you need age on your side.

Let's talk Gloria Jones, best known to soul pundits for her Motown work and, naturally, 'Tainted Love'. We had been friends only a short time when we chatted. I originally met her through Marc Bolan. She had moved here from America to live with him and later bore him a son, Rolan. Imagine my surprise, her delight and Marc's horror when, in 1976, she was spread across Blues & Soul's centrefold wearing nothing but a pink silk sheet!

There are many gifted people I'd love to remember here. Some very special folk, like Linda Womack, one of this world's true troupers with a positive attitude on life. Like Vesta Williams and our lunch at The Royal Garden Hotel when she wore low-cut everything as we chatted over baked potatoes. The effervescent Weather Girls who squashed me in a hotel lift: I didn't think I'd get out alive, that's for sure! The shy Jermaine Jackson for his loyalty and gentle outlook on life. Patrice Rushen and the release of her 'Watch Out' album, a nervous lady but a good interview nonetheless. Sylvester, whom I first met when he came to London to promote '(You Make Me Feel) Mighty Real'. The dearest man I've met; the guy who loved too much with a heart as huge as he was tall.

Also, I won't forget: Syreeta's honesty and kindness; we trusted each other; Martha Reeves and her treasured friendship; Kim Weston and her humour; Brenda Holloway with her openness; Barbara Randolph's obvious delight at being recognised in Britain; the smooth talking Freddie Jackson; the courageously innovative Paul Hardcastle; Ray Parker Jr; The Temptations.... Enough of this, please move on to the interviews.

INTRODUCTION

I'm now on the home run with this and the last words are coming up. All my interviews are treasured; it may sound silly now, but it's true. Many are also precious, particularly those with artists who have passed away—and God knows the number has increased alarmingly since I started researching this book. I've been so lucky to have enjoyed my profession, but even more so because I was a part of the changing musical decades—when music was fun, when money flowed for expense accounts, and when everything about the business was decadently exciting. It was one of the best times in my life, let me tell you.

So, my thanks to Dave Godin for allowing me to include his contribution here. I owe that man so much. He's a darling of a guy who encouraged me to continue writing when I felt my faith had gone. A part of me died with him in October 2004. I miss him so much. All my thanks also to my mate Graham Betts, who published the *Complete UK Hit Singles 1952-2004* which I've used to check chart positions mentioned in the interviews. To the press people who've touched my life including Debbie, Berni, Lorraine, Phil, Sian, Brian, Graham, Karen and Keith. To Motown's Silvia and Daryl, and, of course, to *Blues & Soul*'s Bob Killbourn, John Hassinger, John Abbey, Roy Daniell and Jeff Tarry.

And finally, a big 'thankyou' to Dave Randle and the Bank House gang; to Gerry Constable for dreaming up the book's title, and a huge hug to you, for sticking by me and staying with me now that I've swapped interviews for books. We've grown together; shared music together; argued and laughed together. Yeah, we certainly spread the word didn't we?

And to the artists themselves. The hellos and farewells: the tears and laughter: arguments and reconciliations. The concert where a song is dedicated; the thoughtful phone call or birthday card. The first hit record. The applause of an audience. All those special moments I was so lucky to share. I'll be honest, when the music no longer moves me, I'll hang up my keyboard. Hopefully that day is a long way off.

So, let's chinwag.

Sharon Davis
2006

THE PHENOMENON OF NORTHERN SOUL

by
DAVE GODIN

The music of black America has, since the invention of recording capability, had many differing names used to describe it, and these terms have generally passed into use over here. But, go to the States and talk about Northern Soul and they'll assume you are making a geographical reference to the studios located in Detroit or Chicago. True, many great Northern Soul records did emanate from those places, but the term does not apply to sides which were recorded in the North, but to records which found popularity in the North. And, moreover, not the North of the USA, but the North of Britain! And, just to complicate matters further, these records did actually possess musical characteristics which, though widely utilised in black American soul recordings, only became isolated into a definable genre, passion and cult over here. Northern Soul is an exclusively British term.

It all began in the mid-60s, an era of remarkable creativity which we've all been dining on ever since, and a Golden Age for soul music. (As I wrote at that time, Golden Ages are seldom noticed whilst one is living through them, and it is usually only hindsight—and growing disappointment—that enables us to recognise them once they have gone.) Not only was I writing about soul music at that time, but had also opened the UK's first Soul-music-only record store, Soul City, in London. As well as having a sizeable mail order business, Soul City became a weekend Mecca for soul fans and DJs who constituted the true (but unnoticed) underground of the UK music scene. Gradually the restrictive monopolies of the British record companies were being worn down and it was becoming increasingly easy to import records direct from the States. This was a vitally important factor since only a fraction of American recordings have ever been made available via UK labels, and this gradually increasing flow of imports, together with the soul records that UK companies did issue as a result of their success in the US charts, slowly revealed the fundamental shifts in the nature of soul that were taking place in the States.

Until then, the Motown-type sound with its big, glitzy production values and incredible dance-inducing qualities had enjoyed huge US success, and, as always happens, success bred imitation. Imitation is not copying or plagiarism, but simply an attempt to calculate and ascertain the magic formula and recipe for success. The perceptible shift was increasingly towards what was gradually becoming known as funk. Added to this, serious social changes were taking place in the States so that after a delay of nearly two hundred years, American citizens of colour were beginning to aspire towards upward mobility. In musical terms this found expression in an increasing sophistry perhaps seen at its most over the top in the penthouse daydreams and misogynist musings of Barry White's output. Certainly the last style black Americans wanted to be stuck with was the old-time, down-home, cotton-picking imagery that so sadly preoccupied too many British commentators of that era. Their innate snobbery and repressed racism often manifested itself in a paternalistic over-friendliness that silently signalled the expected code of conduct that put each participant precisely in their 'right' place, with each acting out their assigned role: exotic, slightly wild black performers, helped by their kindly, liberal, white intellectual friends. Since many of these people were in positions of control (either as music press journalists or record company employees), what black America was *actually* doing by way of its thing, and what the British media *thought* it should be doing, were actually at odds. There was also, amongst those who described themselves as 'purists' a chronic and ghastly sort of musical equivalent of political correctness, which in effect said to black America "You are the creators, but we are the arbiters. You may have the talent, but we have the power." Joe Public of course, who bankrolled the whole show with his purchases, wasn't even consulted, and he/she began to develop views of their own about it all.

So, what I began to observe both in the shop of a Saturday afternoon, and from the hundreds of letters I used to get from readers, was that a gradual gulf was developing between the North and the South as to the type of soul that was turning people on. It was then that I coined the term Northern Soul simply to identify the genre the North was favouring. (I also coined the term Deep Soul at the same time, but that's another story.) What then defined a Northern Soul record? What distinguished it from the bulk of soul that was then going down big in the States and in London and Home Counties' discotheque? To understand this in part, we have to look at the history of popular music culture in Britain. Firstly, although it may come as a jolt now to realise and be reminded of it, black American music is an entirely alien musical genre for Europe. It is foreign, and it had to be imported into our consciousness. It is not (despite all the media hype surrounding UK plagiarists who spoke British and sang American) indigenous to our culture, so as a result, it has to be learnt, acquired and absorbed (the same way we learn French or Esperanto). We are not born 'speaking' it. Luckily for us in Britain, a shared common language made it much easier, but let us not forget that when rock'n'roll first seeped into general consciousness, (and nearly all of that was originally black American), it was regarded by many as a cacophony simply because it went counter to all accepted British notions of melody, and, (most importantly), it went against the grain of accepted rhythmic tradition. European music was, prior to this, based on rhythmic patterns which accentuated the beat on which the dancing foot touched the ground (typically seen in clog-dancing, Morris dancing or, even, Knees-up-Mother-Brown), but black American music had invented the back-beat. The bit that was normally silent in European music now exploded with percussive noise. This unsettling and unusual effect delighted some and offended others. Each era has its own spirit, invisible, unspoken values and assumptions which permeate the collective consciousness, which is why some outré fashions are chic and 'in' one year, and the subject of comic mirth some years later. Although cultural artefacts remain as they were originally created, the context of their creation changes through time as people move on. In 1992 it would be utterly impossible to sense and feel the startling impact that a record like 'Bo Diddley' made when it was first issued, and only those who actually bought it in 1955 will know exactly what I am talking about. The power to shock or startle diminishes through time as we become accustomed to newer sensations, but when we discover something we really,

NORTHERN SOUL

really like, we tend to want to stick to it and not let it change. It's the beginning of conservatism! Because therefore, black American music had been such an entirely new, restless musical innovation, many great soul records took quite a while before they registered here. The public was not yet ready for them. This meant that some DJs with aesthetic convictions and a feeling for the creative (and educative) aspect of their profession, persisted with certain sides until their soulful magic reached and moved their patrons as much as it had already done themselves. Record reviews were unreliable since they were always referring back to the past rather than celebrating the new, the different and the innovative, and those like myself who did welcome the new were often regarded as perverse, heretical and 'not one of us'. (The fact that I was also a notorious vegetarian only compounded their certainties about me!). I recall how when Britain had a short-lived R&B Hall of Fame, my nomination for the late Sam Cooke to be enshrined on their Roll of Honour was almost unanimously rejected!

Because, therefore, of this slowish UK acceptance rate for contemporary soul, many of the records which were huge hits on the Northern disco circuit were already by then a couple of years old. (Lest the South felt smug about this, I pointed out that they'd hardly played them at all when they were new and had not received an instant response from the floor!). Long since deleted from record company catalogues, they were invariably up-tempo, urban, sharp and sophisticated soul sides, many of which also told a story! They were also embellished with a very pronounced rhythm, heavenly (or swooning) choral backing, lots of sparkle, and that sheerly optimistic uplifting quality that so exemplified the music of black America when black Americans were at last beginning to feel they did perhaps have something to feel optimistic about! Most Southern DJs (with a few heroic exceptions) didn't see their role in any way the same sort of light as their Northern counterparts. Their creativity tended to be directed towards their own egos and personal popularity. To augment this trip, all one had to do in order to demonstrate how painfully hip one was, was to simply spin the sides that were making it big in the States. That way all the hard work had already been done for them by other people. It was the beginning

CHINWAGGIN'

of the 'disco phenomenon' which was eventually to take such a grievous toll on black America's creativity. Also, other factors played a part, often as trivial and infantile as those which cause some football fanatics to inflict grievous bodily harm on other football fans, or certain political rallies to infer that God is an Englishman! This parochial, territorial nonsense when nearly all the media power bases were located in London, made it all too easy for some to imply that Northern DJs and fans were rustic yokels, hung up on the sounds of yesteryear, and in any case, we all knew didn't we, that London Rools? Well, that was not OK and with admirable individualism the North stuck to the type of soul it liked best. When derision and scorn failed to bring these wayward soulies to heel, the media decided it might just risk checking it out and see first-hand what it was all about. The North always extended a warm welcome to them, but, determined to find something to reinforce their prejudgement, they only saw the admittedly widespread use of recreational drugs.

The next major development grew from my decision to re-issue Gene Chandler's *Nothing Can Stop Me* on our Soul City label, previously out on Stateside. I'd decided to put it out because it was constantly being asked for in our shop, and, as a result of getting so many in-the-past spins on the Northern circuit, it made (to everybody's surprise, not least my own) the UK Top 50! Now major record companies began to send scouts to the North to see what they had in their back catalogues which might merit being issued. Sides which had been changing hands between Northern DJs for £50 a copy (£500 in today's money), were rushed into release and, in order to retain some degree of exclusivity and play-life for their 'specials', Northern DJs began to cover up labels and present them with made-up titles by fictitious artists. In one way this was regrettable since it denied fans the information they needed to get copies, but who could blame the DJs protecting themselves from the brain-picking of some record company johnnie who'd swanned up from London for the night? Soon the market was swamped with re-releases and first-time issues of oldies that had not been deemed worth releasing when they were new. As soon as this happened, Northern DJs would promptly drop them from their playlists and find replacements. For not only did it seem like there were thousands of as-yet-

NORTHERN SOUL

unheard US recordings made in the Northern groove style, but more like millions! The better-off Northern DJs took trips to the States to trawl through the oldies and cut-out bins and bring back anything that was even vaguely Northern. By this time a clear, distinct Northern Soul style had emerged, but, like all musical styles, it was not easily analysed in words. It could be more easily recognised when it was felt rather than thought about. But if Northern Soul sides shared one certain common denominator it was that they were always vibrant.

The names of the clubs where Northern Soul ruled took on their own legendary status, as did the names and reputations of certain stalwart and ace DJs who were determined that what they and their friends out on the floor had collectively said "yes" to would remain distinct, and, above all, autonomous. Looking back now it was inevitable that the Northern scene would gradually change, but when the history of soul music in the UK is written, its contribution to forwarding and advancing the cause of soul over here must never be underestimated. It was immense, and its constancy protected soul from the whims of fans and fashion. I might have coined the term and in my advantaged position as a journalist given it every encouragement, but it took thousands of loyal and ardent soul fans to keep (and spread) the faith, and in doing this, they gave black America their highest compliment and collective thanks.

Without that stubborn, unyielding personal autonomy and the egalitarian treasuring of each and every individual's right to exercise their own tastes, (which so riled the London Establishment by thus ensuring they were beyond their control and manipulative powers), the soul music scene in Britain today might well have been something very different to what it is. For Northern Soul was also about freedom....

DAVE GODIN

CHINWAGGIN'

The above is an exclusive article in print for the first time. My thanks to my mentor and treasured friend, who currently is not in the best of health, for adding his indelible mark on this book. A fitting contribution because it was Dave who recommended me to *Blues & Soul* in the first place and who, in his inimitable style, guided me through the first hesitant steps of my journey into soul music, and trained me to listen, not only to the lead vocals, but to what was happening behind the grooves. Dave also introduced me to Marvin Gaye—need I say more?

ASHFORD & SIMPSON

Dateline: June 1982

Once in a while an interview can be a godsend, a life-long ambition or a total pleasure. All three summed up my feelings when I sat down with Valerie Simpson and Nickolas Ashford before they debuted on the Dominion stage in London during 1982. The couple had signed a recording deal with Capitol Records in 1981 and the 'Street Corner' single was on release, lifted from their first studio album in two years titled 'Street Opera'—an ambitious piece of music comprising a conceptual suite of songs that spanned one album side.

The interview kicked in with 1963 when Nickolas was twenty-one, Valerie, seventeen, and the venue New York City where she was born and raised. "I was born in Michigan," Nickolas explained, "and I came to New York City because they said it was the place to make it. Where I came from it was very, very slow and small. So I just got on a bus and went there. I was kinda destitute and was invited up to this Baptist Church. I went mainly

CHINWAGGIN'

to get a good meal. And that's where I saw Valerie. She was singing with three girls, not in a choir exactly. I thought she looked kinda cute too. After the service she came over to me, but I don't think she knew of my situation." (Valerie: "He looked alright to me!")

"We got to know each other socially and talked about writing. I'd been writing gospel songs all my life: just something I loved to do. I couldn't wait to get old enough to sing in the senior choir. When I met Valerie she was singing in this group and they were invited to perform in this nightclub as a gospel unit. They didn't have enough material so they contacted me and asked if I would write them some."

Valerie continued: "There was never any problem between us musically, but I was attracted to him. However, he kinda let me know that it wasn't happening. I wasn't happening for him. So I thought well, if that's the way you feel, OK!" Nickolas had good reason for saying this as he explained: "I thought she was too young at the time. She wasn't even out of high school and I was out in the world—struggling!" It actually took them eleven years to start a relationship. (They married in 1974.) Instead, they ploughed their feelings into writing and producing songs, secured a contract with Glover Records, and according to Valerie: "Right in the very beginning we recorded two songs, but nothing ever happened ('I'll Find You' in 1964). It let us know it wasn't for us then. We even tried to do a few appearances to back up those records. It was so rough that we decided we'd be better off as writers, which we did. Glover was a little subsidiary of a bigger company which is no longer in existence."

From Glover Records, the two switched to Scepter where they wrote for artists like The Shirelles. And it was at this time that Ray Charles recorded their composition 'Let's Get Stoned' which was a big selling item. Did Nickolas record this?

"Did I?" he asked Valerie. She nods.

"That's right, after Ray Charles did, as a B-side. It's so nebulous in my mind that I actually did a recording of it myself."

It became apparent at this juncture that the duo were unaware of the number of songs they'd actually composed unless a royalty statement dropped on their doorstep. But, as Valerie admitted, the intervention of Ray Charles saw the turning point in their

ASHFORD & SIMPSON

composing career. "We do think 'Let's Get Stoned' got our names off the ground as writers. And Ray is still doing concerts, still singing good, and shows up on American television all the time. He did a lot of commercials for Maxwell House. Everyone does commercials. It's becoming the thing, because everybody's going broke. We did one although we won't do a lot. It's something that's an identification factor...you have to be careful that you don't do too many so that you're known not for what you do, but are known for the commercial."

After Scepter Records came Motown, where they were contracted as a composers and producers. Valerie: "It was a dream come true. I mean, we were just writers, and Motown was Motown. It was the best thing that could have happened to us, it really was." Nickolas: "To us Motown was it. And when they called us, we didn't hesitate. With a whole slew of artists our songs would get the chance to be recorded."

The hits were many—'Ain't No Mountain High Enough', 'You're All I Need To Get By', 'Ain't Nothing Like The Real Thing'—all for Marvin Gaye and Tammi Terrell initially. They then recorded with Diana Ross, Gladys Knight & the Pips and others, before Valerie became a soloist. A star-studded career indeed which prompted me to relate a call I had placed with Motown to obtain information on the company's writers—Ashford & Simpson in particular—only to be advised it wasn't company policy to promote the backstage staff. By way of explanation Nickolas said: "That's just how Motown were. I thought it was really strange because they wanted to keep you in the dark. Everything was Motown. That was all that was supposed to be there. At least we got our names on records; they couldn't stop that, but you never knew who was playing or anything. I think Motown were afraid, because of those contracts, that outsiders would get to you, talk to you, and perhaps wisen you up."

The contracts were, in fact, known as their 'slave contracts', which enabled them to do nothing unless it was stipulated in print. However, Valerie quickly pointed out that they learned so much during their Motown stay and, in hindsight, regretted nothing of the association except the way in which company staffers were kept under wraps, but once freed she felt

23

CHINWAGGIN'

sympathetic to the company's rulings because: "If you've ever had your words taken and changed around, which journalists are apt to do, then it concerns me a great deal. It bothers me because there were a lot of awful things about Motown but there were a lot of wonderful things too. I don't mind if both sides get told, but if the person just wants to paint a bad picture then they can just take that portion of what you say and use it. I can well see how some people are reluctant to talk because you don't know what's going to be said or indeed written."

Returning to safer ground, I wondered if they had thought of saving and later recording the Marvin Gaye and Tammi Terrell compositions themselves, thereby making them Motown stars. "I don't think at the time we could have been," replied Nickolas. "Nor did we have the opportunity. I don't even think we thought of it because we were so thrilled at the fact that some songs we had written were finally out there. We just didn't think of it. I mean, when you have an artist like Marvin Gaye, who's just a phenomenal singer, it's just a dream. We were real writers then and we had this voice that could do something. That was it, that was all the glory we needed."

"I never even asked that question either because I don't feel that we could have used me in that way," said Valerie, when I asked if she felt peeved when Diana Ross enjoyed exceptional solo success with their compositions. "Besides, I couldn't have sung 'Reach Out And Touch'. The public had built an image, this certain commercial voice that pleased them. She had the sound, she's distinctly Diana and we perceived the type of material we would give her which would be more 'pop' than that we would, say, give to Gladys Knight, because we knew her audience was going to be wider and you'd sell more records.... One thing I must say about Diana is that everybody has feelings about her and they're usually strong, very strong, one way or the other. They either love her, or they hate her, it's not like she's ok. I find that very strange."

During the end of their stay with Motown, Valerie became an artist in her own right via the albums 'Exposed', 'Valerie Simpson' and 'Keep It Comin''. From these sublime albums a handful of singles were lifted, but sadly success eluded her. "We actually had extra material at the time that we didn't need for someone else, so we thought we might as well do it on me. Motown didn't quibble about it, but they didn't do much either! So we returned to writing. It's a longer lasting career. Long after we've done our last number on the stage we can still write because we have that established. When you get old and grey you can't continue performing but as long as your mind says intact you're ok."

Valerie smiled when I asked if they received their just financial rewards from Motown or were they, like others, paid a salary. "We got our royalties, but we perhaps didn't get what we should have got. We ran into trouble with things that were not in our best interests. When they had the leverage, which they had because of the contracts we signed, they took advantage sometimes. But I think we got the best end of the stick when I look back at it, even though they tried to suppress who we were. We were considering this thing about being artists and realised that Motown maybe didn't see us as artists. My albums hadn't done very much so they really weren't excited about the idea of doing anything on us. So it seemed the right thing to do. The contracts were up, so we left." The departure was amicable: indeed, Ashford & Simpson returned to work once more with Diana Ross on the 'The Boss' project in 1979.

Signing as artists to WEA Records, Ashford & Simpson found freedom. Nickolas took up the story: "Just to be able to write and produce artists outside of the label, it just opened up a new field for us, like being re-born. Mind you, I like to go home and think 'Oh yeah, I was with Motown.' That's a good feeling. I'll always bring it up if someone doesn't know about it. But the way we are now is the best feeling for us because we do have the energy to pick and choose. We've now got a little thing going with performing and it feels right. I like getting out there after being behind the scenes for so long."

Their American success with WEA far outweighed the success experienced in Britain. "Yes we were conscious of that," said Valerie. "We were prompted many times to come here and work. I don't know what it was that stopped us except that maybe we wanted too much to happen on its own. The idea of coming over here and starting all over again was just a pain in the neck. You feel like you've paid those dues and done those things, gone

CHINWAGGIN'

through all those interviews in the States, and now we've gotta do the same again! It didn't bother me too much that we weren't that well known, except that everybody said it was a whole new market in Britain that we hadn't even touched. So, beginning with our new company, Capitol, we had no choice. We had to come over because it's an area we can't ignore. We wanted to give it a try: if it doesn't work we can say we tried. I don't know what the British like—perhaps they didn't like any of the things we did when we were at Warners. Maybe they released the wrong thing. I don't think it's the public's fault because you need that machinery behind you. If they act like they care about you the people will take more notice, but I don't think WEA put that much emphasis on us. I can't completely blame them because we didn't really want to come."

"Yes, but they didn't say 'we want you to help us in England. We want you to go over and promote your product'," interrupted Nickolas. "If I'd have felt they were trying to make us worldwide, I would have felt some kind of energy between us but there was nothing to make you feel that way. Capitol has made us feel that they're interested in making us worldwide. You know when someone's doing something for you. There's no mistake. You can feel it, you can see it."

Even though their career is the most important part of their lives right now, they plan to continue writing for third parties. Nickolas emphasised that the demand for their work is more than they can handle and that unfortunately some acts would be disappointed. "Maybe we can fit in one or two a year, but with our working schedules too it takes so many months of writing out of any year. We have hundreds of songs in the can but we always like to write afresh."

"We start songs" Valerie added, "We don't write a song all the way. We start hundreds of beginnings!"

Working and living together, I suggested, surely poses good grounds for divorce. They shake their heads. Having a large house, they can be isolated—Nickolas pens the lyrics; Valerie creates the melodies—then they collaborate until the product is completed. However, this arrangement can lead to blinding arguments as Nickolas remembered. "I was in California. In fact, we were writing for Gladys Knight at the time. It was early in the

ASHFORD & SIMPSON

morning and Valerie hadn't got cranked up I guess, and I didn't think she was playing too well. So I told her. Then she said, 'Well, every word that falls out of your mouth isn't golden, y'know.' That blew me away!"

In 1983 I phoned them while they were midway through their three-month American tour, which, Valerie laughed "does seem to take in most of the country. We finish just before Christmas but it's all going just great. We're playing at large and small venues, sometimes before three to four thousand people. We're headlining, although with acts like Maze, we share equal billing."

The duo mostly perform at weekends, leaving them more or less free during the week, but as Valerie pointed out free time is scarce, and what time they do get to themselves is usually crammed into a couple of days. The American trek was to promote their 'High Rise' project but, she explained: "The album has only just been released, so the tour is a little early. Sometimes it's better for an album to be on sale a month before a tour but it just didn't work out this time. The singles usually fall into place as well. We'd love to tour England again, but it's doubtful that a visit will be fitted in this year. The American one doesn't end for a couple of months and we don't really like to be away from home at Christmas. There also has to be a demand for us in England because we can't keep coming over for promotional visits. There has to be a legitimate reason for coming. We have to wait for a certain kind of response for something to happen. We'll keep on trying to break it there but it's proving hard to crack, as you know. It proved hard enough to get recognition in the States, and we're still trying to stay on top; it's very hard work but it's comfortable. It's nice to know that in England our name is kept alive from the old recordings being re-issued and promoted." Nevertheless, like so many acts, the couple pine to be known for their own product and to this end have cut two promotional videos—one for the current single 'High Rise'; the other for the second album track 'Side Effect'.

At this juncture, I'm compelled to admit, the 'High Rise' album is a musical gem: an absolute delight with its 'socially aware' tracks dealing with daily aspects of life. "We took a great deal of time with the material for this release," said Nickolas, when I told him my feelings. "We wanted to say something someone would

CHINWAGGIN'

be interested in. We took more time also in the actual writing of the songs. There are more observations this time. We try to help people by creating music they can relate to, like, trying to give a feeling. We can only show we care and understand through our music."

As with the previous 'Street Opera' project, Nickolas again returned to the streets to gather information, soaking up vibes from everyday people from all walks of life. "Some of the songs say more than others," elaborated Valerie. "Some inspiration is consciously street level, and hopefully there is a combination of a lot of things in the album for people to listen to. Things happen in life, relatable things, and I feel the album is dimensional. It's much deeper, yet much younger, with the feeling of today. It's not upbeat and not in a certain groove. It has a more pop feel, although what message there is, is there. A lot of people like different cuts because those tracks obviously mean different things to them. And that's what we wanted to achieve."

Valerie's particular favourites include 'Experience (Love Had No Face)'. Her partner agreed, adding 'My Kinda Pick Me Up' as close second. For myself I favoured 'I'm Not That Tough', but conceded to loving every track. It's true Ashford & Simpson; the melody lines on the lower-keyed tracks are fashioned with sensitivity and a certain delicacy. The couple work so well together but, of all the areas they're involved in, writing was their preferred occupation as Nickolas laughed: "Well, it's probably the easiest. If I had to choose, it would be that, although we enjoy doing it all. The actual production of the songs this time round was easy because we really prepared ourselves.... We haven't at this point in our career, installed a home studio, rather, have allocated a room for musical workouts. Having a studio is an added expense. We try and keep our operation running as smoothly as possible and besides we're only in them at certain times of the year, so it's more appropriate to use outside studios for that couple of months or so."

Finally, a personal update, Valerie's brother has joined them for the tour. Ray Simpson was, of course, a member of the Village People. Most of their onstage musicians appear on 'High Rise', likewise the backing vocalists. Their eight-year-old daughter also travels with them, although, Valerie said, it's too early to tell

ASHFORD & SIMPSON

whether she'll follow in their musical footsteps....

Two years later I met a tired Ms Simpson at The Gloucester Hotel, London, after braving the city's lunchtime rush hour. We sat in her sixth floor suite, while Nickolas remained in bed. The couple planned to return to the States the next day, following their three sell out concerts at Hammersmith Odeon.

Obviously, the first topic of conversation was 'Solid' which passed gold status by shooting to no 3 in the British singles chart, with its mother album riding high on the back of this success. "I really didn't think the single was going to do what it did," the lady gushed in delight. "Nickolas and I were really surprised I can tell you, bearing in mind it didn't take that long to write, when compared to our other songs. It happened we were working on a group of songs at the time, and we hadn't had an album out for over a year because we decided this time we'd take our time. The main thing we found with 'Solid' was that it gave us access to another public and enabled us to show ourselves in different colours."

The trio of sold-out shows was, she admitted, largely due to the single's success. "There's a whole new breed of people who bought the single, and they think we're an overnight sensation. Hah! An eleven-year overnight sensation! The new crowd we've attracted is obviously enjoyable, but it's our older fans who know us so well, and that's something we'll never overlook."

With the duo's newly found audience and a whole different slew of journalists queuing for interviews, Valerie developed her own unique way of handling this time consuming situation. "When I'm talking to someone who isn't aware of our background, to save saying we did this and that, I give the journalist a biography, thereby cutting at least three quarters of an hour off the interview! They don't seem to mind either. We've done interviews for so long now, and we've told our life story so many times that I've got bored with it. And now I'm sure reporters have got just as bored with us...in fact, I'm running out of things to say—period."

Did I detect then, interviews might be a thing of the past? "Obviously we'll have to cut down, but I appreciate the new market, the pop arena, wants to talk to us now that we've crossed over. But I'll tell you something, we'll never forget or ignore our

CHINWAGGIN'

grass roots. It pisses me off when the black papers that've supported us over the years tend to be overlooked by our various company press representatives. Nickolas and I are a little wiser and older than most artists and consequently we're real careful with our interviews. It's a lot harder for us to forget our friends." Then she stressed, "Sure, we've crossed over for the moment, and it's really like starting out all over again...we fought our way through, but we'd never sell our black base. We've seen a lot of new people and have got access to things we never had before... but how long will it last? I dunno. The pop market is rather fickle, whereas the black market has always been faithful. When it appears the black press is being ignored, it's usually not the artist's fault. It's to do with managers, record companies, and so on.

"As much as I understand and appreciate that national press reaches a much wider audience, and is a necessary part in promotion, there's always time to include black press, as I see it. And I hope that's the way it will be with us. If it doesn't work out that way, then it's simply because we're not aware of the situation. It's usually up to our press people in the record companies to draw up interview itineraries, and we have to be guided by their local expertise."

Ashford & Simpson's stage shows are designed to their own modifications, from stage sets to lights and repertoire. The band has more or less retained the same membership since its birth, and the road crew are now part of their family which, Valerie stressed, makes the arduous task of touring that much easier.

During their Hammersmith triumph, it was noted they didn't mention their song titles, a minor point that, until now, she hadn't given thought to. "The show we did here is what we did in New York and introducing our songs was an adjustment we didn't make. We assumed, I suppose, that we were known more over here. It's a very good point though, and one I should have thought about. Also, there's another thing we noticed. The applause came in different places over here. It's nice but takes a little getting used to. When we were thinking about what show to put on in London we decided to keep the American one because it's pretty varied. The songs go up and come down and we tried to link things together to keep the audiences in the mood."

The opening night was also minus an encore because they

ASHFORD & SIMPSON

hadn't rehearsed another song. "To be honest with you, we didn't expect to be asked to do one. We got off that stage and could hear the audience wanted more. I said to Nickolas in sheer panic, 'What can we sing, we've done it all?' So as much as we wanted to, we couldn't go back out there. We couldn't do a song we'd performed already because people would think, 'Oh, they've written all these songs and they're repeating themselves.' We usually do 'The Boss' as our American encore but I'd used that as part of the show, so that was out. So, the next morning I got everyone in rehearsal to get another song together, and I just juggled the next two shows around a bit. 'Solid' had to be saved 'til the end because it's the capper for us, and obviously a great up tempo song to leave the stage with."

Predictably, this international success brought with it extra pressure for personal appearances. A sighing Valerie agreed. "It's true. We're very much more in demand now than we were in, say, '82. We weren't even able to come to London when 'Solid' was a hit because of other commitments. Time-wise, touring takes a large chunk out of our lives. It's not an easy thing either going on the road because we have to bring a big band. It's also true to say we're wanted all over Europe—we won the Edison Award in Holland, for example—but so far London is the only place we've managed to get to. It would be different if we were just artists because we'd have nothing else to worry about. But being writers and producers as well, we're finding this side of our career taking second place for a while because it's not humanly possible to do it all...unfortunately."

With their composing commitments behind schedule, the couple was attempting to snatch moments while travelling. In fact, three tunes had miraculously emerged from this somewhat undesirable situation and had been submitted to Island Music who handled their publishing. "It's difficult to write while touring. In fact, I don't find it easy to do anything while we're on the road," she confessed. "We tried to write when we were in the Bahamas for some concerts...we even took along our instruments, but it was hopeless. So we haven't bothered any more. It's hard for me as an artist to do a show because primarily it takes a lot of time and energy to make what happens on stage look easy. It's also very tiring. We just come back to the hotel to unwind: I haven't even

CHINWAGGIN'

had the chance to get to a restaurant this time round."

Being part of the music business for so long now, I wondered whether, in retrospect, she'd change anything. Yes, she said, and surprised me with her reply. "I'd probably change the selling aspect. By that I mean the things that go into making us better known to the public. To a certain extent the music speaks for itself, but we're still having to push so hard. Sure, videos help to a certain extent, and do cover for us when we can't get to a country in person, but it's not the same. Balance is what's important now, getting the right balance in our lives. By still promoting ourselves we use up a lot of time, and really that is something that should be done without our involvement."

Apart from their distinctive musical styling in voice and melody, Ashford & Simpson have their own trademark clothes-wise: 'colourful street credible' was one description. They have Kevin Ernard to thank; he not only designs their stage gear but also Nickolas' regular clothes. "Kevin was just starting out when we found him. Now he's just as famous. Originally, Nickolas bought one shirt from him in his store, and it started from there. We might have had something to do with the fame he's got now because Kevin can really make everything, so we don't have to worry about that side of the business now."

In the last interview we spoke about their living and working arrangements, and a smiling Valerie harped upon this once more. "It's natural that we get fed up with each other. But we've got, like, an eighth sense about each other now, and know when each other needs air, more space. We're fortunate that we've got houses in New York and Connecticut, and Nickolas uses the New York place to get away by himself. I think it's something about what we do for a living that makes us this sensitive to each other's needs. Nickolas also gets into the streets, and hangs out to get ideas for songs, and then we work on them together. Sometimes, I'll have a go at him for getting under my feet, but by and large we don't live out of each other's pockets."

Back to the music, and it was noticed that the USA for Africa project which spawned the 'We Are The World' single, a no 1 single across the world including Britain in April 1985, did not include Ashford & Simpson. The reason was only a certain number of artists could be involved and there wasn't room for them! Believe that if you will! I found this particularly ironic because the couple are involved with several charities geared to prevent world starvation. However, Valerie didn't appear that perturbed. "I've never talked publicly about what we've done for charities because I feel it's like asking for a pat on the back, and we're not into that at all. Yes, we have given a lot of money to the hungry...we do charity shows, but always quietly. These things are close to our hearts. Of course, America has its own hunger problems, and this is something else that has to be taken care of. Drug abuse is another, although I think lack of education is the reason we're in the situation we are today. Parents don't seem to want to know, or understand; they don't appear to talk to their children. They tend to veer away from such things, even sex education. Now that's a bit old fashioned. They tend to rely on their children's schoolteachers to tell them about it. It's a matter that can't be changed overnight, more's the pity."

Before bringing the chat to an end, we talked Marvin Gaye. She was quiet, reflecting, perhaps thinking of the success Marvin and Tammi had enjoyed with those timeless slices of pure soulful magic. "We talked about Marvin on our way back in the car last night," she quietly said. "You know we do our medley, well, Nickolas had to catch himself on stage last night...he got so full up that he felt he was going to lose himself. He felt Marvin's presence there on stage next to him, and the emotion was so overwhelming that Nickolas practically had to stop. We've always included a medley in our act and Marvin has always had a part of us through his music. I always felt his career was exceptional early on and he became even more brilliant when he went into 'What's Going On'. His music will be even bigger in his demise but I would rather have the man. He and Tammi were such a strong magnum, and now they've both gone. It takes a lot of thinking about, doesn't it? And, quite honestly, the fact that both of them have gone is something I still can't believe...it just doesn't seem fair...and you know, there isn't even anything in the can that we did with them. It's all been released. I do miss them."

CHINWAGGIN'

On the recording front, Ashford & Simpson failed to repeat the success of 'Solid'. However, during the Nineties two albums of note were issued—'Capitol Gold' (Capitol) and 'Been Found' (Ichiban)—the latter a collaboration with Maya Angelou. They performed for President Clinton at the 52nd Presidential Inauguration, sang at The White House for the CISAC 39th World Congress, and were awarded The Founder's Award, ASCAP's highest honour. They remain in demand as writers and performers; and, personally speaking, I can't thank them enough for the joy they've given me as both.

CINDY BIRDSONG
Dateline: November 1987

I like Cindy Birdsong. She's sincere and friendly, and possesses a warm personality and, until recently, has been the Supreme few people knew. She tended to stay in the background while Diana Ross enjoyed the limelight, and later still, with Mary Wilson.

Ms Birdsong was in London for a short spell to promote her new single 'Dancing Room'—a bouncy, mid-tempo track—where she, for the first time in years, uses her voice to its fullest.

CHINWAGGIN'

Helping out on backing vocals is none other than our own Madeline Bell, a splendid combination.

Cindy was sitting in the smallest of rooms when we chatted one lunchtime. She was dressed casually and her hair was, well, kinda windswept. A half-eaten breakfast was nearby. She looked good, although she offered that she intended to lose weight before embarking upon a string of arranged personal appearances. "I don't really want to lose any more," she said "but my manager thinks it'll be a good thing."

Oh, the problems of being in the public eye, I sympathised, as we both like our food. We hugged and kissed, caught up on some gossip since last we spoke, then talked seriously because the single was foremost on her mind.

"With this release people will know I've not just started out, and because of my experience, I was able to offer suggestions to my producer and I felt I could offer valid improvements. It gives me the kind of freedom in the studio that I never had before."

'Dancing Room' was in fact recorded in Britain on the instruction of her record company, and is actually a track she was due to release on another label. "Oh, that last deal," she moaned. "There were a lot of complications there, and we wanted out. But we were fortunate to get the song back."

Returning to the studio was, she said, an experience all on its own. "It's all more hi-tech and computerised now. And the studio itself was huge. I felt I lost the personal side in such a big place because I felt like a speck of sand in the desert. It was strange being by myself too, it's not the same as singing in a small booth with the others. I was a mile from the control room and couldn't even see the people in there, which really gave me a feeling of being by myself. But I overcame the vastness of it all eventually."

Signing to the smaller label, High Hat, was a deliberate move on her part, she says. "There are a lot of new artists about, and I had a feeling if I went on a label with a lot of acts I'd be overlooked. If I was on a bigger label I felt I wouldn't receive the special treatment I need. It's a big adjustment to make after ten years out of the business. So I thought a small company could give me that kind of treatment and handling."

The ex-Supreme's lengthy hiatus from the recording world wasn't self-imposed as she conceded. "When I was working

CINDY BIRDSONG

around Motown after I left the Supremes, I always wanted to sing again. I used to think about it constantly. It was like a physical thing, like a pressure building up in my chest. I would never have forgiven myself if I didn't do it now. The new music of today was a great incentive because clearly the opportunity is there to really experiment. But, really, so much of today's music is similar to the Supremes' era, and the whole nostalgia of the sixties and seventies has been brought back and the young acts adapt it to suit their styles. They take it to their hearts as their own music, thereby opening the doors for the older acts because we can still do it, and the new generation know we can and accept us."

Cindy's life with the Supremes is one she treasures. A happy, obviously successful time and one she will never regret. Her memories are coated with love...and hard work. "The real essence we had was the closeness when we worked together. We were one unit in three parts. When we toured together, it was us against the rest of the world. It was a definite feeling, very strong, almost as strong as a passion. It was a bond of unity when we got onstage, and occasionally when the passion was that strong we would cry. It was like an electrical charge shooting through us all."

It went without saying of course, that Diana Ross was the star on stage, something Cindy happily accepted and admired. "She had the ability to put whatever annoyed or upset her offstage, behind her. When she was on stage, one of her relatives could be locked up, and she still wouldn't worry about it until the show had finished. That sounds awful and is a bad example, but it gives you an idea of how professional she is. She's a person who will give one hundred per cent and never makes excuses for not appearing no matter how she's feeling. When we went onstage and those lights went up, there was nothing negative about our show."

While admitting they enjoyed a working relationship, she remembered the arguments. "There were times when there were clashes of personality which is bound to happen with three women, although earlier in the group there weren't so many fights. With the name change to Diana Ross and the Supremes, our way of recording changed, and we knew we would separate, and that's when the confusion and bad feelings came in."

Cindy replaced the much-loved Florence Ballard in the group

CHINWAGGIN'

during 1967, a move that provoked great tension, anger and disappointment, to the point of disbelief that Florence had been sacked from the group she had founded. "Mary didn't feel good about Florence leaving because they were so close," Cindy divulged. "Then there were a lot of different working arrangements, like, separate dressing rooms, and we were the backing group to Diana in a sense. Mary felt it more than I because I was new to the group."

Florence's dismissal severely marred Cindy's delight at being the newest Supreme because they had been close friends since Patti LaBelle's Bluebelle days when the two groups toured together and "Florence was very open and warm. We had this thing that people always said we looked alike. At one point I actually went to a theatre where they were playing to see for myself. And, yes, we did look the same." When Cindy received the call requesting her presence in Detroit she had no idea that she was being asked to replace her friend. "All I was told was they wanted me there. I was met at the airport by Motown executives and driven to Berry Gordy's house where the group was having a meeting with him. I had no idea what was going on in the other room. I was still a member of Patti's group and didn't even tell her I was going to Detroit because I planned to return. So, the door of the room swung open and Florence came out in tears. Her mother came out with her. Oh, she was so upset, so shaken, she didn't even see me. It was then I realised I was to replace her. I felt so bad, but later on Florence understood why I did it."

Cindy's version of events is the same told by Mary Wilson in her autobiography published in 1987 which, Cindy feels relayed the facts, although "my viewpoint is different in a lot of areas, but it's only natural it would be. We have had the same experiences but our perception is different. Mary perceived things as she saw them. If I were to write about the same situations I would not write them that way. Probably Diana would come along with a whole different perception. The only way to get the real story is for each of us to write books as we saw our life, and then put all three sides together. Mind you, even with three books out there, you'd still probably not get the whole truth!" She also felt that Mary's book didn't harm the somewhat sacred memory of the trio because "people are going to think what they want to think. Mary

CINDY BIRDSONG

has been quite controversial which, I believe, caused some people to think harshly about Diana. And, sure, Mary got criticised for that. I don't feel she's done any real damage to the reputation of the group because it can stand on its own. The career of the Supremes is strong enough to hold its own."

When Diana Ross was questioned about Mary's damning book, her reply was Mary was entitled to write what she wants, that she obviously needed the money, and although much of what was written had hurt her deeply, she would not enter the public debate. Cindy respected her view. "I'm not saying I saw Diana as Mary did. Regardless of what Mary said, I no longer see Diana as that same person of the sixties. She is totally different now, like night and day. We've all seasoned through experiences, success, failures, marriages, and so on. And I don't feel it was Mary's intention to cause controversy."

Mind you, Ms Birdsong's career to date hasn't be trouble free. She married David Hewlett while a Supreme, but it ended in divorce, breaking her heart. "It broke down because of my career which put a lot of stress on my marriage. When you have to leave your mate for ten months of the year, with a day off here and there, well, it was asking for trouble. It was hard to keep a good relationship going. I had my son David then, and had to leave him at home as well. So his father and our housekeeper raised my son. My husband had a full-time business as well and when I asked them to come on the road with me, he couldn't because of his business commitments. So, our relationship began to decline. You can't leave a handsome man behind to fend for himself. Eventually, we got divorced when my son was two years old and his father lives five minutes away from me. He's lived with him for the last year because he knows I have a career. My husband remarried and people found it funny because he married a girl called Diana and she looked like Diana Ross too. I'd love to marry again, but have no man on the scene at the moment. I just hope there's one waiting in the wings for me. I'd rather like to have another child, like Diana."

Following this single, she plans to record an album to show her varying vocal styles, while insisting no Supremes tracks. "I don't want to establish a sound but rather experience a little versatility. The single is being released in the States, then I'm coming back

CHINWAGGIN'

to promote it here with TV guest spots, personal appearances, things like that. I'm even working with a choreographer, although how much dancing I'll end up doing remains to be seen. But I'll whip myself into shape if nothing else!"

Sadly, Cindy Birdsong's solo career was a non-starter. The proposed album was dropped and she seemed to disappear from the limelight. Always overshadowed by the other Supremes, Cindy rarely had the opportunity to promote herself—a pity because she has a wonderful voice and personality. In fact, during the years I met her backstage, she shrugged off the showbiz exterior to be a regular gal.

Ms Birdsong no longer lives expensively, and, according to reports, owns a small apartment in West Los Angeles, which she shares with her son. Singing only in church, Cindy earns a living as a health care worker. In 2000 Diana Ross was asked to reform The Supremes for an American tour. She approached Cindy and Mary Wilson to join her. Unbelievably, Ms Wilson reputedly was financially unrealistic in her demands, while Cindy wanted to accept the offer, but, for some reason, opted to stick with Mary. Their refusal led to Ms Ross asking two further Supremes, Scherrie Payne and Lynda Laurence. The few shows that were staged were a tremendous success, 'a once in a lifetime occasion', but the complete touring itinerary was not honoured due to contractual problems. Fans believed that had the "Return To Love" tour kicked-off in Europe, many problems would have been overcome; as it is, they were denied the opportunity of celebrating the music of The Supremes with three true members.

JOHNNY BRISTOL

Dateline: March 1981

A man who was responsible for some of the timeless sounds to originate from Motown has just started singing again. His new single 'Love No Longer Has A Hold On Me' has been tickling the chart for a while now and could be the hit he desires. To give a further clue, although I doubt it's necessary, the Motown compositions he wrote or co-wrote included 'Daddy Could Swear, I Declare', 'Do You See My Love (For You Growing)', 'Pucker Up Buttercup', 'These Things Will Keep Me Loving You' and 'Someday We'll Be Together'.

And talking of that last title which was also the final official single released by Diana Ross and the Supremes in 1969, Johnny Bristol—born in February 1939 in Morganton, North Carolina—confirmed the male voice heard intermittently on the song was indeed his, thereby confirming months of speculation, and he told me how it came about. "That was Berry Gordy, Diana Ross and myself recording that song. We had been working on it for hours

CHINWAGGIN'

and Diana was getting tired and a little irritable, so I suggested to Berry that maybe if I went into another booth and sang with her, sing in her ear, y'know...two people singing back and forth to each other, it could just take her mind off her tiredness long enough to make her finish it. So we did it and I did the little things that you hear. Berry liked it so much that he decided to keep it on the finished record."

Well, that was one rumour verified and, inadvertently, Johnny confirmed another that neither Mary Wilson nor Cindy Birdsong sang on that last single. And it wasn't the first time he had included his vocals on that particular title; a fact that surprised him when I mentioned it. "Hey, that's right. Just listen to you. I recorded it when I was in the duo Johnny and Jackey. It goes way back (1961) and was released on the Tri Phi label. The follow-ups were 'Do You See My Love For You Growing' and 'Baby Don't Cha Worry' and the Jackey was Jackey Beavers."

Pausing to reflect on his early days, he continued. "I was in the service, in the air force, when I started singing in the duo. Some guy who was in the service with me knew the Gordy family. He introduced us to them." Berry liked what he heard and asked Johnny to join Motown as a writer. "Motown in those days was very exclusive. When you worked for them, you weren't able to work for any other record company. I stayed there about ten years and I guess I produced just about everyone on the label".

Working with such an array of gifted artists, Johnny believed all had a specific quality which he admired greatly. "They were all very easy and all so talented. How can you say that The Temptations were better to work with than Marvin Gaye or Diana Ross. I really loved them all... all that I worked with I mean, and fortunately I was able to work with all the people who excited me creatively as a producer and a writer. So it's fair to say everyone I worked with had my adrenaline flowing."

Like many of those he worked with, Johnny and Motown eventually parted company. Money was the stumbling block, he said. "It's all about money. I really had no other choice because of the offers they made me. I was one of their top five producers and when they came to me—I never talked to Berry Gordy—about my contract they made me a very insulting offer and I felt I couldn't take it." His feelings about leaving weren't in the

JOHNNY BRISTOL

slightest way vindictive because he stressed. "Please don't misunderstand what I've said to you about Motown because I love Motown Records and I have great respect for Berry Gordy and the people I worked with."

He moved to Columbia Records as a producer, leaving his singing career on the back boiler because he felt it was non-productive. "When I first started singing I just wasn't making enough money and I felt that that was the quickest way to starve. So I decided producing was better and found out that I loved it. I stayed with Columbia for a couple of years before moving to MGM and that's where I started singing." During his stay there 'Hang On In There Baby' (1974) was an international hit, an achievement that didn't really surprise him. "When I wrote it, I said 'now this song is a smash and it doesn't matter who sings it.' It's one of those songs you come up with every now and then. Anyone could sing it and it would sell. So MGM said 'OK, you're already a master at producing, why not sing it?'"

From MGM Johnny switched to Atlantic—a horrendous move he said, without giving any details despite my persistence—and then Hansa, where he feels comfortable, respected, and for the first time in a long while, able to do things his way....

A year later I spoke to Mr Bristol again during his promotional trek for the album 'Free To Be Me' and his current single 'Take Me Down'. It was nine in the morning in Los Angeles; he had been working since six. The sun was already shining, he gloated, while I moaned that the British weather was dark and depressing. That was soon forgotten as he started explaining why his album was recorded in America and Europe. "For the first time I have used another producer, Gus Dudgeon, and he lives in Europe. We hired him to do three tracks (including the single) and it was easier for me to go to him. We tried to capture the English/European sound and feeling—in fact, everything is so different. The musicians over there are definitely talented and everything just worked beautifully."

Included in the musicians he rates so highly are Pete Wingfield (keyboards), John Giblin (bass) and percussionists Ray Cooper and Frank Ricotti. Johnny's attitude surprised me rather because I'd always felt American musicians were superior, having that

CHINWAGGIN'

edge, that particular styling and inborn feel to music. "I think that there was a time when that was true, but English musicians came to the States and spent time here being involved with American artists, went out on the road with them and brought that experience back to the UK."

Despite high hopes when we last spoke, he was disappointed that 'Love No Longer Has A Hold On Me' bombed by national chart standards. "I don't think people listened to it lyrically, because that song was well written. It was for the lonely people and there are many of them, a song they could listen to in their homes to make them realise they weren't the only lonely ones. However, I'm in good hands with the people I work with at Hansa, and I know they're going to make me even more well-known and hopefully the hits will follow."

The Kiki Dee track 'Loving And Free' has to be one of the most endearing songs written and Johnny has included this on his album, saying: "I met Kiki once and the reason why I recorded her song was because it was sent to me from the company. I've not heard it before but I liked it right away. It's nice to sing songs I haven't written. As a writer myself, when I pen a song and sing it I know the freedom I have with it. When another writer sends you a song, one tries to sing it with a certain amount of discipline because it shouldn't be changed too much."

The phone link was soon over but for Johnny Bristol the promotion goes on for at least another two months. He was prepared to do everything that Hansa's publicist wanted and hoped to tour Europe during 1983. "It doesn't matter whether I headline or not. It's more important for people to see me perform. Y'see the public seem to like what I write and that makes me feel I was accepted before I was a performer. So, I would like to be with the public so's they can ask me questions if they want to, shake my hand, and I want to let them know that I really appreciate their continued support. Say, you sound like a cheerful lady. Maybe, when I come over I can take you out to dinner?"

He did tour: he didn't take me to dinner.

JOHNNY BRISTOL

Although Johnny Bristol never enjoyed a UK hit following his duet with Amii Stewart titled 'My Guy-My Girl' in 1980, he continued to release distinguished music, including 'Man Up In The Sky' in 1989, and 'Come To Me' in 1991. Five years later he released the 'Life And Love' album for Japanese release only.

Tragically, Mr Bristol died from natural causes, aged 65, on 21 March 2004 at the St Joseph Mercy Livingston Hospital in Howell, Michigan. He was survived by his daughters, Karla Gordy Bristol and Shanna Mueller, and son Johnny Bristol Jr, following his marriage and divorce from Iris Gordy, niece of Berry.

TOM BROWNE
Dateline: August 1980

At the invitation of Arista Records, I had dinner with Tom Browne, his manager Jimmy Boyd and a few of the DJs who hold between them the titles of the country's best. Tom was hot property, basking on the success of 'Funkin' For Jamaica' lifted from his current 'Love Approach' album. Having devoured a debatable starter of whitebait, I tucked into a healthy steak (I am now a vegetarian) and was squeezed next to the artist who was himself struggling to eat a shrimp dish and sip white wine between mouthfuls of cold black coffee.

With his hair closely cropped and his wispy moustache bouncing around on his top lip as he spoke between smiles, Tom told me he comes from a small family, having one brother. "I had a pretty easy childhood, although my parents had a struggle but, by the time I came along, they were pretty secure. My father is a meteorologist and my mother works with schoolchildren." His musical training began with a year of piano lessons when he was eleven years old, and then he took to the trumpet, which was an instrument his father played. Attending New York City's High School of Music, the training ground of many young players,

TOM BROWNE

some of whom are now featured on the 'Love Approach' album, Tom's passion was classical music. In fact, he says he spent most of his time playing in brass choirs and orchestras. "Jazz is my main love, but before I got into that, I played a lot of classical music and still listen to it now for pleasure."

Jazz and Tom found themselves courtesy of a friend who played him an Ornette Coleman album. At the time the quietly spoken artist was attending the Kingsborough College as a physics major. As his interest in jazz grew, he began sitting in with local musicians, and after a year moved on to Queens College where he began to make an impact in the local clubs, particularly The Village Door. This club has a few notaries to its credit, like, Roy Eldridge, Sonny Fortune, Jimmy Nottingham and Walter Perkins.

His first professional gig in 1975 was with the Weldon Irvine group which played the club circuit along the Eastern Seaboard. "Then I joined Sonny Fortune's group and toured Europe and the States for about two years. We recorded an album together and I found that music was taking me over. So much so that I decided to try to get recognition as a musician on my own." To this end, he left Sonny's group—"and the next month I went to a jam session and George Benson was connected with it. I suppose, I'd been playing for about a month or so and CTI Records offered me a contract."

Here enters Jimmy Boyd who, at seventy-one years old, has been in the business for forty years and is as sharp as a Wilkinson blade. We spent a long time talking of his childhood, the struggles and cruelties poured on poor black families, and how he got into the business. He told me he owned two clubs in New York, a city he can't bear to be away from for too long because he thrives on the pace, atmosphere and the people. However, many musicians had passed through his hands at one time or another, as he helped them fight their drug addictions, educating them on its misuse, paid doctors' bills and returned his patients to a normal life. Smoking yet another cigarette, he admitted. "I didn't even get a thank you....I don't really mind. So long as I feel I've done my bit towards clearing the streets of this plague, I don't mind."

Tom consulted Jimmy Boyd on the CTI contract and was advised to leave well alone because of 'a lot of hidden things'. "Jimmy pulled me aside," Tom explained, "and pointed out some

CHINWAGGIN'

problems in the contract. He was right. I hadn't seen the complications. This was late-1978/early 1979 and he's been my manager ever since. And he still manages George Benson."

Dave Grusin and Larry Rosen, presidents of the newly formed GRP Records heard about Tom Browne's expertise from guitarist Earl Klugh, who described him as 'an incredible young trumpet player'. Grusin and Rosen checked Tom's credentials and immediately signed him. "I went with them because I believe in small companies. In a large outfit my trumpet would get lost in all the other trumpets," he laughed. "Big companies have too many artists to look after and as I wanted to get into the music business I thought a smaller set-up would give me a fairer stab at it. My first album 'Browne Sugar' sold over 100,000 copies in the States. We had a single out from it, but that didn't do too well." The album included original compositions, plus versions of 'What's Going On' and 'The Closer I Get To You'.

His second album, 'Love Approach', now on British release, was only completed in April because: "I toured Japan on a GRP 'All Stars' tour. It was a promotional thing and was great fun." One of the featured vocalists on the album is a nineteen-year-old lady, Toni Smith, whom Tom admired greatly. "This is the first album she's ever recorded. She is the friend of a former keyboard player in my band and I'm so excited about her voice that I've done two tapes on her with the hope of producing her in the future. She reminds me of Chaka Khan but really needs more experience. Toni's got lots of potential and I think has a promising career in front of her."

Of his own current album, Tom admitted he swiped ingredients from most of the current sounds, worked them together and released the result. "I wanted to get an album out that I felt the public wanted to hear, with music that is happening now. I didn't go out to make a disco sound—in fact, I didn't know people danced to jazz-funk over here. I wanted a well-rounded album but I do think my next one will be what I like to play."

Finally, was he surprised at the staggering success of 'Funkin' For Jamaica'? "I couldn't believe it," he grinned. "I am so happy and I want to thank all the people who've bought it and...." A piece of sickly gateau arrived for the trumpeter's attention and that was that.

TOM BROWNE

In February 1982 we spoke again. No meal this time but a phone mouthpiece. This time he was engaged in promoting 'Yours Truly', his new album. Unfortunately, I caught Tom in some rehearsal rooms in New York where he was working out for a couple of pending dates in Pennsylvania and Detroit. He was dog-tired having been awake and working for twenty-four hours and really the only thing on his mind was sleep.

As he mumbled and I strained to listen, I gathered he tried to steer away from dance music with this current release but had failed. "It just works out that way. There is a large audience for that music and I want to keep the people happy. It was finished about two or three months ago, but was a long time coming as I was in and out of the studios. I really had no idea how it would turn out, but I'm glad it's been so well received both in the States and over there. However, jazz was, and still is, my main love."

It didn't surprise me that a fair selection of dance tracks had been included because Tom was amazed when last in London to see how we appreciated funk-jazz (or jazz-funk), and he held this thought when recording the current project.

I had my suspicions that he was recording what his record company dictated, and he admitted he was aware of certain restrictions. "Things are tight. Money is scarcer because no longer are companies offering incredible advances. People don't want to spend large amounts of money on recording albums—those days have gone. The finished album too has to give real value for money. They sell here for $8 to $9 a go, and that's a lot of money for the kids. There's a lot of talent around today but no-one gets to hear about it because, I suppose, of the cut-backs and savings being made by the companies. One thing, though, I always try to ensure my product gives value for money. If I didn't, I wouldn't be around for long. This situation isn't just confined to the States, it's a universal thing, so it's probably hitting England just as much."

His mumbling became more erratic. Hell, there was so much more I wanted to ask, but felt guilty at keeping him awake. Deciding to re-hash my previous interview with help from his record company biography, I did the decent thing and wished him a good night.

Staying with Dave Grusin and Larry Rosen, Tom went on to

CHINWAGGIN'

release the 'Magic' album in 1982. He then switched to Arista Records, where he issued the 1983 album 'Rockin' Radio' and 'Tommy Gun' in '84. He also recorded with Fuse One and Roy Ayers. Moving to Malaco Records, Tom was widely used as a session musician, later releasing three albums during the Nineties—'Mo' Jamaica Funk', 'Another Shade Of Browne' and 'R'N'Browne'—before re-working 'Funkin For Jamaica' for inclusion on the '101 Eastbound' compilation, originating from Jazz FM.

GARY BYRD

Dateline: March 1985

He looked dapper in a sharp grey suit, grey silk shirt and narrow leather tie, when I arrived at The Westmoreland Hotel for a drink and a chat with the King of Rap—Gary Byrd. Actually I was lucky to catch him because he was hosting the Steve Wright radio show and attempting to keep his American business ticking over in his absence. He agreed to see me because of the support given to him by *Blues & Soul* when, as he put it, "I was starting out. And that support wasn't repeated by any other magazine and, for that reason alone, I'll always be available to you. The coverage given to me helped my European career no end, and I'll never forget that." My smug smile widened!

Drinks arrived—for me a brandy, him a juice, hotly followed by a pure ginger ale—as he told me about his association with the BBC and Steve Wright. "It's an odd thing. I wasn't unaware of the music scene in the UK—probably more fully aware of it from '74 onwards. And over the years I explored the attitudes of this market place, and in the last year I've been able to understand what has occurred. Stuart Grundy asked me to contribute towards

CHINWAGGIN'

a radio show on Motown. That was a project I enjoyed, and he then asked me to do some announcements too. He called me after that programme to ask if I'd take over the American Chart Show as Paul Gambaccini was going on vacation. It was at the same time as I was due to do a British TV show, so I could do both things on the one trip. The Chart Show was my first live networked programme and it went fairly well."

From that came his 'Sweet Inspiration' Sunday gospel show, originally planned for thirteen weeks only. He takes up the story. "I was on my way back to the US after the Chart Show, to resume my job with my radio station which during my absence had reverted to gospel music, when Stuart phoned me with the idea of doing a gospel show for the BBC. I couldn't believe it: I guess I was in the right place at the right time.

"The programme was extended and it's now run for thirty-one shows. I tape it in the States and send it over. I'm told it's a very popular show, although up until last Sunday I have never heard it over the radio. And even if I say so myself, it sounds OK to me!"

'Sweet Inspiration' generated a lot of listeners' mail, all of which he reads. It mainly concerns his choice of music, and where it can be purchased. Such is the public interest in the-gospel-according-to-Byrd that an album containing the most requested tracks has been compiled. "I felt very good about that and that's a nice way for the series to end," he smiled.

And now his current situation with Steve Wright, which was born from a week's holiday, is another success. "I was talking to Stuart about having a vacation in the UK for a week. Next thing he phones me up at home: 'Can you come to London because Steve is going on holiday?' So I did. I asked how I should script the programme and what music I should feature and was told 'Do what you like, you've got a free hand.' I never really had time to think about it, or the work involved."

It's quite obvious Gary loves radio as a medium to reach an audience, and, he admitted, his ambition for twenty long years was to be what he calls an international announcer. "I can still remember clearly hearing a tape of a DJ with an international sound. I studied and studied that tape and knew from that moment I wanted to become involved with broadcasting and make it a career."

GARY BYRD

Gaining considerable experience and recognition via his radio shows and breakneck rapping which many have copied but rarely perfected, he worked with Stevie Wonder on 'The Crown'. Released in 12" format only in Britain to soar to no 6 during July 1983, a success that was repeated across Europe, it was never followed-up. "What happened in the UK was exciting, almost a phenomenon," he glowed. "We felt the UK was a very good market for the record but we were really surprised at the subsequent level of success." In America, though, 'The Crown' was doomed, as he remembered. "The single got caught up with Motown's new distribution deal with MCA but there were other things—like they really didn't know what I was about. I have operated in radio and promotion and the record thing before so I know how these things work, and the single wasn't moving in the way I wanted it to in the US. And also if a project doesn't work with Stevie Wonder's involvement, well, you know something is wrong. I've learned one thing about this and it's that many things happen because they're meant to. So I won't make the same mistakes twice. I'll record for the European market and import into America if need be."

Stevie Wonder instigated the 'The Crown' project but the actual recording was a shock awakening for Gary. "When I did the vocal, Stevie first had me running for the voice. He warmed me up in the studio. After that, he pressured me to do segments of the song, to top the song. It was some time, by the way, after the record had been pressed that I actually heard the completed record. Anyway, so I went to hit at a certain place in the verse and I felt a terrible burning sensation in my chest. It scared the shit out of me! It was like a terrific heart attack, or how I imagined one to be. Later, I talked to some Indian friends of mine and they said the burning sensations were called 'shockers in the body'. Your body has certain shocker points and you need a strict discipline to open these points in your body. What happened in my performance was that Stevie had pushed me further than I had myself and had opened up this shocker. I looked at Stevie later on and saw the kind of emotional level he was looking for on a record. He pushes himself to this high artistic level each time he sings. He showed me what being an artist was all about, and you hope you are going to get to that level at some time. The high

CHINWAGGIN'

artistic level these people want is something you don't even see.

"I was always conscious of Stevie's stature. He is a creative genius and it really is an honour just to be in the same room as him when he's playing music. It's a total personal experience of historical context and he opened me up to another world of creative possibilities."

With the BBC work now completed, Gary Byrd once again turns his attention to television, documentaries, his daily show on WLIB, his syndicated show 'Star Quiz'....yeah, he's an intensely busy guy. "At one point," he grinned, "I wasn't getting any sleep. The only way my company and I could get projects done on time was by not sleeping. In the meantime I kept writing—I write something every day. But I wouldn't change a thing, except, perhaps, to cut down on making new programmes. What I'm enjoying now is, I'm sure, thanks to being in the right place."

And I had a feeling I was in the right place at the *wrong* time, for Mr Byrd's early night was now an hour overdue. I left quietly but grateful for his time.

Gary Byrd never followed-up 'The Crown' because his proposed deal with Motown International failed to materialise. To this day, he continues to compose and host his own extremely successful radio shows in America.

NATALIE COLE

Dateline: May 1989

A last minute cancellation saw me running down Piccadilly in the pouring rain trying to find The Mayfair Hotel before I got soaked through. Why would anyone do such a damn fool thing? Natalie Cole was the reason and she was in London on a short trip

CHINWAGGIN'

to promote her new single, the beautiful ballad 'Miss You Like Crazy', produced by Michael Masser (a top two British hit).

In the few minutes I had to myself before meeting Ms Cole in her hotel suite, I managed to change from a rain-sodden wreck into something resembling a human being. Natalie, of course, looked great. Dressed in a black jacket and high-waisted matching ski pants, a cheeky black hat and a pair of multi-coloured boots, it was hard to tell she was suffering from jet lag. We talked first about her music.

'Miss You Like Crazy' is taken from her new 'Good To Be Back' album released this month; crammed with goodies like 'Rest of The Night', 'Gonna Make You Mine', 'Don't Mention My Heartache' and a duet with Freddie Jackson 'I Do', but more about that later.

This new project follows her runaway hit album 'Everlasting' which many have classed as one of the ultimate soul albums. It also spawned four British top thirty singles. How on earth does anyone follow that? "I don't know," she answered, "You don't really think about it. First of all, when we did 'Everlasting' we didn't think it would be such a big album. It struggled a bit over here. They released 'Jump Start' twice and 'I Live For Your Love' twice, which I thought was really funny. You can't do that in the States. But it worked. I didn't even think 'international' with the album but with the new one I was thinking more of Europe."

She admitted the two markets are totally diverse and cited American music as 'silly' while Europe tended to be more sophisticated because "The young people I see that are doing stuff over here are different. For some reason they seem to have more of a knack for performance; they're more performance orientated, and they don't follow trends. They're also more unique; the way they dress, the way they move, and with the songs themselves. Even though they may not make a lot of sense, they're still more unique than the songs over in the States. We've got a whole slew of young girls coming out in the States right now and ninety per cent of them cannot sing!"

We discussed the state of music generally, then she astounded me by saying she had praise indeed for Stock, Aitkin and Waterman. "Why does everyone make a face when I say that?...

NATALIE COLE

My manager was considering working with them, but I don't think they're for me. I think perhaps I'm a little sophisticated for that." She could hear me sigh in relief.

Of late, Ms Cole has recorded a fair number of ballads—all superb. Not a deliberate move on her part, although she insisted: "They were not ballads for ballads' sake. I choose a song that tells a story. I find that when I do too many up-tempos you can't hear what's going on and it's the beat that's the star and not the lyrics. I'm not happy with that. I'm not just a singer, I'm a story teller, a stylist. 'Miss You Like Crazy' is representative of this. It's kind of a sad song especially if you have someone in your life that you're used to being with, or they're out of town or whatever. The way we're doing it live is very much like the video. I'm sitting in a make-believe studio, and at the end of the song—on the record it goes on and on—we end it very quietly, and it's very sad. It's the first sad song I've done in a long time."

Not all her repertoire is based on her personal experiences but, as she smiled: "I've probably been through everything so I don't think there's anything missing. I tell you my life and career haven't been boring at all! Someone asked me did I have anyone I was singing 'I Live For Your Love' to. I didn't, so I just pretended. I think if anything it was more spiritual. I was thinking about God. But I was also thinking to myself most women are devastated to think we just live for a man's love. No man should ever know that a woman lives for his existence. But it turned out that so many loved that record; many different interpretations were put on it, but it doesn't matter now."

Talking of men, her duet with Freddie Jackson was the only one on the new album: a happy liaison as she recalled. "Freddie and I worked together on a number of occasions, and then when he went to Capitol Records, it was really a matter of politics. Capitol is like my sister label now, so the record company thought it would be a great combination. Freddie was real cool but I'd say the producer was the boss at the session—unless he did something we didn't like. I think that an artist and a producer have to be a team with no one in charge."

Apart from producing and co-writing 'Miss You Like Crazy', Michael Masser penned a second track 'Starting Over Again'—a future single which took nine months to complete! "It was a

CHINWAGGIN'

nightmare! Michael is a perfectionist, a little on the neurotic side when it comes to producing, and he couldn't make up his mind what he wanted. He didn't like the way some of the musicians played on it, so he went home and re-did it. He did a lot of work in his home studio then he came back—this all started in March '88—in August the track was totally different. It was better, and I must have done it sixty times. In early January I did it again. And by then I was sick and tired of the sight of it. Then Michael re-added some synthesised strings, not real ones—on 'Starting Over Again' we used real strings, a room full of strings, just like the old days—then it took forever. It's certainly the longest song I've ever recorded. I certainly hope that after all this it will be a hit. If not, we're doing something really wrong." (It was a top sixty British hit in December 1989)

Michael Masser has worked with Diana Ross and Whitney Houston, among others; did Natalie feel she was in competition with, say, Ms Houston? "I thought about it, but there's nothing I can do about it," she candidly replied. "Michael wasn't thinking of Whitney when he wrote this song. We've worked together before on the 'Don't Look Back' album on the 'Someone I Used To Love' ballad. So, I basically knew his technique. We had a serious conversation about sounding like Whitney. Y'know competing with that sound and he said, 'Don't worry about it. She's who she is and you are who you are. You both are differently talented.' But Whitney sure is popular. She's working on her third album and already she's sold twenty million albums. Young people buy her records because to them she represents Middle America. There are members of the black community, and black radio and the black industry who question her approach to music, and wonder where it is that she's going and what she's trying to accomplish. But I don't think Whitney's trying to accomplish anything.

"Whitney and I are friends. We have a lot of respect for each other. I've heard that she's been persuaded to start writing, which, I think will be a great step for her. If she was allowed to do her own thing, people might view her differently, and that might happen if she starts writing her own music. She might end up writing nothing like the stuff she sings now. At the moment her songs are chosen for her and I don't really think she has as much say as I do. I like to think I have one hundred per cent control over my work. But realistically, have about seventy-five per cent. I'm not totally independent because I am contracted to a record company, but if this new album goes multi-platinum maybe I'll start my own label."

Ms Cole has had her fair share of tragedies; first her father, Nat 'King' Cole, and then her husband died. Later she survived an horrendous trip into a drug-induced world which many say she was lucky to come through. However, as she told me so many times, she weakened: "But the people around me just wouldn't let me give up the battle. Or something inside of me would say 'who the hell do you think you are, how can you give up just like that?' It would have been so easy but my conscience wouldn't let me. I was still signed to a record company and they wouldn't let me. Oh sure, they were ready to give up on me too.

"It was pretty bad because what happened for a while, especially after the drugs, was nobody wanted anything to do with me, and that can be very hurtful and damaging to one's ego as well as your career. In fact, you can forget your career! People were afraid to take a risk to hire me, record companies were afraid to have contracts with me because they really didn't know if I was gonna cut it or not."

It took a inner strength to go public with this—not a lot of artists would have—and at the time of this interview, Natalie didn't know why she had so openly spoken of her nightmare, while admitting—"It haunts me everywhere I go. It's really not anybody's fault that they want to know so much about it. There's just something unique about a person who has been through the fire and emerges victorious. I went to hell and back and survived, and I guess that takes a lot of courage, although I don't know how much courage I had at the time. I think I was more afraid of being left behind than anything else. I just wanted to be able to hang on, just a little longer, and that was my biggest fear. I just couldn't see myself dropping off the face of the earth. It's not my style and I didn't know how strong I was until it happened to me. I feel great now."

Returning to music now and what many claimed to be her 'comeback' single—'Pink Cadillac'. A top five British hit in March 1988; a milestone in her career, she said. "It was important to have a hit. I think the *kind* of hit songs you have are more important than just a hit song. People really liked 'Pink Cadillac' because it was fun and didn't say anything in particular. It didn't raise any consciousness, it wasn't a political song. It was a fun summer song and even to this day people can have fun with it. For it to come from a girl, and a black girl at that, and for it to be a Bruce Springsteen song...well, all these elements went together to make it what it was. Plus it had a great arrangement and I think all that together made it very special."

As this was the first taste of success Ms Cole had had in a while, the media naturally treated it as her 'comeback' but, as she laughed, she'd never really been away! "They have to say something. I know the media don't mean to be malicious or negative but it does get a bit boring after a time. I just wish there was another word that one can use but I racked my brain and I couldn't think of one, other that re-birth or rejuvenation. You could say born-again I suppose. But just because I haven't had a hit record, it doesn't mean to say I haven't been working. That's the business for you. If they don't hear from you for a while, you must be lying in a dump somewhere. So, yes, in that respect, having a hit is important.

"However, what is more important, especially for young artists, is that having a hit song doesn't mean anything if you can't sell it. Radio can play it all day long, people can love it to death, but if it doesn't motivate people enough to go to the store and buy it, it doesn't mean anything. And that's what you have to look at—will it sell? Let's say you have a huge number one song, then you come with an album that's just OK. That album is going to hurt your ability to go out and get work because it means you only have that one huge song to offer your audience in an hour's show. And then there's the nightmare following up a hit. I think that's why these days artists try so hard with albums, ensuring they hold enough good songs to keep a show together. After all, that's where you earn your money unless you're also writing your own material. Just think how much money Whitney will make when she writes her own stuff.

"But, there's all kinds of things that can work against you. For example, you have your hit, your album is OK, and your next album is bullshit. That's the end of your career—and that's only

NATALIE COLE

with two albums! That's exactly what's happening now. Everything is very trendy for right now, and you just milk everything you can, which is a wicked thing to say. You just try to get out of it what you can, then after that I don't know what you do. Go back to wherever you came from I suppose. The whole thing is sustaining power; maintaining consistency and longevity. Those words are very valuable to me....I've proved I can sell records, but Jeez, I still get so scared. And it gets scarier—it doesn't get any easier. Even doing albums gets more scary. I can spot a good song, but what makes it a hit isn't necessarily the fact it is good. I've heard some incredibly creepy, crappy songs becoming hits."

Natalie is fortunate. With the position she holds in the industry, composers come to her with their best work. However, it wasn't always that way. "When we did the 'Everlasting' album, we couldn't get anyone. Everyone was too busy, either working with a Whitney or an Anita Baker, and nobody wanted to be bothered with me. After 'Everlasting' started to really grow legs and we were ready to record this album, we got calls from all kinds of people. And it was nice because we turned them down! For me to get songs from a writer who has written fifty smashes isn't as important as me getting one great song from an unknown writer. I almost go out of my way to get unknown writers to submit songs to me, as was the case with the people who wrote 'I Live For Your Love'. It was really their first big hit and they love me dearly because of that. They also wrote the title song for the new album, so now we have a real rapport going. Michael Masser, the same thing. Just because he's given Whitney great hits, it doesn't necessarily mean he'll do the same for me. That's not why I chose him. I chose him because he's a great songwriter."

The Michael Masser conversation steered towards Diana Ross which led to Thelma Houston who sang the demo version of 'Do You Know Where You're Going To?' (the title song from Ross's second movie 'Mahogany' released 1976). I only knew this, I said, because I'm fortunate enough to have Ms Houston's version in my collection. "That's right! And do you know who else did demos for Diana? Stephanie Mills. She told me she did a lot for her. Stephanie was signed to Motown for a while and she said when she heard the final product, Diana would be doing the same

CHINWAGGIN'

lyps that she did. Not a lot of people knew that Diana's demos were sung for her. So she didn't have to work too hard. All she had to do was go in and sing the songs. This totally dispels the illusion, but that's OK because people need to stop being attracted to the illusions of the business."

Before ending our chat, I asked the Capitol star how she felt about performing in the 1988 Nelson Mandela charity gala, staged at Wembley. "That concert was something really different. I've never done anything like that before. I was glad I could contribute, but I've really had to cut back on my charity work because I think it's got a bit much now. Once you start, you're always asked to do loads more and you don't make any money. And let's face it I do have to make money—the baby needs a new pair of shoes!"

The Mandela gala obviously attracted international television coverage, but even if it hadn't, she'd still have appeared. "I've certainly done a lot of things that were worthy of national exposure that weren't given it. The experience to perform over here to an audience that's not familiar with my music is a challenge whether it's televised or not. Just the idea of performing in a stadium with that many people there, was great. It's funny because in a place that big you don't really know what kind of effect you have. I could only see a few people and couldn't really tell what was going on. You can only tell afterwards when you get the feedback. They told me to go out and have fun which was just as well because I was so nervous. I'm glad I did an up-tempo song because nobody could see or hear my nervousness.

"There were a few groups who were on too long in my opinion, as much as I love Eric Clapton and the others. I also think that every artist could have done at least two or three songs because the show lent itself to that. And by it not being like that it looked like a plain case of racism; they even put us in a section." (Natalie appeared with Al Green, Jonathan Butler and Ashford & Simpson) I agreed with her, white acts *were* afforded more generous performing time than their black contemporaries.

Admittedly, Natalie's music has now flown the soul/black nest to sell vast amounts in mainstream music; a market which, she felt, was extremely fickle compared to the loyalty shown her in black music circles. She justified her current position as such.

NATALIE COLE

"I'm a singer of songs now, I don't know that I'm a singer of only soul songs. I know I sing with a lot of soul, and that there's something in my voice that makes people want to listen and that's what is important. I just wish the States had a little wider approach in music the way Europe does, because America is so segregated still."

Another journalist was on the verge of being ushered into her suite, so I reluctantly left to face the pouring rain, which was gradually transforming Piccadilly into a river.

Natalie Cole, a star indeed, with all the qualities befitting her heritage and status. Recording-wise she continued to release exquisite albums including 'Unforgettable, With Love' in 1991, 'Take A Look' two years later. During the late-Nineties she issued four albums— 'Stardust', 'Christmas With You', 'Snowfall On The Sahara', and 'The Magic Of Christmas'. Her most current album, 'Ask A Woman Who Knows', a showcase of her enduring artistry, was released by Verve Records.

CAROLYN CRAWFORD

Dateline: August 1990

Motown connoisseurs have delighted in Carolyn Crawford's talents since 1963 when her first single 'Forget About Me' was released. She was fourteen years old. This title was followed by her evergreen 'My Smile Is Just A Frown Turned Upside Down' and 'When Someone's Good To You', both a year later.

So, over twenty-five years on, we met for the first time to chat: her début UK interview as far as she can remember. So, following her instruction to "Shoot away babe," we wandered through the years as if they were yesterday, thanks to her excellent memory.

At thirteen years old Ms Crawford won a talent contest jointly sponsored by a Detroit radio station and the Tip Top bread company. "You had to enter with a tune that you liked," she

CAROLYN CRAWFORD

remembered. "If you were picked for the finals you had to go out and collect bread wrappers! I went around restaurants, cafés and hotels for these wrappers—boy, you had to work hard as well as sing! After the contestants had got all they could find that would determine whether we got into the finals or not—where Berry Gordy was one of the judges—I decided to sing the Mary Wells' song 'Laughing Boy' and added an extra verse. Not only did he like my singing, he said, but he realised I had a little writing talent as well."

Before she could catch her breath, Carolyn was a Motown artist in the studio recording her first single, which she also wrote. "I had a contract from '63 to '67, but I came in the middle of the company changing over their business operation. I got lost in the shuffle so to speak. I don't think anyone knew what to do with me so I was pushed aside and by '65 I was through.

"For two years I sat around and did nothing. I couldn't go to work because I was still signed to Motown. My family didn't have a lawyer to get me out of the contract; we didn't have that kind of money. So I sat out my contract, which I regret. I felt Motown could have given me a release."

When eventually free, Carolyn sang jazz tunes in Detroit clubs where Hamilton Bohannon spotted her. "I worked my first gig for him on New Year's Eve 1973 and after that I was back and forth with him because he was a little temperamental at the time." In between the Bohannon experience, she sang with other units until she wormed her way into Philadelphia International by walking into their offices demanding to see (Kenny) Gamble and (Leon) Huff. They weren't in their office that day but their secretary promised they would phone her. Oh yeah! Thought Carolyn. But they did, and within weeks she was recording 'If You Move You Lose', Leon Huff's first solo composition and production. From that she recorded nine titles with McFadden & Whitehead. Then quite unexpectedly, the bubble burst, as she remembered: "I had walked into another company changeover! Right smack in the middle without knowing it. Philadelphia International were preparing to join the CBS family and once again I didn't have a record company.

"I worked with Chapter 8 from '75 to '78. Anita Baker replaced me when I left because of a personality conflict. I've got a little

CHINWAGGIN'

musicianship in me as well as singing but unfortunately not a lot of male musicians are prepared to take advice from a woman." She returned to Hamilton Bohannon until 1979 when—"I developed nodules on my vocal chords from singing too hard. I thought I had cancer and had the choice to leave them alone or have them removed. I chose to leave them be, but I had to stop singing for some time. I took nine-to-fivers after signing on to an employment agency. Boy, that was depressing because I really wanted to sing and wasn't allowed to."

As an aside here, when Ms Crawford gigged around the American club circuit, her mother was her companion. She laughed as she recalled those early days. "Yeah, it's true. She travelled with me during my Motown stay when I went on some of the Revues. She kept me alive, made sure I looked good. She was very particular about my dress—like, all my clothes had to match. I couldn't get away with anything." She giggled as she recalled one incident when she was on stage and her mother noticed her slip was hanging down below her dress. Instead of rectifying the problem when her daughter came off stage, mum instructed the show's emcee to boogie across the stage to tell her daughter to hitch up her petticoat. He did just that, whispering in her ear as she was singing. "I couldn't believe she'd done that," Carolyn shrieked. "I was so embarrassed and so was the emcee!"

With mother in attendance on tour, keeping an ever-watchful eye, I asked if it kept the men at bay? She laughed again—"Girl, I never had to wait until I was on the road to do that! I did that at home. No, what I mean by that is, I grew up like a normal kid and found out what I was gonna find out at home. I did get married when I was older to the lead singer of Chapter 8. He wanted to stay married and I didn't. I got a divorce easily as he was always out of the country. Then I married again. This time to a non-singing, sensible sort of guy. But I've got no kids, didn't make that and I doubt I will because I'm at that age."

Carolyn Crawford might have given up on motherhood, but her career has been rejuvenated thanks to the British based Motorcity Records, opened by Ian Levine. Following the release of her debut single 'Timeless', she had updated her 'My Smile Is Just A Frown Turned Upside Down', one of eight new tracks on her album 'Heartaches'.

CAROLYN CRAWFORD

At the time of this interview Ms Crawford was one of numerous ex-Motown acts to join Motorcity. The future looked extremely encouraging for all. However, in true Crawford fashion, Motorcity Records closed before she enjoyed the hit she craved so much.

I'm told Carolyn continues to perform and, of course, her Motown material is spasmodically re-packaged on compilations. The pity was she never realised her ambition to become a hit-making artist with Motorcity.

FOUR TOPS

Dateline: February 1984

I seemed to have spent most of my adult life talking and writing about the Four Tops. Indeed, as a teenager living in Sussex, I ran their fan club for several years before joining the ranks of *Motown Ad Astra* (a fan club encompassing all Motown acts)when I moved to London. Through the transition from countryside to city, I'd spent so much time with the group during their UK visits that I felt rather special. Therefore, the following interview is not what I had expected, I'm sorry to say.

It had been some years since I'd spoken to my darling group, so with a happy heart I skipped to their London hotel to rekindle our friendship, which I held dearly.

Unfortunately, my happy heart became heavy when only Duke Fakir was available, and although he endeavoured to compensate for three absentees, this interview isn't one I'm proud to present.

FOUR TOPS

The ambience was unsociable; we sat on a bed in a smallish hotel room with Motown's publicity guy in attendance—who also felt obliged to contribute—with Duke appearing to have a pressing engagement, judging by the several times he checked his watch.

Don't get me wrong, Mr Fakir is a charming man, always has been, but I worshipped Levi Stubbs and when I enquired as to his whereabouts, was told he was sleeping. Lawrence Payton was writing, and I was given no reply as to Obie Benson's location. However, when I later left the hotel, I spotted him in the foyer. Hell, I was so paranoid by this time, I hadn't the nerve to approach him. All I wanted to do was go home.

Originally known as the Four Aims, all four group members were born and raised in Detroit, where they still live, as Duke explained. "We got to know each other as kids and grew up in the same neighbourhood. We liked the same things—and still do—and now our families and kids are very close. Obie and I live almost next door and the others aren't too far away. Sure, we get tired of each other's faces, and when that happens we just don't see each other for a while. By and large though, we have a happy life together."

Most of the Tops' recording is now confined to Los Angeles due to Motown's move there. Taking their respective families with them, Duke said, makes recording sessions less like work—"They can have a holiday, enjoy the sun, but more importantly, we can all stay together".

The Four Tops secured a 1956 recording deal with Chess Records and worked with Billy Eckstine as his backing group. They learnt a lot about the business from Billy who was more of a father figure than an employer. The group first signed to Motown's subsidiary label, Workshop, where in 1964 they recorded 'Breaking Through' and 'Hello Broadway'. The two albums were jazz influenced, a style they later dropped. "We weren't really into jazz anyway, but we wanted to try out most types of music to see where we could excel," a lounging Duke explained. "The idea of recording an album of standards, easy listening tunes and some jazz hasn't been ruled out for the future. We're always on the look out for different songs and ideas, so who knows...."

Last year Motown celebrated its 25th anniversary: this year the

CHINWAGGIN'

Four Tops celebrate their 30th! An astonishing feat for any group, but even more so for the Tops as its membership has remained the same since its inception. No celebrations were planned though, said Duke: "As it seems everyone is having anniversary celebrations these days. We don't have any plans to record anything in particular. We are going into the studios to record our next album once our tour with The Temptations has finished. The idea of putting us with the Temptations came about from our appearance on the Motown anniversary gala. It's great working with them. We laugh a lot but work hard. There's no real competition between us of course. We each perform our respective shows, then join forces for the finale."

Once off the American touring trail, Duke confirmed they intended to finish a musical about their life and career as the Four Tops. I don't remember whether the musical will involve the group members but did note that black Detroit-based playwright Ron Milner was involved. "We've partly written the script and Ron's keeping the whole project together for us. He's known us for years, and it will be finished within a year."

The conversation petered out as Duke once more looked at his watch. My enthusiasm waned and I wanted out of the situation; we were getting nowhere. I felt he was talking to me through obligation and it showed. Breathing in the fresh London air outside the hotel, I told myself it wouldn't have happened if I'd seen Levi....

Sadly, I never had the pleasure of talking to all the Tops together again. Their career, of course, continued to spiral with the 'Indestructible' project. In 1990 they were inducted into the Rock And Roll Hall Of Fame, and seven years later Lawrence Payton (the quiet, talented Top) died from liver cancer. It was an unexpected tragedy. The world mourned his loss. Theo Peoples replaced him, and the guys continued to tour alone, and with The Temptations, where their British dates were always sold out. My dear Levi hasn't performed with his mates since 2000, following a mild heart attack and stroke. He was replaced by Ronnie McNeir for touring purposes, but the group's performances are often lacklustre without Levi's distinctive, powerful leads. However, in

FOUR TOPS

2004 a special event was held in his honour—'It's All The Way With Levi—50 Years And Still Going'—at Detroit's Roostertail Club. A host of Motown stars paid homage to the group who were also celebrating their 50th anniversary. To this end Motown released the 2-CD 'Four Tops Anthology', a magnificent tribute to these guys. More sadness followed on 1 July 2005 when the smiling Top died. Obie Benson had been battling against a sudden onset of medical problems when he suffered a heart-attack following the amputation of a leg due to circulation difficulties. This led to a diagnosis of lung-cancer, for which Obie had begun an intense chemotherapy programme. His last significant US performance was on 'The Late Show with David Letterman', and his final UK appearance was as a contributor on BBC2's highly watchable 'Soul Deep', weeks before his death. His onstage replacement is his son, Roquel. The group's most recent release, 'Lost Without You: Lost & Found' is, as the title suggests, packed with previously unreleased gems. It's quite lovely; I'm listening to it now.

JAKI GRAHAM

Dateline: July 1984

Travelling to London by train from Wolverhampton is something Jaki Graham is now used to following the release of her debut EMI single 'What's The Name Of Your Game?', released on the Capitol subsidiary. The journey is monotonous, but she doesn't complain as her visits to the capital involve promotion work for her fledgling career. "I would have loved a hit with my first single but I understand that the public takes time to accept newcomers, particularly in the market I'm in. So I'll be patient." Ms Graham is now keeping her fingers firmly crossed that her second outing 'Heaven Knows' will do the trick.

Born in Birmingham, Jaki was one of six children and was raised by her grandmother who, it seems, was largely responsible for her interest in music. She took the youngster to concerts and bought her records until Jaki left school to work at a variety of jobs including secretarial positions. As a hobby, she sang part-time with her pal Ruby Turner and from there came her

JAKI GRAHAM

involvement with groups like Medium Wave.

Although she's a newcomer to actually recording her own product, Jaki's no stranger to the recording studios having been a session singer for acts like UB40, Alexis Korner and David Grant. In fact, she's now a member of David's tightly operated management family with Brian Freshwater as the boss. She explained further: "I was kept busy working with David, while Brian was keeping a look out for the right song for me. He knew what he wanted to record but until recently he hadn't heard the right tune. I'm new to this business, at least this side of it, and relied on him entirely. Once he found 'What's The Name Of Your Game?', we cut a demo and things began to happen very quickly. The next step was working on my first album with Derek Bramble from which the first single was taken. Everyone is treating me so well and as I'm the new girl I'm broken into different areas very gradually.

"I'm delighted with Capitol's enthusiasm about me, particularly when you think of how many big names are signed up in America. It doesn't seem possible that I'm on the same label!"

A year later we met again. It was one of those muggy July afternoons outside EMI Records' press office. Inside, the place was buzzin' as younger acts—one with a charted single, and two with potential hits—chatted amongst themselves, talking shop, swapping jokes and drinking coffee and mineral water. It was like the old days,. when artists and record company personnel gelled, and I thoroughly enjoyed myself, that's for sure.

Jaki and I snuck off into a quiet office because she was working to a tight schedule. In her unassuming way she muttered, 'Are your serious?' and 'Thank you very much,' when greeted with 'You've got a monster smash there, Jay,' from everyone who interrupted her three o'clock lunch of sandwiches and crisps. That future hit is, of course, 'Round And Around'. (UK no 9)

So, dressed in black pants and jacket, the singer munched her way through my questions, starting with her debut with David Grant titled 'Could It Be I'm Falling In Love', her first top ten single. Naturally, she was excited but explained, "If it hadn't come along I'd like to think my turn to have a hit would have arrived one day, because I think I could have done it. In this

CHINWAGGIN'

business nothing is certain, and predictions don't mean a lot either, do they? Even though these guys have been kind enough to say good things about 'Round And Around', well, it might not chart at all, might it? If it does, I'll be dead chuffed, I can tell you." The duet won't make her wealthy, she sighed, because she's in debt, but if her current single sells, she'll be back on the right track.

She cited David Grant as an inspiration, although was now concerned that she would be competing against him for single success. "He's a very considerate guy...he not only coached me and guided me, he pushed me, if you like...because I'm not really a confident person. I get by by doing my own bits and pieces."

Enjoying the hit with him also meant a spot on BBC1's *Top Of The Pops* which wasn't as daunting as she'd expected. Tiring, yes. "You get there at ten in the morning, then there's several rehearsals, dress rehearsals and more rehearsals. Then about five or six o'clock it's done for real. I think that was about the time 'cos I left at seven to catch my train. Offstage, though, I had a great time; Phyllis Nelson was there, and The Cool Notes. We all met up in the canteen; it was like a small family of us, and it's wonderful to know that we had all made it at the same time. We looned about and it took the routine of the show away.

"It's most extraordinary now. People actually stop me in the street, and I get stared at a lot. I really feel uncomfortable about this. Makes me feel like I got a run in my tights or something's hangin' down—do ya know what I mean? I'm not aware of having thought about being recognised but I suppose I must have realised things like this could happen. I'm just going to have to look at my life differently now. Tony, my husband, overhears conversations in the street more than I do. Like 'Isn't she that girl that sings,' or 'Isn't she that Jaki Graham with whatshisname?'. It all makes me smile...but it also makes me want to curl up in embarrassment. You know I've always used the train and bus; now someone's told me I shouldn't do that anymore 'cos I'll get hassled. I said he couldn't be serious. Who would want to hassle me? I'm just like everyone else."

With all this travelling about causing potential problems, wouldn't relocating to London be the answer? She agreed on the one hand, but on the other explained: "It'd be great moving here,

JAKI GRAHAM

and I've often thought about it. However, I know I couldn't stand London life—like the traffic for instance. Man, that'd drive me bonkers. I do like returning to Birmingham to get away from it, returning to normal life, if you see what I mean. Also, I have Natalie to take into consideration; she's four years old and she's just started nursery school. If I was in London and had to go out who would take care of her? And, we also have a house in Birmingham. It's not a mansion, or anything like that, and we've just started doing bits to it. Decorating, doing the garden, generally doing it up, and with the summer coming on, we want to build a patio, so I'd feel very reluctant to give it all up. And besides I'm not financially secure enough to take the step. I know I wouldn't get anything in London like our house for the same money. So...I guess I'll have to keep on with my travelling for a while yet."

Jaki is very much like her fellow singer (Sid) Haywoode in many respects, even down to the last minute panic of buying clothes for appearances. Jaki laughed. "I'm a nightmare. I get all my stuff in Wolverhampton, and it really is a case of blind panic when I have to do a TV show because I rush out to find something suitable. I have to swap and change clothes about for shows 'cos I'm poor! If this single takes off maybe I can get some credit at the shops.

"I'm full up now. I think I'll save the rest of this food for my journey home because I'll be starving by then." And with the swirl of the long black jacket, the singer was out of EMI House, clutching her plastic bag crammed with records, T-shirts...and, of course, her half-eaten three o'clock lunch!

By the time we talked again, Ms Graham and I were firm buddies. She phoned me from the *Soul Train* studios in September 1985 to tell me she felt rough through lack of sleep. She'd just returned from Switzerland and was now stuck in the studio until early afternoon, before more evening promotional work.

With 'Round And Around' now breaking through Europe, following its top ten British entry, the singer has spent more time in a 'plane than in Birmingham. "Girl, I've been to Germany, Holland, Belgium, and all over just recently. I'm seeing a lot of

CHINWAGGIN'

countries and new places I never dreamt of. And I'm meeting a lot of different people. In fact, everybody I've met has been really nice to me. And I've not come across any of those big-headed stars that people talk about. I'm just having a great time. But, you know me girl, I just do what I'm asked to do, and I don't think about having hit singles and stuff like that. I don't think about being successful. I'll never be what people call a 'star'. God forbid, I'm not made like that...you know what I'm saying? But I am thinking I'd like to be around for a long time!"

Jaki's first album has just been issued and I was surprised it wasn't called 'Round And Around', to cash-in with the hit single. She didn't know either; nor why it had been named 'Heaven Knows' (after her current single, struggling in the UK top sixty). Was she pleased with the result? "I am, girl, but I can't really talk about it because I haven't listened to it as a whole because it's been part of me for so long. It's now up to the people to judge. But, what I do know is, the version of 'Heaven Knows' is different to the original release."

With UK tour dates recently being advertised, Jaki's immediate future was devoted to rehearsals. She told me her support band was already ensconced in the rehearsal studio, but due to her promotional commitments, she wouldn't be joining them for another week. "Half of me is nervous about the tour, the other half is excited. There'll be ten of us on the road, and the band—they've been with me on TV—are really like my family now, so it promises to be a laugh if nothing else. Some of the guys sing as well, so backing vocals won't be a problem. I'm used to gigging, although over the past two years it's been mostly PAs, which are very different. Oh, and I'm not going out as Jaki Graham and a backing band. We are a unit, we're working as one to concentrate on the album, bunging in some other odds and ends, like cover-versions. One of the guys will duet with me in place of David. And—listen here—I have the final choice of repertoire. My, I think I am going to enjoy this...we're gonna kick arse out there, girl!

"I don't like being away so much from my family. Natalie knows what I do for a living but sometimes it's hard on her not knowing when her mum is going to be home, or when I am at home, that I have to dash off again. So that's why, where I can,

JAKI GRAHAM

she comes with me. My family, too, are moaning they don't see me as much these days, but they do understand why I'm not at home like I used to be. And, of course, they're well pleased with how I'm doing, and I think they're a little proud an' all."

And, no conversation would, at this stage in her career, be complete without a mention of her regular train trips to and from London. She giggled: "Well, I haven't exactly got mobbed yet. What does happen is that someone will come and sit next to me and ask if, like, am I Jaki Graham? and start a conversation. I'm asked for advice on how to get into the music business; I seem to attract all the budding singers and musicians on the train. And I feel awful as sometimes it's as much as I can do to talk because all I want to do is sleep. And back home, when I go shopping. I can't do it like everyone else. People...they don't just come up to me, face to face, they follow me around. They stare at me, like they're burning a hole in the back of my head. *I hate it.* Being followed about is very unnerving, don't you think so? I get hustled for autographs too...that doesn't bother me at all because it's a lovely feeling. It's being followed—that's something else altogether."

During August 1988 we settled into one of EMI's offices for a serious interview, having met, phoned and talked in between times. It was a changed Ms Graham I met: she was more mature and confident, and her husband, Tony Ormsby was now her manager. She admitted her musical style had changed, prompting a worrying time in her career, and she was on the promotion trail once more in support of her 'No More Tears' single, extracted from her third, as yet untitled album. (To date Jaki had enjoyed further solo hits with 'Step Right Up', 'Set Me Free' and 'Breaking Away'; and with David Grant the runaway hit 'Mated')

"I've not been dossing around girl" she replied, when I asked her where she'd been for the last fifteen months. "I've been touring in Europe, recording the album, a video...sorting out my professional life, writing some songs and generally getting my life together. I can't believe it all took so long!"

And she toured with Michael McDonald on his recent British tour. "No-one was more surprised than me when Tony sorted the deal out with the promoters. Michael was looking for a girl singer

CHINWAGGIN'

to take the place of Patti LaBelle on 'On My Own'. When it was first mentioned to me I didn't take it seriously...how could I sing like Patti? Anyhow, I went along to meet Michael, we hit it off straight away, and his opening show was in Birmingham, my hometown. The audience was brilliant to me, and I thought this is a fluke. A standing ovation from my hometown! It was a dream come true... we did ten dates, ending at Hammersmith. Throughout the tour he gave me more numbers to sing. At first I thought he meant backing vocals, but he was offering me solo spots. I couldn't believe it. He wanted everything to be right because it was his first British tour, and I was astonished when he confessed he was suffering with nerves!"

Jaki's third album will be released two years after her last. This time, however, she worked with a host of writers and producers in London, Los Angeles and New York. Her longstanding writer/producer partner, Derek Bramble, was already in the States, so Jaki joined him. Once installed in New York, she became reunited with Michael MacDonald and duetted with Philip Ingram on the track he co-wrote for the album. She then switched to Los Angeles to work with Richard Burgess, before returning to New York to record two tracks with Mantronik. She then flew to London to work with Pete Wingfield and Derek Bramble. Working with Richard Burgess was, she said, a nostalgic reunion because she had once been a session singer for his group, Landscape. Being in the studio with Mantronik proved nerve-racking because it was the first time she had worked with outsiders, so to speak. "I was thrown in at the deep end but it was a great experience."

And, as if that wasn't enough for the singer to contend with, she had switched American record companies. "I was with Capitol but now I've swapped to Manhattan, which is still EMI. When we talked to Manhattan they were quite enthusiastic, which was a totally different attitude than Capitol who said they couldn't do anything with my last album."

Like so many artists, Jaki spent years struggling to enjoy that all important break in the business. Many times she felt like giving up the fight, but something inside her kept urging her on. Even the tiring, boring train journeys and flopped singles failed to dampen her enthusiasm. Her arduous tours promoting singles in

JAKI GRAHAM

night clubs, record shops—anywhere, finally paid off. Now, Jaki believes it's payback time and plans to return to those night clubs to thank the punters who supported her.

The upheaval of changing management is always a worrying prospect, but Jaki felt the time was now right for her. Working and being with her husband all day, every day, hasn't presented any problems, as they've known each other since their teens, "and the relationship works very well, despite some negative reactions from some quarters. We work things out together and I know Tony has my best interests at heart. We both know that I'm almost starting my career again because of being away so long and because of the change in my music. It seemed right to me to expand and work with other people."

To be honest, I don't care if Jaki records in London, New York or Outer Mongolia, because (to me) she's not changed one iota. I'm very fond of her: she's one of the gang. Sure, she's taken a gamble now; most artists do at some time or other. But this time round, she's older, wiser and aware of the pitfalls in this business. Actually, there is one thing Jaki lacks—ego! Behind the public face, she's still a wife and mother at home in Wolverhampton. And, I suppose, it came as no great surprise to learn she still treats food with the greatest respect; still travels to and from London by train, and doubtless still has a half-eaten sandwich hidden away in her handbag...just in case!

Ms Graham continues to record and tour regularly, particularly in Japan where she's a top selling artist. She also enjoys her regular stints performing on cruise liners, and her guestings with Michael McDonald and others. Performing for Liza Minelli was another coup for her. When engagements permitted in 2004, he returned to the recording studios to record for her daughter, Natalie's label and, in 2005, appeared on ITV's music show, 'Hit Me Baby One More Time'. Believe it or not, it's 20 years since Jaki's first chart single, 'Could It Be I'm Falling In Love'. Hell, we're old friends now!

SHARON (SID) HAYWOODE

Dateline: September 1984

I hadn't seen Sharon (Sid) Haywoode for some months and was surprised at how thin she was. She'd just had glandular fever, she mumbled, which had confined her to bed. On reflection, she had never carried a great deal of weight—lucky sod! To her credit, her last charting single 'A Time Like This' hit no 48 during 1983. Now she was hoping to repeat that success.

Now back on form, she was glad to be back to work promoting her new single 'I Can't Let You Go'—a song previously recorded by Talkback—now on release. (UK no 63) We shared lunch, and my cigarettes. Sid, now a vegetarian, was taking a break from two days of interviews to relax. Some she enjoyed, others not, she told me. "I used to get really het up about talking to journalists. Y'know, taking care not to say the wrong thing. And I didn't know what they could possibly find interesting in me. I don't do anything out of the ordinary, or anything outrageous or unusual. I'm plain me! Now, I don't worry about what they print about me. I get asked some real strange questions, many far removed from me and the business, and I find myself in the middle of a subject I know damn all about. I now worry about being put on a spot with questions I can't answer, not about the journalists themselves!"

The new single has been a long time coming, she said, because her record company rejected her original title. "I wrote and recorded 'Tease Me' but no-one liked it! I was very proud of it—it even had a violin solo on it—but CBS felt they couldn't promote it. In the end I decided to hold it back. It would have been silly to have taken such a big chance, or gamble, so early in my career and what's the point of releasing a track no one could work. I was disappointed at first, sure, but eventually what the company said made sense, and as they have been so good to me I went along with them.... The fact that they cared enough to be interested in talking this over with me made me feel even more happy with our relationship. No, this isn't a publicity push for CBS either!"

Sid lives her life in an unaffected way and deplores it when artists change attitudes and personalities after enjoying a hit record. "I've thought a lot about how I would be should I become a star, and I can honestly say nothing about me will change. I've been in this business since I was a child (her father was a member of The Fantastics and she used to tour with the group) and I knew I was going to stay in it when I got older. We should always remember we're only as good as our last hit, and if more artists took care to bear that in mind they'd think twice about being pigs.... Just because some people sing that doesn't make them any superior a person from, say, Joe Bloggs who's a waiter. After all we all breathe, wash and go to the loo. It's people who make people different and turn ordinary people into stars for the public. Publicity and marketing try to prove artists are better than others. I'm doing a job of work which, I'm happy to say, I love, and I consider myself fortunate to have the chance to be extremely happy in my work. I don't like people being promoted into

CHINWAGGIN'

something they are not. My feet are on the ground, always have been and always will be, thanks to my Jewish nature and upbringing."

Sade is her CBS stable-mate and, I suppose, both careers can loosely be compared. Did Sid hold any jealousy over Sade's success? "Not at all" she retorted. "Quite the opposite in fact. Sade is a very beautiful woman with lots of talent, but I'm not in awe of her. I hope one day to be as successful as her. She's got a lot going for her and looks to go with it. I'll have to make do without her beauty though! She's also a star and conducts herself as one, but I imagine underneath she's an ordinary, normal girl who won't let the glitter of the business spoil her. I wouldn't mind a number three album though!"

I teased Sid by reminding her that CBS's press handout compared her to Diana Ross, amongst others—well? "*Diana*? No, never! I could never be like her and I don't think I'd want to. For example, I could never feel comfortable in long gowns singing the type of songs she does. Also, I'm not the kind of artist Las Vegas would fill houses with, but I'd like to think I could move into other types of music as I got older ensuring I could make a living from singing. I can't really remember being influenced by any particular artist, although I do enjoy most types of music."

I asked her about drug taking in the music business. "What drugs?"she interrupted . "I haven't seen any. If it comes to that, I don't use any.... In my younger days I used to smoke a bit.... I stick to my drink—occasionally I can't handle that either. Sex? Yes, I agree with that and enjoy it regularly. I know you're going to print something outrageous so I'm keeping quiet on that one." And she did!

I like Sid Haywoode. In fact, have done so since watching her début club performance when she looked so small and vulnerable wearing her over-sized straw hat and tightly fitting clothes. From that time we often crossed paths at some bar or other, both leaving on a higher plane than we'd arrived, but decidedly happier having put the world to rights.

Our next official chat (in April 1985) took place in the CBS offices in London's Soho Square, where the twenty-three year old was waiting to hear the chart position for 'Roses', which was currently sitting in the top eighty. She said she was used to having singles around this position, but to rise above that would make her day. At five-thirty she was told the single had shot to sixty-five. The girl was ecstatic! "Other artists worry about whether their singles get to number one" she gushed. "Me, I'm in a state about getting into the seventies! Come on Shar, let's celebrate. Let's have some tea!" *Tea*?

'Roses' is, I ventured, quite a departure musically. "I mixed the 12 inch single with my friend, Radford Quist. I've never done any mixing before in my life, but we needed a 12 inch. We took out bits here, pulled something else, and so on. The 12 inch is really an extended version of the 7 inch but it's not intended to be a heavy club track." Reviews were mixed; sometimes the single got slated. Did that bother her? Did it hell! "I don't get upset with bad reviews, never have. I'm fortunate that I'm able to take criticism easily, and I always listen to other people's opinions. I believe in what I do, and I want other people to like it too. I don't really care what they think about me."

Having been a recent support act for Imagination at Hammersmith Odeon, was she now hankering to tour the country? "As soon as I have a hit, I'll be out there. When I did support for Imagination the audience actually didn't stay in the bar as so often happens with support acts. They came out to see me. I performed to taped music because, to be honest, I couldn't afford a backing band. Sure, I could get some guys together to play with me, but I didn't want to do something so important half-heartedly. I did five numbers in all, including 'Single Handed', 'A Time Like This' and 'Roses', and thoroughly enjoyed myself. I used to watch my dad from stage side and I thought how on earth can he get on stage and sing in front of all those people? It takes a lot of guts. Now I'm doing it, and it doesn't bother me. Mind you, God knows what I'd have done with my life if I didn't sing."

When we next met in November, Sid was a new woman! Her public image was different: she'd smartened up to promote her new outing 'Getting Closer'. For our meeting, however, she was dressed as my friend—baggy T-shirt, boots and swept back hair, with an over-sized bulging bag at her side, her usual companion. Part of her new look, she said, was due to her new managers, as

CHINWAGGIN'

she told me: "I was getting neurotic and after 'Roses' I needed a fresh input from someone else. I owe a lot to my previous manager, and I wouldn't be here today without him. He worked his butt off for me. I was difficult then—very nervous—but he started me off and I've been very loyal. With this single it's a fresh start for me. My new managers look at things from a different perspective. They were looking for a female singer because they take care of groups like Fine Young Cannibals. So I'm the only female they've got and they've worked with me on the way I look now."

So, to this changed image. Let me tell you, Haywoode no longer gads about in nightclubs to all hours; instead she's now totally committed to her career. Her new gear, a smart black suit, was made by Princessa and a young, unknown designer, André created it. "I suppose you could say I'm being polished up again because I'm a bit tacky when left on my own. And that wretched hat has gone for good. Did I really go through all that?

"Talking of clothes, do you remember that red rubber dress I wore for 'Roses'? Well, it went down a storm, didn't it? But I've got to tell you, I was doing this TV spot in Paris and had to have several takes. I was wearing the rubber and, believe me, it was really so hot under all those studio lights. Well, when it came for the final take, water was running down my legs! Heaven knows what the cameraman thought I was doing!"

We started talking about the achievements of British acts, and the resurgence of home grown talent—long overdue, we felt. But she took over. "Everyone is entitled to have a bash. People thought I was naff when I first started, but everyone deserves that chance. We're all equal. However, British acts do need so much support, and there's no room for snobbishness and all that. It's the music that matters. I'm really pleased for our black acts because everyone is trying and having a go. The press and DJs have always been supportive of me—everyone I know has been rooting for me—so that can work for other people too. I thought instead of moaning about my singles only getting into the seventies, be grateful for that. And I think it's wrong the way all black artists are being bunched together. It's like saying all cars are the same. Everyone is different and they are doing their own job, doing their best. And I'm sure they'll have nasty things said about them, the same as I did, but that's all part of being in the public eye. You get over it."

I can now divulge the reason for her new, calm, positive presence—Buddhism. She elaborated: "Look, I was so neurotic and uptight all the time, and over the slightest thing too. I really needed to calm me down, to put me right. I went along to one of their meetings about three months ago. It was nothing heavy and I joined in the chanting. I now chant twice every day by myself and it's like a life force building up inside me. After two weeks I could feel it working for me. I only wish I had done it ages ago. I'm not now dependant on other things to make me happy, and I don't let certain things control me anymore. I'm positive and am enjoying my life now, more than ever. Oh, sure, some people think I'm mad, but I don't care. We don't worship a gold god, or pay any money... it's an avenue to improve your life. And I'm a Jew, so needless to say, my mother's not that pleased.

"Anyway, I won't keep on about it. You could say I've been a closet Buddhist all these years!"

During the next three years Sid and I fuelled our friendship; we partied, giggled, gossiped, and generally had a wicked, uninhibited music business life. By 1986, I'm delighted to say, she had enjoyed her first top ten single with the re-issued 'Roses' and had released her album 'Arrival'—the perfect vehicle to promote her music. She had also switched from CBS Records to Fresher Records; dumped her management and, after several attempts, packed up smoking. Oh yes, we had a lot of ground to cover here.

The parting from CBS Records seemed a good place to start. And, as usual, she was openly frank. "You knew my situation with them was a bit iffy. When I think about it, when I signed I didn't have a clue really. I knew nothing about the business and didn't even know what a manager did! During the time I spent there I really learnt so much and I think this, and the mistakes I made, will serve me well in the future. By the time I discovered they were used to having control of everything—well, it was getting a bit dodgy because they were coming up with songs I hated; and what I wanted to do, they didn't."

But the company released the 'Arrival' album on you, I started.

CHINWAGGIN'

"Yes, but it wasn't an album as such, like, a let's sit down and talk this through record. It was an album of singles and I was a bit disappointed to tell you the truth. I wanted to do something that was more representative of me."

After CBS, Sid was wary about joining another major company because she felt she needed more of a personal involvement that, perhaps, a more intimate set-up could give her. "I was offered a few things but I needed to find someone who thought the same way as I did, like, not giving me a song to do and me not having a say in it. There's no point in putting singles out for the sake of it, and I wanted to talk about doing what I wanted, like getting together with a team to form a strong base of people working with me. That's when the idea of an independent company came to mind."

Fresher Records seemed to fit the bill. "I actually met Brian Freshwater when CBS told me to go and find a manager, but he was getting involved with Jaki Graham and wanted to concentrate on her. I really liked him—he was straight, very respectful, but he couldn't handle me and Jaki at the same time." When Ms Graham split from Brian Freshwater, Sid filled the gap, adding "I couldn't step into her shoes. We're two completely different artists, and I'm sure Brian doesn't look at me as a replacement. He knows how different I am to Jaki. We discussed it when we started out. Like, I'm a bit more commercial and poppier, and he's never been down that road before. He's always been more on the soul side of things. And before you ask, no, I don't think I'll be duetting with David Grant either!"

'He's Got Magic' was her new release on Brian's label and she felt her future looked more positive, even though the photo on the single's sleeve was a year old. While Sid waited for a new deal to materialise, she wasn't idle. For instance, she started writing seriously, experimenting with ideas she'd nurtured for years. She also passed her driving test after three attempts. A traumatic time indeed. There were problems with her voice too, which necessitated an operation to remove nodules from her throat. "I'd been having a problem for quite a few years, and I'd been to see a throat specialist. He told me to rest a bit. But my voice kept cutting out, and after a day in the studio I couldn't speak at all. Then I was told I had nodules and had to have them off.

Thankfully, they weren't cancerous, and I'm fine now."

And, of course, Sid's dress sense hit our conversation. She was now pleased with her image, although it's not an aspect of her career that consumes her waking hours. "I dress the way I feel at a particular time. Everyone has an image and some people's are stronger than others. Image is part of success so I always make sure when I'm working that I look *presentable*, if that's the right word. I'm into hot pants right now, but in two months' time I'll change my mind and wear something else. So I'm the last person to talk about image! However, I now go on stage with two guys... I love all the glamour and theatrics of the stage. Sharon, you're talking to the girl who saw Michael Jackson four times! Oh, can you get me tickets for Diana Ross?"

And that's how we parted. Sid to the next interview, me to the cab rank. I thoroughly enjoyed our friendship while it lasted because we certainly gave the Eighties a good hammering.

I'm sorry to say I lost touch with her completely when I left London. However, I hope that whatever she's doing, she's happy with her life. Also, hope the gal is still having f-u-n!

NONA HENDRYX

Dateline: June 1984

The subdued voice I heard on the phone wasn't what I expected to hear from Nona Hendryx whose powerful, gritty vocal chords explode from the turntable, frightening me half to death. She laughed when I told her, and hastily explained that off-stage she is quiet and retiring, something which throws many people off balance. Quite so!

Ms Hendryx has just unleashed her second solo album 'The Art Of Defence' which is a belter—especially the current single 'I Sweat (Going Through The Motions)'—in support of which she was pounding the obligatory promotion trail.

Let's backtrack. When Labelle split up during 1977, Nona secured a solo deal with RCA Records. Her debut eponymous album was well received by critics and public alike. However, the experience of recording alone actually terrified the New Jersey-born lady, as she explained. "I had a lot of doubts, especially fears on stage. I'd never done it before and to confront an audience

NONA HENDRYX

without having Patti or Sarah to hide behind was nerve-wracking. Always being part of a group before really made me naïve. In the studios too, I had other people to back me up when I wanted to voice my opinion. Now I have to argue with the musicians alone. But I did gain a lot of experience with the girls, and gradually I became more comfortable both in the studio and in front of the public."

As a member of the mighty Labelle, Nona discovered her talent for composing but always with Patti in mind. "Writing for her was easier than writing for myself. I'm my own worst critic though, and I'm always looking for a new approach and new thoughts. After all, there are only so many things you can write about. I get influences mostly from day to day things. Even my fantasies are down to earth and part of life's routine!" she laughed. "And my insanity is now part of everyday life. You must be insane at least a few times a day y'know."

Lyrics and music usually form simultaneously—"It's difficult to write one without the other"—and her favourite inspirational moments, she said, included at the dinner table when out with friends, on a subway, a bus, but she laughingly recalled one instance of 'plane' inspiration. "With my portable recorder on my arm I was flying to my next gig when a melody chanced to come to mind. Not wanting to aggravate the other passengers by singing and humming into the small mike, I went to the toilet to record. When I got home and played back the tape all I heard was the sound of the plane's engines. So that was a whole wasted effort!"

Nona Hendryx was born and raised in a ghetto with four brothers and two sisters—"It was quite an undesirable place to live in"—and life was hard with such a large family. "Y'know, when I came across an only child in a family I really thought something was wrong with these people. It seemed strange to me. Now I know better!" The young girl had no desire to sing because her ambition was to be a teacher, as she recalled: "I was about to go to college when I became involved with some people in a singing group. I sang with them for fun and we got to sign to a record company. So, my ambition to teach got lost along the way, but I try to utilise those ideas in music. By the way, I wanted to teach ancient history—the Egyptians and Romans—anything that took place a long time ago, because it was different to my own

CHINWAGGIN'

time.

"The singing group comprised six, I think, and was called The DelCapris and we earned nine dollars for our first show; two dollars of which went to our manager! With me in the group was Sarah Dash, who was to join The Bluebells with Patti and Cindy Birdsong. And, through Sarah, I became part of the group too. I didn't know the others."

Always an enthusiastic and vital group member through the name changes to LaBelle, Nona believed this was her niche in life. But as quickly as she thought this, so she changed her mind—the group environment bored her. "It became something to do, although the forming of LaBelle was right and it happened at the right time. We were excited about our work but towards the end I felt I was asleep for at least a few years. I became lethargic and had no burning desire to continue. I don't like change normally, but it was inevitable that something had to happen."

Throughout her career so far, Nona's music has been decidedly rock-based, a throw-back to her influential years when she soaked up Chuck Berry, Elvis Presley, Pink Floyd, The Beatles and David Bowie, although she confided Jimi Hendrix influenced her the most. "I love rock music. This has been created from the streets, and is really different to what we've known. It's created out of a vacuum and paves the way for future music. Large record companies then sadly exploited it: it loses its street credibility thanks to these corporations, offices and accountants. And it all gets boring. The only answer is to return to square one again. With young people not having the money to spend on other things, they make and enjoy their own entertainment. It's real music, but at the end of the day it becomes big business."

Naturally, with her love of rock, Nona's stage act is hardly sedate, as she laughed: "I'm really a different person on stage— it's the music—and some people say I'm aggressive. But I hope my audiences experience something when I'm performing, get the same feeling as I do. It doesn't matter if I'm performing before an audience of twelve or twelve thousand, the thrill is still the same. And that's how I know whether what I'm doing works or not. I don't know where the energy comes from. It's just there. I need to perform to use up this excess energy. I've always had such a lot. That's why when I'm not performing I have to work out for at

NONA HENDRYX

least two hours a day. I think it's a controlled energy, a natural energy...and I need to be close to my audience for total satisfaction. With each song I perform, I try to adopt a different personality. Off-stage though I'm totally the opposite, and I can relate to each life equally well. I couldn't live with my onstage self off-stage—it would be exhausting!"

We eventually reached the topic of her new album, which was, of course, the purpose of this interview.

"'Art Of Defence'?" I asked. "Physically or mentally?"

"Well, defence is a moment to moment awareness, hiding from the truth, indifference and manipulation. The whole idea stemmed from the world's attitude to defence and the importance of owning guns, putting up walls and killing. It's also about people defending themselves emotionally. When we don't want to get hurt we put up defences. I'm totally against premeditated violence. For instance, when two countries sit down and decide to go to war on each other, instead of taking up arms and dropping bombs, the two countries should talk some more and find a solution by conversation.

"There are moments of course when people do lose control and I can't say whether that's right or wrong: it depends on the situation, although it's invariably a political situation and decision. Nothing that is wrong is justified. Children are being killed every day, and people are affected by people who don't care about them. It's always the innocent who suffer and no-one benefits. It's all power and money and someone else's opinion.

"Very gradually people will stand up and say 'we've had enough' but it is a situation I'm constantly aware of. It's part of my life, it's part of your life, and it affects me as badly as anyone else."

A year later we talked again: this time to promote her third RCA album 'The Heat' from which 'If Looks Could Kill (D.O.A.)' has been extracted as a single.

However, before Nona could say I word, I rudely gushed that 'I Need Love' was quite possibly the best track she had recorded. "That's the one I like above the others too," was her response. "Thank you. I can tell you too it will be the next single. We decided to go with that one because everyone chose it—like

CHINWAGGIN'

radio, people in the field, my record company and so on. People are used to me releasing rock singles and at the moment I've got to give them what they expect. At home, black radio stations don't really play songs, just grooves, dance grooves. So it was decided to go with 'If Looks Could Kill'".

The new album, she said, was overdue because of the need to find producers sympathetic to her recording needs. "I started writing for the album in October last year (1984) and went into the studio during March through to June. And, whereas my other albums have had a sort of central theme, this time I wanted to record a group of songs, with each having an individual feel. So, finding producers took up a lot of time. I started with Bernard Edwards but he was going off to do his own stuff, so I had to look around, dig into backgrounds and listen to other things."

Developing an interest in Arthur Baker's work, she decided to approach him, even though she didn't know him. The meeting paid off. "I knew he had a thousand other things to do, but all he listened to was 'I Need You' and said 'what a great song. This is the one I want to do with you'. Well, when he said that I was overjoyed and thought to myself, 'This guy's got taste!' One thing about Arthur is he likes his food and he likes his money. And he needs lots of money to keep him in food!"

Also, the track 'Rock This House' features The Rolling Stones' Keith Richards on guitar. In retrospect, this isn't that surprising as Nona is a long-standing friend, following an American tour with them. She wrote this song with the Stones in mind, but later decided she wanted to keep it. "I've always loved their music and when I started recording this track I thought I'd see if Keith would like to come and play on it. It was at the time he was waiting for his baby to be born in New York. So I sent him a tape of the song, and he said once the baby was born he'd love to do it. Getting someone like him was a real coup. Keith is such a nice guy and has a really kind heart. I'm very fond of him. Sure, he's had his problems, but he's still one of the finest guitarists ever.

"Anyway, once we'd done the session, this huge package arrived for me. It was two dozen red roses from him. They were fabulous. I kept one and pressed it after the others had died. And there was no money involved either, which makes a change. Someone else like him would have asked me for a lot, I can tell you."

NONA HENDRYX

The conversation switched to British music where Nona was quick to point out that this country was always willing to try something different. More so than America, she felt. However, there was a downside because thanks to dance music's explosion, too many records were being released. "It's up to the record companies to choose acts and records with care. If not, they themselves will blow the market. A&R departments should have a very good ear if they're to function properly, and should liaise with artists all the time. The trouble is that now much of the industry is run by accountants.

"It's imperative that good ears in the industry are left alone to do their jobs. Many acts are signed purely because the lead singer looks good, has skinny legs and wears tight pants. What about music? People have to be conscientious; that's the most important thing."

From music we turned to her love life. Nona still tight-lipped about her private life, did drop her guard, albeit slightly, when she said. "Yes, there is someone in my life but it's very private. It's an on and off affair, if you like, and has been going on for a long time now. No, I've no plans to settle down. I think I'd go crazy being with one person constantly. I have to travel a lot, which I do enjoy, and I like doing things on my own. I also like to get out and meet new people and form new friendships.

"Actually on thinking about it, I don't think I'm capable of settling down. I don't know about me going crazy with someone else around—I think I'd drive him crazy too! Even when I'm old and grey I won't be alone and even if I was I don't think I'd mind a great deal because I enjoy my own company. And I've got lots of friends. I need people all the time, but it's nice to go home alone."

Ms Hendryx continued to release albums of quality, including 'Female Trouble' and 'Skin Diver' during the Eighties. 'You Have To Cry Sometime' and 'Transformation' were Nineties releases. During 2001 the artist toured Europe and America and penned material for the Broadway musical 'Blue'. Later, she collaborated with Bootsy Collins to write the score for a further Broadway-bound show 'Ball', before authoring the classical

CHINWAGGIN'

score for Kathleen McGhee Anderson's play 'Oak And Ivy', and singing on the soundtrack of Denzel Washington's movie 'The Siege'. Nona went on to form her own label, Rhythmbank, to score the soundtrack for the movie 'On The One', and tour Europe with The Daughters Of Soul who included Lalah Hathaway and Joyce Kennedy.

BRENDA HOLLOWAY

Dateline: October 1987

It's a very lucky writer who gets to meet a lifelong hero or heroine. Well, that's exactly what happened to me when I met the voice behind the songs that, even today, are so treasured I'd fight nail and tooth to keep them in my collection. Our meeting took twenty years to arrange; yet time seemed so immaterial when, in the early morning hours, Brenda Holloway and I talked. And we later spent so much time together that I felt she'd been a long lost friend, and not simply a voice on Motown vinyl.

Historically, the beautiful Ms Holloway was Motown's first West Coast signing on the Tamla label in 1963/64. She was born in Atascadero, California, and her sister Patrice is also a noted singer/songwriter. Brenda's first single was the classic slice of emotion, 'Every Little Bit Hurts' in March 1964, followed by a string of masterpieces that included 'I'll Always Love You', 'When I'm Gone', 'You Can Cry On My Shoulder' and, of course, 'You've Made Me So Very Happy'—all of which encouraged the tears to flow and the soul to flutter.

CHINWAGGIN'

Brenda's voice was far superior to any at Motown and her talent outshone most, yet her stay was far from perfect. The support and encouragement showed to her turned sour, until the decline led to her leaving the company on impulse.

'Every Little Bit Hurts' was an American album release in 1964 and 'The Artistry Of Brenda Holloway', the only British issued album, in October 1968, where the front sleeve pictures the singer growing a violin on her chin! While the artwork may have been tacky, the contents certainly weren't.

This was the singer's first British visit, despite enjoying a cult following here since her début release. Unlike other Motown acts, Brenda knew her work was released here—"because as a writer as well as a singer, I knew where all my songs were going. I always dreamed of being in London but never thought I'd end up here." She explained that Mary Wilson had tracked her down for Ian Levine, who wanted to capture her on record once more for Motorcity Records. "I've never been asked to come here before and if I'd known it was this far, I doubt I'd have come," she laughed. "I really wanted to cut a gospel album, which I'll probably produce as well, but when I was asked to come over, I thought I'd give it a go. I did a day of praying about it because it was a crazy situation to be in. I didn't know where it was going to lead me. I was going to a country I'd never been to before, to meet a man I didn't know. But somehow it all felt comfortable to me. My daughters have never seen me as a professional woman, so they're waiting now to see if 'mom can crack it'. They sing like the Clark Sisters as it is, so I've got competition."

Brenda Jereal Holloway (so named after a comic strip character) has four children from an eighteen-year marriage to Alfred Davis. Theirs was a strange mixture of background and personalities that gelled, as she told me: "I came from entertainment and he was a preacher. I suppose you could say I was trying to save my soul by marrying him! He had also led a sheltered life; his parents were very strict, and I don't think my husband had experienced a woman before me, so we had a lot of growing to do together. It started out as a shaky marriage, but it did smooth out, even though I left him five times. I'm still finding out his strengths and trying to discard myself of my weaknesses, but I hope we can stay together."

BRENDA HOLLOWAY

The couple married in October 1969, following a first-love encounter, although Mrs Davis stressed, "Love was something I had to learn about. It's not an immediate feeling, it is something you acquire. I don't believe you can start a relationship with love; you have to have a mutual respect first. So, I learned to love my husband, and I believe he loves me."

When Brenda joined Motown, she believed the company's founder, Berry Gordy was attracted to her, not her voice. Recalling that time led to shrieks of laughter. "As I grew up I could see I had a good body developing, so I wanted to be noticed. I wanted to be attractive to men, even though my mother said Patrice was prettier. Berry treated me differently from the other artists, because he recognised I had a talent and he actually signed me up himself. Sure, he was a womaniser and he was suggestive in his approaches to me. I told him I either had to be his woman or I sing. After that he never really pushed me. But a lot of the girls there were jealous of me because I would stay with Gwen, Berry's sister, and his parents. Berry had told them whatever situation you're in, Brenda can mix."

After her initial American success, Motown had problems in promoting the singer known as Brenda Holloway because, she said, she was a black singer with a white voice—"A perfect pop voice. So, when the company marketed me they de-blacked me, so that nobody could tell I was black. When I went on tour with The Beatles, the kids asked for me to go out and meet them before the shows. When I did they said 'No, you're not her. Brenda's white'. Hah, I was born black on the outside and white on the inside, which is a complicated state to be in."

On another evening, we sat in the Chalk Farm Tavern's restaurant where the cuisine is extensive and mouth watering; Brenda wanted to try good old-fashioned fish and chips, because she'd heard so much about the dish from touring Americans. She also demolished a huge fish starter and closed with a specially mixed 'BH Cocktail' complete with spitting sparklers and floating pineapple slices bobbing about in her glass.

We left the restaurant to show her London by night, stopping briefly at the more historical landmarks, and surprising her by driving safely and quickly "...on such narrow streets." Arriving at her Bayswater apartment, which was now full of flowers from

CHINWAGGIN'

fans who had discovered her address, she glowed: "Everyone has been so kind to me. I never expected anything like this at all. So much love and warmth from people I don't know, yet who by some miracle have remembered me. I can't really take it in."

Returning to Motown and *that* rumour—where her stage act was too risqué for British audiences! "Yes, it's true" she giggled, flopping into a huge armchair as she kicked off her shoes. "I was very sexy at one time. My skin couldn't breathe unless it was exposed. My costumes were made for sex appeal, and definitely not for women. Actually, they wanted to pull me off stage and knock my teeth out because they thought I was flirting with their men. Tina Turner and her sex appeal influenced me, and I wanted to keep it. However, when I was touring the Southern States, trying to be like her, Smokey Robinson told me not to copy her again. He said, 'You have a voice. You don't need to act like her. You want the guys to hear you more than they need to see you.' So I tried to tone down my act after that, but it didn't work for me."

After a strong and regular flow of singles, the releases became spasmodic due, she said, to Motown's policy of building one act at a time. "When The Supremes were taking off, the company would pull in records so that The Supremes could go for a million sales. When I asked why my records were being pulled, Berry Gordy just kept telling me, 'Wait your time'. My records would go out of stock and stores were told to re-order. It was usually at a crucial point when the singles couldn't be got, so they weren't played and didn't go into the charts."

The singer didn't earn a fortune at Motown either, despite millions of dollars being earned by the company. If Brenda earned $1,000 a week, she received $500. "Motown would take money for recording costs, promotion and so on. Now my work is being re-released, I still get artists and writers' royalties. But to be honest, I do feel Motown really exploited and used me. I'll give you an example. They let The Supremes study my tapes and take songs from me. And, as I come from a different cultural background to the others—I liked to play the violin and 'cello—it made me appear strange to them."

She also experienced a strained relationship with Holland, Dozier and Holland, although they were later to come to her rescue, as she explained. "I didn't get on with Eddie (Holland) but I don't know why. I think he liked me as a woman though. I was treated like dirt because they didn't want me to be as big as the others. They tried to label me as a troublemaker because I was outspoken, and a lot of times I came across as being too masculine to men. When they couldn't handle me, they stayed away." Nonetheless, it was Eddie who stayed in her corner. "Yes, he got me out of my contract, employed me and paid me a salary for two years."

The decision to quit Motown was an accumulation of frustrations, some of which have been highlighted, but the way it happened wasn't planned. "I was actually in the middle of a recording session with Smokey when I ran away to Los Angeles. He later called me there and I told him I didn't want to be with Motown anymore. There was no future there for me, because there was a long span when I was doing nothing. And when Gladys Knight came in to record my songs, it was the straw that broke the camel's back. Motown didn't live up to its commitments."

So angry was Brenda, that she took Berry Gordy to court in 1969/70 to ascertain exactly what she earned. "I don't know where I got the courage to do that. My contract was up and Motown wanted to pick up the option. Success meant getting out of that contract in one piece. I was afraid to go to Detroit for five years after I left because I wanted to wait until Berry Gordy had forgotten me." The company's publicity people hurriedly released a statement prepared by her saying she had 'decided to quit for God.' It was partly true, as she told me: "I did sing in church and still do, but that wasn't the reason I left. I actually recorded a gospel album with Holland, Dozier and Holland but it never came out, which was a shame because they were good writers and the songs were excellent too."

And to the present time, the Brenda Holloway of the eighties. She's matured through marriage and time, of course, and like most mothers is at odds with her daughters who are growing into independent misses. She had also quit her receptionist's job to travel to London, but was quietly confident she'd easily secure another nine-to-fiver upon her return.

And me? I was delighted beyond words; my legend was

CHINWAGGIN'

everything I dared to hope for... and a lot more.

Ms Holloway has always been on Northern Soul's A-list; indeed, she performed on the circuit during 1995, the same year that she resumed public performances in America, notably with Benton Wood. She's also a guest on Motown revues. During 1999 Brenda recorded 'It's A Woman's World' for the revived Volt label, which, apart from a 1980 gospel album, was her first American release in nearly 33 years! In 2004, Sanctuary Records released David Nathan's compilation 'The Sisters Of Soul' on which Brenda's contribution is 'Some Quiet Place'.

In 2005, Brenda (with Kim Weston and Frances Nero) performed at a Motown Legends weekender at Great Yarmouth. The photo of Ms Holloway was taken by Paul Nixon during one of her performances.

CISSY HOUSTON

Dateline: February 1987

With all the acclaim showered on her daughter, Whitney, Mrs Houston has taken a back seat to plough her experience and support into the young singer who, in ten years time, could well be classed as the new Diana Ross.

Despite the fact that Whitney Houston has taken the pop world by storm with a stunning debut album and has performed to sell-out audiences across the world, the proof of longevity is in the ability to sustain and progress on record.

However, for a change, this is not about Whitney, but the power behind the throne—her mother—Cissy Houston, a singer I've idolised since the Sweet Inspirations. She doesn't merely have a good voice; she's gifted with rich, creamy smooth and silky vocals that can rise to mountainous pitches. Some of her recorded performances are spine-chilling and take your breath away: her talent has been a significant force in our music for more years than we—and probably she—would care to remember.

CHINWAGGIN'

During 1978 Mrs Houston was classed as a legend with the release of her eponymous Private Stock album. Blues & Soul's John Abbey wrote: "Her past has been steeped in honours, she is my type of singer...her high pitched wailing is frequently heard above all others as lead background singer with many of our music's greats."

The last album in my collection is EMI's 'Step Aside For A Lady', produced by Michael Zager circa 1980. An uninspiring release when compared to her previous couple—'Think It Over' (from which the title—a heavy dance track—was lifted for single release) and 'Cissy Houston'. Nonetheless, she was, and still is when time allows, a hard-core gospel singer, born and raised in music.

Prior to forming the Sweet Inspirations, often cited as among the world's finest vocalists, Cissy was a session singer in her own right, adding her vocals to the works of Wilson Pickett and Solomon Burke, amongst others. Before she was much older, her voice was heard alongside the likes of Esther Phillips, Maxine Brown, Chuck Jackson, Nina Simone, Bette Midler, Elvis Presley (who insisted she and her Inspirations support him on his 1968 comeback tour), Brook Benton and Dusty Springfield (on her Atlantic Records' sessions).

Cissy also worked closely with her dear friend Aretha Franklin on her 'return' album 'Jump To It' on the tracks '(It's Just) Your Love', 'If She Don't Want Your Lovin'', 'Just My Daydream' and the album's title. In her sleeve notes, Aretha wrote her thanks for "Cissy Houston's sweetest touches," and it's reputed she also gave Cissy the following advice: "Pick a song for an album or for a performance because you like it and believe in it, and it will come across to the listening public regardless of whether it's rock, blues or gospel."

With the Sweet Inspirations (so named by Atlantic's Jerry Wexler), Mrs Houston toured the world and enjoyed terrific hits like 'Sweets For My Sweet', 'Sweet Inspiration' and 'Reach Out For Me'. At one time the group comprised Cissy's nieces Dee Dee and Dionne Warwick, and Judy Clay, who were also integral members of the famous Drinkard Singers—New Jersey's finest gospel outfit. When the Sweets disbanded and before Cissy signed to Private Stock, she recorded for Commonwealth United

CISSY HOUSTON

Records during the seventies. That album 'Presenting Cissy Houston' was issued here on Major Minor Records. Producers Charles Koppelman and Don Rubin signed her to Commonwealth where her brilliant 'He/I Believe' was extracted as the first single. It was a powerhouse of sound, which prompted Johnny Carson to book her on his *Tonight* TV show. One performance led to another—Cissy Houston was in demand. "Cissy's unique vocal presentation is derived from her awareness of what an audience wants," Charles Koppelman explained. "Gospel singers improvise most of the time and it is this ability which makes her a most unique talent."

Also included on this extraordinary album is a blinding version of 'I Just Don't Know What To Do With Myself'; a deep throated 'Be My Baby,' and extra special Cissy interpretations of 'Didn't We?', 'The Long And Winding Road' and 'When Something Is Wrong With My Baby'. Her daughter could well take note of these tracks—listen and learn girl! Moving to Janus Records, Cissy recorded the original version of 'Midnight Train To Georgia', which gave Gladys Knight and the Pips a monster hit single. "My previous experiences with record companies left me discouraged and disappointed," Cissy said. "After the Janus experience, I decided just to concentrate on doing background sessions and commercials."

So in demand was she, that her voice was the most heard on American television and radio, and it was heard on British TV over a Texas oil commercial. She preferred this avenue because: "There was so much hassle attached to being on the road and you don't end up making that much money after you've paid your musicians and everyone else. And when you have records out, you do have to go on the road, so I decided to shelve that side of my career for the time being."

However, that phase of her career was to end when Michael Zager contacted her to record an album with him. Cissy takes up the story: "I needed something stable, that would work out. So we met with Larry Uttall (of Private Stock Records) and it seemed that all the things I wanted I could get there, so we started picking material."

During 1976, the singles 'Love Is Something That Leads You' followed by 'Tomorrow' were issued. But these were, many felt, overshadowed by 'Your Song' and 'Make It Easy On Yourself', both featuring her own choir. "This was the first time I've ever worked with sixty people in the studio at the same time. The choir originally had fifteen members, and then we grew and grew. We cover all age groups, and it takes a lot of work because you're really cultivating voices, lay voices, people who haven't been in the business, and who don't necessarily read or write music."

Coupled with this, Cissy is also the Minister of Music at her local church in Newark—"But that doesn't mean I'm a preacher or that I've been ordained. It means I'm in charge of the music there." And she helps potential singers with her private tuition. "I used to give lessons way back before 1967 when the Sweet Inspirations officially came into being. But then things just got too busy. I tried to teach things like breathing, which is extremely important and is something that an amazing number of people don't even think about. Then, delivery, and above all the 'feel' of things. It's all about being able to convey what you feel through your voice. Practicing constantly is the only answer, after all, your voice is another muscle and if it isn't used properly, it won't work."

The other Private Stock album, 'Think It Over', was, as far as I know, the first to officially recognise Whitney as a backing vocalist on most of the tracks including the set's title. Another terrific compilation produced by Zager, including 'Warning—Danger', 'Somebody Should Have Told Me' and 'I Won't Be The One'.

Naturally, Cissy chooses her repertoire with extreme care, as she commented: "I won't do any material that I can't feel, and there's never been a time when I've had to. Sure, there are some songs I like better than others, but I've never cut anything I didn't like. I have to be true to myself and I must relate to the song, which is why lyrics are so important to me. I do want success for myself but I'm not willing to compromise or sell out my talent to get it."

Nowadays, she works regularly with her choir and continues to work tirelessly with Whitney, who acknowledges her mother as a guiding force in her career. Indeed, on her debut album, Cissy can clearly be heard on 'How Will I Know', while Whitney wrote in the sleeve notes—"Mommy, I love you with all my heart. You

CISSY HOUSTON

know how it began for me and for many others too. But I had you all to myself and got the best of all of you."

Whitney Houston could not have a finer act to follow; yet it will be years before she'll possess the magic of her mother's talent. However, with the renewed interest in the Houston family, perhaps Cissy will be persuaded to record once more. When that day arrives, Whitney could well realise what competition is really all about!

Mrs Houston appears to have devoted her life to Whitney, whose career reached unprecedented heights as a singer, performer and actress. However, the world of drugs grabbed her from the spotlight, which undoubtedly devastated Cissy beyond words. So much talent is now dormant while Whitney fights her demons. We mourn that loss. In 1997 Cissy won a Grammy Award for her gospel album 'Face To Face', and a year later she published 'How Sweet The Sound: My Life With God And Gospel' to rave reviews.

THELMA HOUSTON
Dateline: April 1977

It was early evening when Thelma Houston and I sat in London's Serpentine Bar, hovering over vodka and tonics, brandy and cokes, for an interview that should rightly have been conducted in her hotel room. However, upon my arrival the singer was desperate for a change of scenery, so we did what any girls on the loose would do—we hailed a taxi to the nearest bar to celebrate the recent success of 'Don't Leave Me This Way', a top twenty British hit earlier this year.

Her new album 'Any Way You Like It' was her second for Motown—the first being 'Thelma Houston' in 1972, one of the first to be released on the newly formed American label, Mowest. It was British released in 1973. Prior to these, she recorded the critically acclaimed 'Sunshower' album for ABC/Dunhill under

THELMA HOUSTON

the guidance of Jimmy Webb, which Motown had now purchased for future release.

In the singer's own words, here's a brief resumé of her career so far. "I was singing around Long Beach, California—must have been in '67. I was booking myself in and was totally ignorant of the music industry. Mind you, I had a regular job singing at the weekends. Then I met Marc Gordon, somewhen in '69. He became my manager and recommended I sign with ABC, which I did. I met Jimmy Webb and we did the album together. ABC said it was going to be a hit. When it wasn't I was really disappointed.

"Anyway, ABC and I split on friendly terms and I told Marc that I wanted to go to Motown. But he didn't like the idea. Y'know, it's not often that I make major decisions; when I do I've thought about the situation very carefully and weighed up the fors and againsts. I always wanted to go to Motown...even my instincts told me it was the place to go. So I did, and I've never regretted it." However, on joining the Motown ranks, Thelma and manager parted company.

"I'm very happy with Motown" she offered, "They are good to me and have taken a genuine interest in me. If I want to do anything, I ask, and they don't make me do anything I don't really want to do. They haven't pushed me into the studio, for instance, cos they know I'll go when I'm ready. I wanted to go to acting lessons, and Motown paid for me to do that. I also wanted to do an album in '75 for Sheffield Lab and they let me. The album was called 'I've Got The Music In Me' and I honestly loved doing it."

Asking about the delay between her recordings, she replied. "Why put out another album until you've got something right. In '72 I did the 'Thelma Houston' album for Mowest, and of course there was 'No-one's Gonna Be A Fool Forever'. That was a turntable hit...and I was more than pleased about that. I was also nominated for a Grammy with 'You've Been Doing Wrong For So Long' in the best R&B female performance category—Aretha Franklin won it. There's been several singles released in the States, the last of which was the theme for the movie 'Norman...Is That You'. So I've been pretty busy."

Like many artists at this time, Thelma had ventured into the disco market, but not from personal choice. "I've been in this business for a while, and I do have other things in my catalogue. I can, and have, released other things and haven't followed a particular trend. So, no, it wasn't my intention to become involved in discos. I feel that in America particularly, you're only as good as your last hit record. Unless your name is kept in the public eye, people tend to forget...and as I haven't been around for a while, I guess everyone thought it a great surprise to find me with a hit single! I haven't had this feeling from Britain, and Australia, or Japan, or even other parts of Europe as my admirers are all so faithful. They still talk about 'Sunshower' after all this time—it's so amazing. If you think back, the latest single isn't the first time I've aimed at the disco market... 'Jumpin' Jack Flash' was." Point taken.

Not many people are aware, but Thelma cut the original 'Do You Know Where You're Going To', which Diana Ross recorded as the theme track to her second movie *'Mahogany'*. I purloined a copy just recently and was thrilled to hear her different interpretation. Naturally, I was curious to discover how she found herself in the position of demo-ing for Ms Ross. It seems the song's composer/producer, Michael Masser approached Thelma to record it. "So we did with just the basic background. It was never finished off properly and I guess was hidden away. Certainly it was never issued in the States. Then *'Mahogany'* was in the works and Masser was asked to write the score. He resurrected the song for the title track, and as Diana was the star of the movie, it was only natural that she would sing it. I didn't feel denied. Let's put it this way: if I was the star (a word she hates) of a movie, I wouldn't expect someone else to sing the credit. I'd want to do it for myself."

Anyway, she had movie plans of her own: the Bessie Smith biography. At this juncture, the director was still undecided, but, she said, it was to be a joint project between Motown and Columbia. "I'm not actually playing Bessie Smith—I am Bessie Smith. Acting is something I always wanted to do. To me I felt that acting and singing went together. That is until I started acting lessons and found out that the two were actually totally unrelated. With the film it's my intention to make more people knowledgeable about Bessie. Already people are saying to me 'what makes you think you're qualified to do this?' Well, I learned very early in life, regardless of how or what your intentions are, that someone's not going to be in agreement. I'm going to do my best in this film, that's all I can do.

"That reminds me...I was in high school, 10th grade, and these two girls just didn't like me. I hadn't done anything to them and was hurt 'cos they didn't actually like me. I honestly didn't know why they felt this way. Funny I should remember that...in fact, I've never told anyone that before..."

It had recently been announced that Thelma was involved in a recording project with Jerry Butler. This was possibly another attempt by Motown to recapture the magic of Marvin Gaye and Tammi Terrell, or indeed Marvin and Diana Ross on record. Jerry Butler was quoted as being an enthusiastic partner, while Thelma took on a more idealistic view. "It's coming along well, but we're taking a long time because it's a case of, one day we'll say we'll do something in the studio and be pleased with it at the end of the day. We'd then take the tapes home. Come next day we'd do it over again! I suppose one of the reasons is that I'm a different person each day. No matter what, we have to get it finished for release in a couple of months. Incidentally, before you ask, it was Berry Gordy's idea to do the album." ('Thelma & Jerry'—1977; 'Two On One'—1978)

As the drinks mellowed us, Thelma confided she had had another career upon which she rarely commented, because she was a social worker who was unable to stay in one job for long. When she'd finished telling me about it, I could see what she meant. "My first job was in a hospital as a nurse's aide, emptying bedpans, changing beds, all that kind of thing. Then I went to another hospital. I think I was eighteen and worked on an 11-7 shift at night. Actually, I never worked in a job long enough to get a vacation. I just got kinda restless and lost interest. I've worked with geriatric patients, worked as a telephone operator, then at a school for physically handicapped children, in physical and occupational therapy. The longest I've stayed in a job is six months. Dreadful isn't it?"

Twice divorced, Thelma has two children: a son aged twelve, a daughter, fifteen, and they both live with her. "We live in Los Angeles in a tiny apartment, have done for about four years. It's nothing luxurious but it's cosy, suits us and is home. I love it; in

CHINWAGGIN'

fact, I'm completely domesticated but I also enjoy going out and having fun. Don't think I'll marry again though. One of my biggest weakness.....I love clothes, especially woollen ones. My apartment is bursting with them. Although I'm a Taurean, I'm not typical of the sign as really I'm not that materialistic. Don't go out to buy expensive things so that I can look at them. People are far more important to me."

The conversation abruptly ended as our taxi arrived. On reaching the hotel, we were reprimanded by Motown's publicity manager for playing hookey. Apparently, he'd been waiting there for most of the evening to talk to Thelma. Ooops!

We next met in January 1989 at The Norfolk Hotel, Kensington, when Ms Houston was part-way through an exhausting but successful club tour. On this, her rare spare afternoon, we sipped coffee and talked. She was as I remembered—bubbly, vivacious and looking magnificent. She'd also shed weight and was deliriously excited about her new single 'Lean On Me' released by WEA Records. "The single is from the film 'Lean On Me' due out in March. It's about a high school principal, a black man, Joe Clark, and based on a real life situation. He goes to this school on the East Coast, New Jersey I believe, which is overrun by gangs. Joe goes in, he's a strict disciplinarian, and turns the situation around with the kids' help...and 'Lean On Me' is going to be the first single. I'm singing it with Marvin Winans. I know this is probably the third time round for the song but we've done it as a ballad because we wanted the lyrics, which are very meaningful, to be heard."

After hearing the song through her personal stereo, I was stunned at Thelma's vocal adaptation of the classic—she's turned it into a gospel/R&B song, which soars and falls as she pours emotion into the lyrics. Marvin's vocals were, she said, to be added when she returned to America. She came to record the track through Richard Perry with whom she'd been working for about two years, following a deal with his Planet Records set-up. This move followed deals with RCA then MCA, where she enjoyed the hit 'You Used To Hold Me So Tight' produced by Jimmy Jam and Terry Lewis.

Thelma explained the sequence of events. "Following the single

THELMA HOUSTON

I was kicked off the MCA label—you can put that in—maybe not kicked off as such, but they told me they couldn't use my services anymore. This business is so weird, politics and all that get involved. If this person signs you to a label, and this person is no longer there, then you're kinda like excess baggage to the person coming in. They already have their ideas about what they're gonna do with the label. So I was stuck in the middle OK? And for whatever reason—I was never given a satisfactory explanation—they didn't want me on the label.

"At this time the record industry was changing considerably, and people were more interested in images, and not what you sound like. The fact that it had been proven that I could sell records didn't seem to matter because I hadn't sold on MCA. It didn't matter that there was nobody there to promote me! Even though I thought I did well with 'You Used To Hold Me So Tight'—MCA followed it up with one more song—then nothing else was done after that. I did a video, the whole thing, so it's a great puzzle to me."

This set-back deterred her not in the slightest, she smiled. "Sure I've been out there but maybe not as successfully as with 'Don't Leave Me This Way' in 1977. Everybody can relate to that song. People still come to me to say it made a great change in their lives—gay guys tell me they came out of the closet or whatever, straight people told me they decided to marry. I was really amazed because you never know the effect of the songs you're recording. You just think you're going in and singing, and you hope it'll sell and that it's good. Someone even requested it to be played at their funeral! Isn't that something!"

'Don't Leave Me This Way' opened other avenues for the singer although she made little money from it—"Let's say I never received a lot of royalties"—and it's follow-up title bombed by comparison. This time, though, Thelma knew why. "At the time that song happened I was changing labels and that had an effect. 'I'm Here Again' was manufactured to be the same as 'Don't Leave Me This Way'. I didn't really like it but I felt obligated to do it. Then after that was 'Saturday Night, Sunday Morning' which I thought was a far better song. You think about things like this, try to analyse and figure out why something happens, but in the end you decide no one thing can be blamed."

CHINWAGGIN'

Before Thelma met Richard Perry at a book signing party for Mamas & Papas' Michelle Phillips, who was promoting her 'California Dreaming' book, she had spent her time composing and acting. "When you don't have a record deal and you're not out there for awhile, you begin to think maybe I should do something else," she told me. "I have a good friend Bunny Hall, and she's a songwriter who has established herself over a period of time by writing for Stacy Lattisaw. She also wrote 'I've Got A New Attitude' for Patti LaBelle, whom I've known since her Bluebelle days. And she's been encouraging me to write for years, but I've always shied away because of how you have to discipline yourself. I couldn't put up with the frustration either. So I felt this time I'd better get over that and try.

"One of the songs I worked on with Bunny and her brother Jeff—who I might add is up for Record of the Year for co-writing and producing Brenda Russell's 'Piano In The Dark'—was 'Be Yourself'. Richard Perry really liked this one and the others we'd done, but somehow we never got round to recording them. So I sent 'Be Yourself' to Patti. She liked the song and I ended up doing background on it. Now, I've just found out that not only is it going to be included on her new album, but is the title track. Yeah! Then, when Richard said the time was right to record it on me, I had to tell him it was too late, Patti had already cut it. Usually when you write your own songs people expect you to record them. However, if you write something, and somebody, like an established artist, chooses to do it, then that's even bigger to me because that's going to establish me as a composer.

"I also restore furniture and design clothes. Know anyone I can be of use to?!"

When we last met twelve years ago, Ms Houston was engaged in acting classes. It came to nothing. Undeterred, she decided to try a second time, but was unprepared for the pitfalls, as she explained. "When you're acting and known as a singer, they say well, fine, she's a singer but can she do stand up lines. You also have to be available to go out and meet the casting people, and you have to get known for having a bit of hunger in your eyes. No, not the casting couch! ....Y'know, that's never happened to me and it got me thinking...what's wrong with me? Seriously, when you stop to think about it, I wouldn't want to sleep myself to the top. You never want to do that because it's not a very stable basis. When that goes, everything else falls into a shambles.

"Anyway, I appeared in *'Cagney & Lacy's Christmas Special'*, *'Simon & Simon'*, and I've done some after school specials. The most recent thing I did was appear in my first feature film *'And God Created Women'*, which was originally done with Brigitte Bardot, with Roger Vadim directing. He did a remake of that in the States with Rebecca De Mornay. She's what they call bankable."

How did Ms Houston rate her own acting abilities? "Mm, yes, I think I'm a good actress, because any good singer—and that's not bragging, please don't think that—can interpret a song. When I sing something I try to get people not only to listen but to believe what I'm singing, because I'm telling a story. From the acting viewpoint, it's the same thing, except you don't have the luxury of music so that if you forget your lines, you can't hum your way through and make up the words. I've done that so many times. I've even made up a whole song by adlibbing, and then thinking where did that lot come from!"

Recording and filming has another similarity. In a studio a singer can go through the same verse at least fifty times before the producer is satisfied. Well, it's the same with movies. Thelma sighed, then laughed. "You have to do things from different view points. The camera looking at you, then the person you're talking to, from the side, from the up and down, from under your skirt. I mean everything—and sometimes it's only for a five second shot which can end up on the cutting room floor! Sometimes I've had to do lines when the person isn't even there. But I don't care how much you study, actually doing it is the best way to learn."

Although the lady is interested in meaty, satisfying roles, there's one thing, she stressed, that she would never do—and that's strip for the camera. "No! I would not! Not even if the part called for it. No, no! Not even if I had the most beautiful and gorgeous body in the world, which I don't. I can say this because I know what my body looks like. Not even for a million dollars, let me tell you. So, if you ever see my head on a naked body, you know it's not mine!"

Let's move on. In 1977 Thelma was married for the second time. Now she's on her third husband. "See, what happens? If I

CHINWAGGIN'

don't work I get married. But I'm still good friends with all my husbands. I had New Year's Eve dinner with my children's father. I had them when I was seventeen, so I was more or less growing up with them. My daughter works at an elementary school and she's going into counselling. And my son works at a hospital in the X-Ray department, but he's also a drummer. My daughter sings as well, she's more into gospel. Sometimes she does back-up on my records and at my shows. I used to really push her, but my mother suggested that I stop because she said she didn't like it all that much. My daughter felt I was really going too far. But, when I see talent, I like to see people doing something. She'd seen the ropes of the business through me and I guess that put her off."

Obviously, mother had to leave her offspring to tour, although, Thelma insisted, she never left them for longer than six weeks at a time. "There was one exception to that though, when I toured with Teddy Pendergrass and I think we were out for eight weeks. But I was always home to do the PTA, make the cookies, pick them up from school, take my son to his football practice, things like that. And when I was out on the road, my mother was there. So I did see my children growing up, and I was the one who did the disciplinary things and so on."

Thinking back, there were pangs of guilt, not because she was away from the family, but because most parents experience them at some time or another. Said she. "You always think 'I didn't do enough'. There was a lot of guilt but as my children have grown up they're saying things to me, like, how they felt about it, and how they didn't feel they were neglected. So that's the main thing. I had to work, but when you have children, something happens that you automatically get guilty! And that goes along somehow with being a parent.

"I'll tell you this...the best way to make money is to make something to sell to children. Manufacturers know parents get guilty. They all are, from the minute their child is born. Mind you, I spent a lot of time by myself as a child. There's eight years difference between me and my sisters. My mother used to say 'my Louise (Thelma's middle name) isn't like other kinds. She can be trusted. I don't have to worry about her starting fires, doing this and doing that. I guess she made me feel like a grown up and you don't do something that's gonna make you look bad. So you have to get along with yourself, except she doesn't know about the times I slipped away. I was a sneaker, she didn't know that! I'd go and find the kids, or went to the cinema."

Finally, we talked about her new slim-line figure, her healthy, fresh complexion—the result of strict diets and back-breaking exercises I reckoned. But not really, as she pointed out. "To lose weight wasn't my objective because, even though people have been telling me for years I should drop a few pounds, I always felt I shouldn't have to be judged on what I looked like. I became more health conscious really, and started working out, running—I ran in marathons and things like that, so it was the result of that. Now I enjoy hiking for pleasure.

"I love food, y'see, and still eat when I want to. I'm not about to give that up. I have much more energy on stage now; I'm not huffing and puffing anymore. I won't talk about age, but when I was seventeen the thought of running in a marathon...well, pleeease! Running? I wouldn't even think of walking anywhere!"

Ms Houston continues to tour; from Las Vegas to Chile, Malaysia and Singapore, over to Australia, Spain and Japan, where she enjoys a loyal fan base. She's also forged herself an acting career on television. Her most distinguished album of the Eighties, 'Qualifying Heat', was co-produced by Jimmy Jam and Terry Lewis. Working as an elected governor of NARAS (National Academy Of Recording Arts And Sciences), Thelma explored avenues to interest new musicians, before working on her one-woman show.

FREDDIE JACKSON
Dateline July 1988

Yep, I've at last met the celebrated and successful singer and what a delight it was.

Freddie Jackson popped into London to perform at the Nelson Mandela birthday celebrations at Wembley. He performed in a soul set with Ashford & Simpson, Natalie Cole and Al Green; so short was this

FREDDIE JACKSON

section that one blink and it was over! This was the first subject we tackled in this off-beat interview. "I believe in justice," said Freddie. "I have my freedom to go where I want and believe everyone else should also. Apartheid is a sad and bad thing. I think it's horrible that children are growing up to hate and kill. Nelson Mandella should be freed, although it will probably mean more bloodshed initially.

"I just wish Apartheid wasn't there. This birthday celebration is important to me, and through songs I'm sharing my feelings. We're all living on borrowed time, and we should try to make it a better world with that time. We're told to believe what we're told but there has to be something else going on. I know what I've been presented with—it's war, killing people and so on. Nobody in this world has the right to take lives. We're not allowed to even take our own lives, so why should we take others? There's a justice system but who does it stand for? I don't know.

"My purpose for coming to London to perform is not for the free airtime, nor to sing my new single. It's my way of saying 'thank you' and offering my support. To stand with others to show the world we are against the appalling South African situation. There's a statement that needs to be made, and we're doing it. I'm actually mid-way through rehearsals with my band in the States and coming here will drastically put back my schedules...but...so what! Anyway, these are my reasons for doing this. There's a time and place for everything and now is the time, and all the artists are here for the same reason. So, this is not something I agreed to do for the sake of it: it's worthwhile and very important.

"I can't speak for the other artists but I hope the concert will show the people in South Africa that they're loved and being thought of, and there are prayers being sent to them. The South Africa situation could happen anywhere...in New York, anywhere. And as a lot of people listen to artists, like, I have almost two million fans out there and I'd like to think that if they know I'm interested in South Africa, it might make them think, and do something about it."

Mr Jackson also used this visit to talk about his new album 'Don't Let Love Slip Away' which, like his past projects—'Rock Me Tonight' and 'Just Like The First Time'—is crammed with

CHINWAGGIN'

sensitive lyrics, sweeping, lilting music and the seductive Jackson voice. The first single out is the luscious 'Nice And Slow', where Najee contributes his stunning sax playing, as indeed he does on another title 'Don't Let Love Slip Away'. However, equally impressive are 'One Heart Too Many' and 'Hey Lover' with my (and his) favourite being 'Special Lady'. "I wrote that with Paul Laurence ten years ago, and he bought it to my attention for this album. The original title was 'Helluva Lady' but we felt it was a bit risqué, so we kept it clean and changed the title."

Unlike most of his contemporaries, Freddie refuses to use computers in the studio. "Call me old fashioned if you like but I'm a graduate of Julliard. In junior high school I played the violin. This is my music and it makes me feel really proud. Actually, it took four months to record this new album because I was trying to find the correct type of music. So I relied on my tested formula of the music I enjoy, which people will enjoy."

He based this on his audiences—and he's been before more than a few just recently. Last year he spent five months performing a staggering 135 shows. "Now I feel I know what my audiences want to hear and this time I hope I've given them what they want."

One of Freddie's keys to success is the way he plans his music with ladies in mind. He smiled when he said this, flashing that cheeky grin. "I think about that lady who's just over a relationship and needs to be comforted, or the lady who's just got married, or to tell someone she's special to me. If her guy can't tell her certain things like how he feels, I can tell her on his behalf, through my music. Many guys have, in fact, thanked me for my albums so I guess you could say I'm part of several love affairs. Women brought along their babies to my shows when I was promoting 'Rock Me Tonight', so I must be doing something right!"

Judging from his lyrics, one could be forgiven for thinking that Freddie was the most jilted guy in town. Not so, but he admits to having had his heart broken more than twice. As a rule though, when he's writing, Freddie puts himself in somebody else's place, to feel different emotions and to tackle those emotions from another angle. "A lot of women come into my life because they feel I'm begging for them and for love in my records. She'll say

FREDDIE JACKSON

she knows me and she's just the woman for me, and so on...just because she heard a particular song. I try and explain to her how I came to write that song and that it didn't necessarily reflect on a personal situation."

Being in love did present Freddie with some major problems, as he admitted. "In the first year I was going on stage at night and my mind was on the other side of town. Why am I here? I kept asking myself. When I perform I have to give my all, and I felt like I was cheating my audiences because I wasn't committing myself totally and I don't think my audiences deserve anything less than one hundred per cent. So I had to take myself aside and talk seriously to me about combining personal and professional lives."

His laid back, soothing music is, he said, a direct reflection of his own personality and nature. He rarely raises his voice or gets riled and it's this placid nature that stands him in good stead when embarking upon a string of gruelling one-nighters or facing stressful sessions when a recording just won't flow the way it should.

At home in his seventeen acre estate in Poconos, on the outskirts of Pennsylvania, Mr Jackson prefers a quiet atmosphere and values his seclusion. His little des-res, has four bedrooms and bathrooms, pool room, den, big kitchen (because he loves to cook) and so on. The grounds include a beautiful lake inhabited by a variety of ducks; a creek that runs at the back of the house; deer that walk on his porch; stables for his two horses, and a guest house with three bedrooms. "I am a very personal person, and I don't go crazy if I don't see people every day. I can be alone and be totally happy. I also like to make my own decisions but, should I decide unwisely, I'm guided by my managers and Hush Productions. Should there be a dispute somehow they know Freddie Jackson wants it done his way. I'm very blessed to have people who care about me."

Hush Productions also have a hand in choosing his material, as he told me. "They are concerned about what I sing because they don't want to be embarrassed about what I do. They know music and they also know good music, but I choose the singles because I have the better musical ear for me. Sure, we scream and yell in heated arguments, don't talk for several days, that kind of thing, but I say 'I have to perform these songs and if I don't feel good about a song, I can't expect anyone to like them either. Well, I have a bit of a bossy side then. If I believe strongly in an idea, well, I want to go with it. I'm the type of person that if I feel that strongly about something it has to happen. I can be a bit aggressive but certainly not egotistical, that's not in my nature. At the end of the day, I have to put into perspective all the things that make me successful. It isn't just me, it's the corporation that makes it work. If I was arrogant it wouldn't work, and that was how I came into this business in the first place."

Born and raised in Harlem, Freddie Jackson, an ex-word processor operator and member of several groups including Mystic Merlin, became a session singer for Melba Moore, amongst others. Through his school friend Paul Laurence, Freddie was introduced to Ms Moore and she persuaded her management company, Hush Productions, to sign him. That led to Capitol Records securing him.

In the past two years his success has been staggering—two multi-platinum albums and a run of number one singles in America including 'A Little Bit More', his duet with Melba. "There are millions of things I could say about Melba but 'I love her' should cover them all. She taught me many things. It takes an artist many years to grasp all the aspects of this business and I was very fortunate to have someone like her to help me, to help polish me up. She's a friend, there's nothing in the world I wouldn't do for her. She calls me her baby, and she'll always stand in my defence. I'll be forever grateful. Melba is a strong lady, she knows what she wants; she's articulate, and I'm glad to have the chance now to let people know what she's done for me.

"One of the most important things she instilled in me was that you're never too big to give an autograph, because the people who're asking you helped to put you where you are. And I'll always remember that."

In November 1988 we met again and I really wanted to start the interview saying I shared an intimate candlelit dinner in a London restaurant's cosy corner. But I won't lie. However, I did dine with Freddie Jackson but it was in broad daylight...lunchtime, and the restaurant was packed!

FREDDIE JACKSON

He was in town following a sell-out tour of Japan to help promote his 'Crazy (For Me)' single which peaked in the top fifty. (His highest UK placing was at no 18 with 'Rock Me Tonight (For Old Time's Sake)' in 1986)

As we tucked into smoked salmon washed down by an Australian wine (his choice), Freddie said he was honoured that so many people had supported the single but thought his recent British tour had a lot to do with it. "When my first two albums were released," he explained, "it was a very hectic time for me in America and perhaps I didn't support those albums as much as I should have in England. There are people who want to make things happen for me and I realise now that I have to help them. I'm the one who can make it happen, I guess, so I'm determined to be more accessible now. I want to be an international artist so there's still a lot of work to do."

Still on a high from his first Japanese stint where, by all accounts, he went and conquered, Freddie shyly admitted his four shows were sold-out. "The first was in Tokyo, and the people there are so damned polite. I was upset 'cos I couldn't understand why they didn't stand up, sing and shout at the concerts. I'm used to total mayhem going on. But I was told it was their way. Quite honestly, I didn't know what to expect, let alone if they would actually like me. Also, I didn't know if they'd understand me, so imagine my surprise when during the second show the audience sang my songs with me. Doesn't that prove music needs no translation...wish everything could be like that."

The people he worked with in Japan showered him with gifts, wined and dined him, until he was sick of the sight of the local food, and the effect the continual flow of warm Saki had on him, particularly as he refuses to drink alcohol when he's working. "I'm very strict with myself. My musicians say, 'We don't see enough of you.' But I tell them if I went out with them after a show the next show would have to be sacrificed because I can't work and drink." Wise words.

With his popularity now worldwide, the singer finds he's travelling more than ever. He claims he loves all the trappings of being a star, but once he's homeward bound, heads for his mother's house. "It's true," he insisted. "I'm able to wind down there and become her little boy again. My mother caters for me

CHINWAGGIN'

and I feel warm and secure when she wraps her arms around me. In fact, being held in her arms is far better than a massage. She really is my heart and soul and there's something about her home that's compelling....my mother taught me to look after myself which I'll always be grateful for. I have often resorted to washing out my underwear in the sink or popping clothes into the washing machine. I'd hate to think that a housekeeper had to wash my underwear. I'm not one of these artists who throw away underwear for the sake of it. I hate buying new ones because they take a lot of getting used to. I like underwear I can feel comfortable in. So, yes, I'm real glad I was taught to be independent." His mother is also the only lady with a key to his Poconos estate—"but she never pops by unexpectedly. I might be entertaining, and it might not be her kind of entertainment!"

Does he plan to marry? He laughed. "Yes, but not now. In the future I'd like to dedicate myself to a lady, but it's not possible now because of my career. I don't want to get into a Mike Tyson situation and marry the wrong woman who, at the end of the day, might only be after my money. I can be quite vulnerable...some women see me as the image on stage and they're attracted to that image and not the man underneath. And, women can end up dominating you, and it all starts with one date and ... let me put it this way, look at Tyson. He took knocks and punches for his wife, and I don't want that. I've actually met Mike: he's a very nice guy, a bit unaware, vulnerable, and when this dreadful divorce happened for him I really felt sorry. He deserves much better.

"I lived with this lady for three years ... it was almost like a marriage. I was still working on word processors and singing in my spare time. She persuaded me to quit the job and concentrate on music. Up until that point we split the costs down the middle but now as my regular cheque wasn't coming in she took care of the bills. One thing led to another and, as she'd wanted the upper hand for a time, she'd now got it. Some ladies like their men on a string, but I couldn't live like that. I had to leave her, we couldn't work it out. I left in the cold, with just the clothes on my back. I didn't take anything from the flat, so all I could do was go back to my mother's place. The silly thing is I loved this lady so much and if only she'd stuck by me, hadn't changed so much, she could've shared my better times. I never cheated on her because I

FREDDIE JACKSON

believe in a one man/one woman situation, but, on reflection, she might have been cheating on me.

"I like being in love, don't get me wrong, but it also hurts a lot. Now I've learned only to extend my heart so far until I feel confident the lady is right. Then I will give her my heart if she'll give me hers."

The conversation switched once more, to perhaps a different personal level, because many felt there's a passing resemblance in the style of Freddie's music and that of Marvin Gaye. My mentioning this didn't surprise him, although he insisted any similarity was coincidental. However, he related the following tale which, he said, had made him think. "When we were in Japan, we were walking down this street and passed an out-door cafe. From inside, music was playing and my colleague stopped and said 'Freddie, they're playing your music.' It wasn't me, it was Marvin, and we both stood, mesmerised on the sidewalk, listening to his voice. It was then I realised what people had been saying. It was uncanny, although I didn't feel uncomfortable about it...but that was the first time I acknowledged the comparison. Maybe the 'Rock Me Tonight' album sounded similar to Marvin's work because Paul Laurence produced that and he's a big Marvin fan.

"I never studied Marvin. I was into Donny Hathaway. I never properly locked into Marvin until 'Sexual Healing', although I adored 'What's Going On'. I used to sing that in school. Marvin had a unique sound, I've watched his videos, and there's a smooth, likeableness about him. Women went crazy for him and I think that image was something he was really selling, although not intentionally. And I feel that's what made people like him when his music went off. I am, therefore, very flattered at the comparison; he was a great artist and a great voice, but I wouldn't be able to conduct my life in the way he did."

There's something about Freddie that's instantly likeable. He's a good conversationalist, a caring host and is downright honest. So it's really easy for me to understand why women flock to be in his exclusive company. However, why does he think this is? "I guess it's because I do treat ladies like ladies. I'm old fashioned like that and when I say they're special, I mean it. I believe in romance and when I date I take my time. If I don't get a

CHINWAGGIN'

goodnight kiss on the first date, I don't worry, I'll wait for the second date."

As it wasn't a candlelit dinner, any visions of being escorted home, kissed on the hand to watch him saunter into a London sunset, were squashed. In reality, Mr Jackson walked me to a taxi, kissed me on the cheek and bid au revoir until next time. When, who knows what'll happen!

We didn't meet again, (damn it) but I continued to follow Freddie's career with great enthusiasm. During the Nineties he released five albums—'Do Me Again' and 'Time For Love' for Capitol Records; 'Here It Is' for RCA; 'Private Party' on Street Life-Scotti Bros; 'Life After 30' on Orpheus. In 2003, 'It's Your Move', which took Freddie a month to complete, was issued by his new management and record company, the Martland Entertainment Group. The album explored the complexity of love—naturally!

JERMAINE JACKSON

Dateline: May 1984

He hadn't changed at all. Slightly thinner perhaps, but the hugs and kisses made it seem like yesterday when last we met. In fact, it was a few years ago, but who's counting. Jermaine Jackson was back in London, albeit briefly, and sitting in his Inn On The Park suite with the hot sun pouring through the patio doors, the location could have been anywhere in the world.

He said he last saw his wife and two children, Jai and Autumn, at the beginning of April when he kissed them goodbye to promote his signing to Arista Records across the world, which included a video shoot with Pia Zadora in Rome. He was also taking care of business for his pending tour with his brothers, and, believe me, there was a helluva lot to sort out before they stepped on that blessed stage.

Jermaine Jackson left Motown in 1983 to join Arista where his debut releases are now available—the 'Sweetest Sweetest' single, followed by the 'Dynamite' album. He's a friendly, yet painfully shy and quiet guy, and speaks in a whispery, stuttering voice. An honest and straight-forward singer who, like his brothers, particularly Michael, has a business mind that equals any executive. I don't know whether he works from the same office as Michael (which is on the seventh floor of the Motown building) and stupidly I forgot to ask.

One of the questions that needed answering was why Jermaine left Motown, bearing in mind his wife, Hazel, is Berry Gordy's daughter. That might have caused some problems I suggested. "No, not at all. Hazel supported me when she realised my mind was made up to leave," he assured me. "I just felt I wanted to be on my own, to be out. We talked it over for a long time, then went to Berry and told him of my decision. We looked at it from all sides and he understood. He said he wanted me to be happy and if this move would make me happy I should do it."

Admitting there was an aspect of Motown he couldn't stomach, he decided to fight against it no more and move on. Arista boss, Clive Davis, and Jermaine had been friends for years and when a deal was discussed Mr Jackson had no hesitation in accepting the offer, saying: "It is a place where I can communicate directly rather than having to go through a committee. Also being with Clive Davis who's a record person makes a lot of difference. We can talk together about the structure of songs, lyrics and the recording of good, commercial material. Arista in that sense is very much like Motown."

"How's Rockwell doing over here?"

I explained about the single ('Somebody's Watching Me') and the recent promotional trip.

"Oh, you met him... did you like him?"

"No, unfortunately I didn't see him, Jermaine."

"He's a nice guy, he's Berry's son...do you think the single sold because of us—Michael and I? I thought it was a hit record as soon as I heard it without our vocals on it".

Jermaine has the habit of breaking off his conversation to ask questions, often unrelated to the subject at hand. He's always been like that, but, well, I still haven't got used to it.

Anyway, his own 'Dynamite' album isn't totally a solo effort as Michael duets with him on 'Dreamin''; and 'Escape From The Planet Of The Ant Men' features the Jackson family. "On that track Tito and I wanted to do something different. And it's turned out to be one of my favourite tracks. That's Tito's voice in the introduction. We wanted to try out some new things in the studio, make up some real weird noises, which we did."

From recording to touring and the pending Jacksons' American spectacular. While Jermaine was promoting his career in Europe, his brothers were feverishly rehearsing their stage act without him. The show will be split in three, he says, one third devoted to him, one third to Michael and the remainder featuring the brothers as a group. But, he laughed, he'll probably return to the States to find it all changed around! "The final dates haven't been confirmed yet, but it's thought we'll be touring until the end of the year or thereabouts. Then I'd like to tour by myself because I've never done that, you know."

Teaming up with his brothers for Motown's 25th Anniversary Gala (staged at Los Angeles' Pasadena Civic Auditorium on 25 March 1983) was Jermaine's idea, although he added: "I would have performed on the show without them, but when I asked could I join them, they thought it was a great idea to perform together. We had a couple of short rehearsals, but the idea was to keep the performance very free and spontaneous. I loved it."

"But you looked like you were crying when you hugged Michael," said I.

"Yes, I was. It was very emotional for me—the whole evening was emotional for us all. It really felt like being home again."

The public reunion, and the audience's standing ovation, prompted Jermaine to think of the past, when his brothers departed Motown, leaving him to fend for himself, although, he insisted, that wasn't quite what happened. "It was a bit tough. I really didn't know that much when I was left by myself, and I had to learn as I went along. I learned how to produce records, how to trust the right people, and those people who would help me for the right reasons. I was young and was open-minded, but part of that learning started by getting abused."

His solo career has taken him around the world, and in certain countries like Germany, Paris and Amsterdam, he received the same adulation as he did when a member of the group. His passion while travelling is real estate. "I look at houses. Actually I saw one outside London I liked and saw one in Switzerland. I could commute back and forth to America because I'd like my

CHINWAGGIN'

children to be schooled in Switzerland. I won't move out of America for good as all my family live there, but I'd really like my children to grow up in a different environment and learn other languages. Europe is changing all the time and if everything goes OK—and once this tour is out of the way—I can do what I've planned for a long time. To open up a company in London."

The phone rang. It was Jackie. Fifteen minutes later, it rang again. Another brother. The next was Michael. For an hour Jermaine's hotel suite resembled a telephone exchange, while his lunch of strawberries and bananas, with a side serving of prunes remained untouched, getting drier by the minute. Eventually he ended the call to his younger brother to continue. "Michael and I have always been close and he still needs a lot of loving. He is under strain right now, so many people want him to do so many things. Half of the stories printed about him are untrue, and this does upset him. He tries to keep himself to himself but he's not a lonely person. At the moment, he's living with my parents in Enico with the youngest member of my family.

"It's real difficult for him to lead a normal life, and even to go outside of the house's grounds is difficult because he gets mobbed. Entertaining is the only life he's known and we all give thanks we've been successful, but it sure does have its downside." Jermaine clearly adores Michael yet not once did he hint at any jealousy at his success. Instead, he's supportive. "He's worked hard and as much as we were all surprised at the way his career has gone, it couldn't have happened to a more deserving guy. We're all delighted for him and will always support him. He handles his career alright, don't worry about that, because he knows exactly where he's going and what he wants to do. A very shrewd business man."

Although Jermaine is probably the second Jackson sibling in the popularity stakes, thanks to his solo career, his success hasn't reached the heady heights of the Jacksons nor indeed Michael. He says that's the way it was meant to be and when asked why the brothers were so unique in their talent, he reckoned their training in music had helped—"but we were all very serious about the business and, of course, we already knew how to act on stage before joining Motown. I think we were possibly the only group in this business to do what we did, as quickly as we did, and that's a great feeling for us. We have always loved what we do, and now we are branching out into other areas. We've formed our own companies, for instance, and the love and trust we started out with remains to this day."

Before bringing the afternoon to a close, Mr Jackson enquired after my family, especially my niece Carly Sian and nephew Daniel Jermaine. We laughed when I related a conversation I had with ten year old Daniel. I had just purchased the 'Thriller' video for £18 and told my nephew this. His reply was: "My mum must have a better one than you because she paid £19 for hers!"

It was really lucky for me that Jermaine phoned me when he did in December 1986, for within an hour or so he was taking his family for a Christmas holiday in Fiji. This was his only real holiday for the next year, and nothing, he said, would make him miss it. But he wanted to call me before leaving.

His next Arista album 'Precious Moments' is finished and: "I'm so excited about this one because I feel it's ten times better than the last one. There could be at least six or seven singles on it. I've been gearing up for this one for so long now and have put ten tracks on it, instead of nine, because I felt they were all good enough. I've written some of them, and, yes, I am really excited... but so glad it's finished."

When the first single was extracted Jermaine planned to visit London to promote this and the album, before starting six weeks rehearsals for his first solo European stint in April. Calling it the Precious Moments tour, he'll be supported by his own hand-picked band, the members of which will be both musicians and vocalists. "Once I've finished Europe, it's back to the States to tour. Then I'm off to Japan and Africa. Because I'll be away from home so long I might take my wife and children along with me for some of the time, but I haven't sorted that out yet. This tour is part of a long-term plan for me. Once our Victory tour was over (with his brothers), I went straight into the studio to record my next album. The next step was the promotional tour, followed by a proper tour. I'll be a bit scatter-brained with all this going on, although I do get to have a couple of days off now and again!

"Like, at the moment, I'm trying to do as much American press as I can before going to Fiji. I've got a new press agency because

CHINWAGGIN'

I want everything to be right for this tour. On the Victory trek too many things were taken for granted, and a lot wasn't taken care of at all. There wasn't a strong organisation to work with, so this time there'll be no pitfalls. We've planned all this so that everything happens at the same time."

The Victory tour was the overall title of the Jacksons' much-publicised American tour, with performances that were astonishingly theatrical, opulently expensive and unbelievably exciting. Why no British dates, I moaned, especially as some were pencilled in on the original schedule? "Primarily it would have meant too much to do at the time and in the time available. The whole tour took too much production, a lot of organising...the stage sets were massive to travel around with and the security was a whole different problem of its own."

With the recording, planning and touring more or less finalised, Jermaine can concentrate on a personal project. Called WORK (Worldwide Organised Record Kompany), he explained that Hazel actually ran it. "She's got a brain like her father's; she can handle it. I'm very much involved with the label by taking care of the creative side, like finding the talent. As WORK is an international label, acts from all over the world will be signed. Like so far I've signed a group The Boys Next Door. There's one girl in it and they're self-contained... and they're from Detroit. I'm possibly going to sign Reactions, a group from London, and another unit from Atlanta."

When Jermaine was last in London, during a Radio One interview, he asked for artists who were looking for recording deals to submit their tapes to him c/o BBC. He's got them all now—"and I've listened to them all too. A lot of stuff wasn't that good. Some of the tapes had no music, some no lyrics. It seemed to me that people just put anything down on tape. Well, if they don't care about presenting their work, why should I? Whatever's going well on the circuits, in the club scene and such like, and if those acts involved are looking for a deal, that's when I want to have the chance to hear their music. I'm looking for people like Human League, for example, and quite honestly, anything that's carefully thought out. However, I was surprised at some of the tapes—no talent and a waste.

"I wanted WORK to get a good world-wide distribution and

JREMAINE JACKSON

MCA were willing to do that. We're working towards a launch in England as soon as we can this year. There'll be loads of publicity, a big spread, so it will all be done properly. Then we'll open up our London office to co-ordinate everything."

Where, I gasped, are you going to get time to cram all this into your life? "Hazel will take care of the running of the label and I have an enthusiastic team working with her. No, I don't think I've taken on too much. I've got to do this myself, and with so much careful planning in advance, I know it'll work out. But, I stress, I have no intention of leaving Arista. I want to make WORK a strong label, and I have my own career to take care of. But, who knows what will happen in the future, and that's all I'm gonna say."

For some reason, our conversation veered towards Marvin Gaye, and the fact that Jermaine spent so much time with him. When he was shot dead by his father on 1 April 1984, the world mourned. I could hear Jermaine sigh down the phone. "He has left a big void in my life because he influenced the way I work and it's this influence that has kept me going. When I was younger we used to play basket ball together and I'd see him in the studios, working away. I really admired him so much, and I can't tell you just how much he meant to me."

CHINWAGGIN'

It's a real shame but Jermaine Jackson's solo career never peaked following his international single 'Let's Get Serious' in 1980, although he continued to chart in Britain until 1989. He was earmarked to play Marvin Gaye in a biopic; to date, that hasn't materialised. Personally speaking, it appears he became a Muslim in 1989 following a tour of Middle East countries, but in the most recent years has been publicly defending Michael through his campaign against Sony Records' Tommy Mottola, claiming he was a racist which, in turn, led to dismal sales of the 'Invincible' album. Later, Jermaine became the Jackson spokesman, defending claims of child abuse against his little brother.

MILLIE JACKSON
Dateline: October 1986

It's been a while, but the Queen of Sass and Class is back with a new sound and a new recording deal. Yes, folks, pull down your shutters. Millie Jackson has returned!

Talking to this dynamic singer initially seemed a daunting prospect for a tender-hearted journalist like myself, but the lady was a pussy cat when compared to her adult, X-rated recorded work. The most disconcerting aspect of the interview was the speed with which she talked; just hope I've caught everything

After spending her career signed to Spring Records, Ms Jackson secured a deal with the Jive company. Her new single 'Hot! Wild! Unrestricted! Crazy Love!' is lifted from her pending 'Imitation

CHINWAGGIN'

Of Love' album—a tamer selection of songs than those featured on, say, 'For Men Only' or 'I Had To Say It'. "There's a reason for taming down the material," she croaked, having been asleep before we talked. "That's airplay. I've always been expected to include one of my raps on albums, and this time I wanted to record one without using profanity. I also wanted people to listen to my singing and not concentrate on my naughty raps which have always been a drawback as far as airplay is concerned." Never fret, Jackson fans, this doesn't, she assured me, mean the end of her much-adored saucy material, nor was the exclusion of the naughty sequences a directive from Jive. It was done through necessity this time.

Millie had good reasons for joining Jive Records, a small tightly-run operation and not a major company. She explained, I listened. "I like the simplicity of a smaller company. If I want to beef about something, I want to go directly to the president of the company. I don't want to have to go through three or four different people to get to the top. In my experience, by the time the top man gets to hear my story, it's all changed, like a Chinese whisper. So, now I can pick up the phone and get straight to the top."

Her long stay with Spring Records though, created the enigmatic and dynamic Millie Jackson who, with their dedicated promotion, maintained her high public profile. Another reason, perhaps, to query her move to Jive. "I'm in charge of everything I do and have done. Nothing about me has changed since I started out. I don't regret anything in my career, not really, because I try not to make mistakes. Moving to Jive is a positive move, and one which I wanted to make."

'A Child Of God' was her first single for Spring, which gave the public a shrewd idea of what was to come. Then during the early seventies she was voted the Most Promising Female Vocalist by NATRA following the release of her debut album. In 1973 her 'It Hurts So Good' was featured in the *Cleopatra Jones* movie soundtrack, and Millie never looked back. Her working relationship with Brad Shapiro led to her achieving her first gold record with 'Caught Up'. In time, this combination added more gold to her collection with the albums 'Get It Out Cha System' and 'Feelin' Bitchy'. With these releases, Millie was nurturing

MILLIE JACKSON

her own style of stage presence, which her American audiences worshipped.

She laughed when recalling her first visit to Britain, which confused and thrilled her. The year was 1972: the venue, The Playboy Club. "I was so accustomed to my audiences joining in, screaming and shouting and carrying-on during my show, that I was so amazed at the British. I had prepared this fifty minute show and had a certain amount of songs rehearsed for it. I didn't have my own band; it was a British group. I'd sing my song, there'd be a few handclaps, and I'd go on to the next one. It was very strange, because in America I did much more than fifty minutes because I'd be talkin' and messin' about with the people.

"So, here I am...I finish my show, and the audience start hollering for more. I didn't have no more! I hadn't rehearsed any more songs. So I told them, 'You should have let me know that you liked me during the show, not leave it till the end, 'cos there ain't any more!' Anyway, we compromised and I sang a couple of songs we'd already done. Now, I know differently because my British audiences act like the ones at home...real crazy!"

For the uneducated, Ms Jackson's stage shows are quite an experience; usually sexed up, both daringly sensual and promiscuous—and certainly not for the easily offended. Dirt and song, because, let's not forget, the lady has one helluva powerful voice. She sighed. "It's hard to please everyone in my audience. For example, one reviewer moans I talk too much, I'm too naughty and don't sing enough. The second one says I sing too much, don't do enough rapping. Reading these reviews gives me the impression of two entirely different shows. It's just down to the individual person, and the only way my shows can be judged is for a person coming along and seeing for herself or himself.

"It's hard planning a show for one and a half hours which is my normal running time. I think it gets boring for the audience to listen to one song after another. So I decided to introduce rapping which, when all is said and done, is simply my sense of humour and I decided to share it. Then when I come to the end of my act, the audience doesn't realise the time has gone, and still wants more. Also, people do come along to hear their favourite song and I don't sing it. That lets them down. Or, if I do sing it and ruin it, that makes them disappointed too. So by including the rapping,

CHINWAGGIN'

I'm not forced to sing a whole catalogue of songs and risk upsetting a lot of people."

During our conversation, I noted her most likeable nature, while maintaining an uninhibited and honest attitude. Much of this was shared with her public, yet I wondered if she was the same woman offstage as on. "Yes and no," she laughed. "I'm not as naughty offstage, but I still have my coarse humour. People say I'm not as rude offstage, but y'see, I don't see it as being rude. I call it mischievous, that's all." Introducing this to her public wasn't meant to offend. She did, however, notice that her audiences were mostly female at first. The men came later. "I haven't caused arguments, nor broken up any marriages," she stressed. "I have had things told me, like, I was the reason for making a woman think twice about making a commitment to her man. Or, men have come to me saying 'Lady, you're the reason why I've been thrown out!' I say 'It had nothing to do with me, you couldn't have been doin' whatever it is properly in the first place!' Mostly, I've brought people together, and turned ordinary relationships into something better. Glad to be of service, I say!"

Away from the bright lights, Millie Jackson is a sharp business woman, heading up Double Ak-Shun (her publishing company), her production and management operations, all under the parent Keivsal Enterprises. She told me. "I'm a workaholic. I get bored when I've nothing to do. I have an office in my house in Georgia and I head up these companies. It's like a family operation, although I don't spend too much time in the New York offices. I have lots of phone conversations, rely heavily on express mail, so nothing escapes me. I have several men working for me too, but they know I'm the boss. My band too...they call me 'm'dear'. That's like another word for 'mother', so we have no problems there either."

And she's a mother herself. With a daughter, Keshia, aged twenty, and a son, Jerroll, nine years old. "Keshia is in university so I only get to see her three or four times a year. Jerroll, he's with me, and is probably the worst. He tours with me, and all he lives for is music. It's affecting his education. I've even got to the point of almost singing his lessons to him. I don't object to his interest, far from it, but anything in excess is bad."

No MJ interview is complete without mentioning her two major

MILLIE JACKSON

duets with Isaac Hayes and Elton John. In my opinion, the 'Royal Rappin's' album with Isaac is immortal, and the imagination ran riot at the prospect of these two sex symbols in the studio for at least a month or so. Not so, I'm sorry to say. "Isaac and I only spent two days together. I had never sung with anyone else before, and I thought it was going to be so hard. But, hell no, Isaac is so professional. It really was quite an experience. I had produced all the songs and sent them to him. He then came in to do the vocals, and when we'd finished we were actually $25,000 under budget which pleased a lot of people. Those were two great days I can tell you and that man is such a pure gentleman."

Elton John and 'Act Of War' were different. "Well, not really the total opposite to Isaac" she confided. "Isaac was all straight and we were a little mischievous, you could say, we played a little. With Elton we got on with it; got it done, yet really we were two kids having fun. The song was originally written for Tina Turner, but she turned it down. They approached me. I liked it and wanted to do it. It was Tina's loss!"

Despite two major stars being on the record label, the title wasn't a premier hit, although it did reach the British top forty in 1985. In America it was a different matter. "Singles have to fall into particular categories, and no-one really knew which category to put this single in. Elton is a pop singer and I'm not. So it couldn't go into mainstream. I'm R&B, Elton's not, so it couldn't go into that market. If it had been handled properly it should have been promoted as an R&B song, got into that chart, then crossed over into pop. That seems to be what happened in England. Still, I enjoyed doing it, and that's the important thing."

Should the day ever dawn when retirement looms, Millie reckons she could be a competent 'agony aunt'. "Most of my mail used to be 'Dear Millie, what should I do about so-and-so.' All were asking for my advice on romantic or sexual problems. I received so many that I couldn't possibly have answered them all. So, yes, I could be an agony aunt for some magazine or other, but it would have to be something like Playboy or Penthouse. Oh, and there'd be no photos taken either, that would be something I'd insist on right from the word go.

"Posing in the nude is definitely where I'd draw the line, honey!"

CHINWAGGIN'

Of the many songs released by Ms Jackson, her 'Phuck-U-Symphony' is the most requested and re-recorded—I wonder why!—and her last UK chart entry was with Elton John in 1985, when they duetted on 'Act Of War'. Despite here chart absence, Millie's career has diversified greatly. For example, she appeared in the 'Wigstock' movie, was dubbed the 'Mother of Hip-hop' by Da Brat, and recorded the Sprite tv commercial. For four years she toured America with her own show, 'Young Man, Older Woman', a musical stage play which she created, financed, directed and, of course, starred in.

Following this success, she appeared in American tv sitcoms, then turned her talent to radio, where for the past several years she's hosted a daily show in Texas. More recently, Millie recorded again, this time for her own label, Weird Wreckuds, where her debut single, 'Butt-a-Cize' was lifted from the 'Not For Church Folk' album. What's that all about, MJ?

LEEE JOHN
Dateline: December 1985

Tracking down artists this time of year is usually a fruitless task so I was extremely grateful when Imagination's Leee John gave me a call to give me the latest gossip. The soul trio had been travelling around London on an open-top bus, singing Christmas carols to all who cared to listen and then stopped off at various hospitals to pay a festive visit to the patients and the hard working staff.

Prior to this, much media attention was given to Imagination's recent meeting with Prince Charles and Princess Diana following a huge concert at the Royal Albert Hall. The trio performed alongside other luminaries like Phil Collins, Sade and Paul Young and, he gushed "everyone who performed came to the party afterwards, including Charles and Diana. We chatted about fashion and the drug problems here with Diana, then talked to Charles about the racial situation and his love of music, particularly jazz.

"He's very much aware of the problems that do exist with ethnic groups, shall we say, and this is the first time anyone like him has shown so much interest. There's no-one in this country that people can associate with, like in America, where people can become involved with the president and so on. In England all people seem to shout about is against Margaret Thatcher, and that they never get the support they need. Well I think that's all been changed now with Charles and Diana."

When Leee spoke to the Royal couple about his plans to become involved in the fight against drug abuse and Imagination's plans to help stamp out the feelings that run rife about ethnic minorities, the Prince and Princess of Wales pledged their help. Oh yeah, says I! "That's what I thought initially" Leee agreed. "But they kept their word. The Palace phoned our office officially to confirm the Royal help. Now all we have to do is get our ideas together and present them with a working plan. My mum's involved in this kind of thing, so I'm going to get some ideas from her. This is something Errol, Ashley and I want to do, and being in the public eye I feel it's something we should do. I like what Stevie Wonder is doing and what he's able to put across. He's a public figure and he cares.

"Listen, I don't want to be a Bob Geldof and all that goes with that. I just feel Imagination are in a position to do something that doesn't need a hit record to succeed."

Life for Imagination is busy; so much so that the solo projects Leee has had in hand for some time are still simmering in the background. For example, Daryl Hall asked for his songs, "But I haven't done this because Imagination takes up so much of my time. Not only over here, but in Europe. Like next week we're performing at a party for the Mayor of Paris. We've been voted the number one group there for the last year and a half and the whole lot's being filmed. Then we're doing a gig at Finsbury Park before Christmas, so that doesn't leave a lot of time, does it?"

Into the new year of 1986, Imagination will concentrate on promoting a new album before Leee pursues an acting career, a move he promised himself some years ago. The end of Imagination I asked? "Hell no! It's true the group is under so much pressure, particularly as we've always got something happening in Europe. But as far as disbanding it, well, to go solo these days you need to think twice, I can tell you. Financially, it's better of course, physically it's easier, but it's still one helluva

LEEE JOHN

risk. Take Michael Jackson. He's doing solo work, yet he still has the group, having the backing and convenience of the group.

"Imagination are all doing their own thing at the moment. Ashley has his studio set up and is involved in all sorts of projects. Errol is producing his girlfriend's group called Just Girls. They've been doing a lot of gigs around London and are actually recording in my studio upstairs. I've got a little demo studio here in my house. But we, as a group, will stay together because having outside interests stops us from becoming stale."

One extra special date has already been planned for 1986. On 5 March at the Royal Albert Hall Imagination will be celebrating five years in the business as a group. "We're really looking forward to that, dear," Leee told me. "Apart from us, we're hoping to get David and Jaki, Junior and so on to join in the celebrations. It's hard to believe it's been five years, but it is, and we'll be celebrating in good style."

One of the fundraisers that Leee John instigated was to raise funds for SCAR (Sickle Cell Anaemia Relief). Sickle Cell is a disabling and often fatal blood disorder, which is prevalent among Africans, Afro-Caribbeans, Asian and Mediterranean peoples. It attacks the red blood cells, taking on the appearance of a sickle - hence its name. So far there's no known cure.

On 27 July 1986 some of this country's top soul artists flocked to the Sarm West recording studios in London to record 'This Is My Song' (written by Leee and Ashley). The single, to be released under the collective name of PIP—People In Progress—included Junior, David Grant, Mark King, Phil Fearon, Haywoode, Kiki Dee, Lenny Henry, Janet Kay, Sinitta, Dark Secret, Paul Hardcastle, Dotty Green, Sharon Benson, Tom Robinson, O'chi Brown, Brenda Fassie, Ray and Sharita Shell, Aswad, Carol Thompson, Bill Fredericks, Miquel Brown, Mike Nolan, Patti Boulaye, Juliet Roberts, TC Curtis, Errol Brown, DC Lee, among others. On top of the sixty or so artists, there were film crews numbering fifty-plus, television crews, radio folk, photographers and journalists. The recording session was being filmed for a documentary (editing alone will take up to five weeks), plus interviews with key people working behind the scenes.

Anyway, let's backtrack. Leee decided to form PIP after

CHINWAGGIN'

attending an Artistes Against Apartheid meeting where Harry Belafonte was present and told him. "You are involved: as the world turns, you turn with it." So moved was Leee by these words that 'This Is My Song' was born. He then asked me and others to pit their organising and administrative skills to ensure the recording of the song was a success. Everyone asked to contribute, including Sarm, gave their services free of charge. The song was, incidentally, first performed at Imagination's fifth anniversary concert, and later at a charity dinner for the Sickle Cell Anaemia Relief organisation. "I had a large number of people who came and said they wanted to sing it with us. This shows how we care for both our own community here and the unity of people around the world who are certain that it can work."

Before reporting on the organised mayhem of the Sunday recording, I should explain that the two principle charities to benefit from PIP's single are—SCAR, who, with other organisations, offer support for practical and financial help to victims and their families, to bring this disease to the public's attention and to raise money for much-needed research. And CCETSA (The Canon Collins Educational Trust Of Southern Africa) which concentrates on funding literary projects in the refugee camps of Africa. It also provides funds for students studying in Africa, Britain and elsewhere, as well as providing money for teachers working in these African camps.

Once everyone had checked through Sarm's reception, with each visitor autographing guest books, posters and T-shirts to be auctioned later, a bee-line was made to the downstairs lounge and catering area (strictly no alcohol) which soon proved inadequate: but nobody cared much.

The lead vocalists including Kiki, Junior and David were called into the main studio at regular intervals throughout the morning until Leee and Derek Bramble were satisfied with the results. Haywoode was also a lead vocalist; but she was nowhere to be found. ("I always seem to be late for important things," she whispered to me as she rushed through the studio). By four in the afternoon the majority of artists were present but, prior to launching them into the studio for the chorus and main parts, an impromptu session from Lenny Henry took place. He, with a film

LEEE JOHN

crew at his heels, roamed through Sarm talking and joking with attendees. Meanwhile, the BBC crew encouraged DC Lee, Phil Fearon, David Grant and Leee to adlib the single's chorus before rolling cameras. Once again, Haywoode was not around (probably in the loo, someone suggested). As she arrived, flustered and shaken, a minder lifted her in the air and flung her down in the middle of the seated singers, causing one cameraman to drop his equipment in fright!

The outside filming caused the inevitable chaos with the residents who eventually decided if you can't beat 'em, join 'em. For some reason, a few policemen arrived and just watched. All the artists congregated in a nearby children's playground, designed like a huge castle, to sing 'This Is My Song' once more. In one corner the straight version was heard, in the other, Aswad led their own alternative version. Dotty Green jumped about to the music so much her blouse slipped off to reveal one boob, much to the delight of a nearby cameraman, while children skipped and laughed about, adding an unexpected special touch to the proceedings. Getting this large number of people to work as one wasn't easy, but somehow the long human snake wormed its way down Basing Street to return to the studio. Film crews and photographers hung from parked vehicles, stood on car roofs and shuffled about at ground level. One poor chap got trampled underfoot but rose again; cables from a shoulder-held camera became tangled around a parked car and someone's legs, bringing both camera and operator to an abrupt halt!

Moving into the actual studio—and it's bursting with singing bodies, film equipment, cameras, and media folk. The walls sweated as music was pumped around, followed by a plethora of voices. An electrifying, exciting and tense atmosphere which overrode any pangs of discomfort. By mid-evening, after a long, sweaty confinement, the overheated singers wearily left the studio in search of fresh air.

"PIP is the seed, the seed is just the beginning" a tired, but happy, Leee John told me as he bid me goodnight.

Well, no one can accuse my mate Leee of dragging his heels. His life is full to capacity. For example, during February 2004 he

CHINWAGGIN'

was in France recording his first jazz album for Cristal Records. The sessions were filmed for later DVD release. Also in the pipeline this year is an Imagination DVD retracing the trio's incredible history. Probably the last time Leee was seen on prime time television was as a worthy contestant in 'Reborn In The USA', and hell, didn't he deserve to win! Behind the scenes, he works with other artists. For instance, he collaborated on Shakatak's album 'Blue Savannah' after contributing to The Morne's 'I Can See For Miles'. He tours the Continent regularly because he and Imagination remain high profile artists there, and this is reflected in their record sales. We're still in contact with each other, and he is, I believe, writing his autobiography. When he gets chance to draw breath that is!

(left to right) T.C. Curtis, Dotty Green and Paul Hardcastle

MARV JOHNSON
Dateline: September 1990

He's a likeable chap our Marv. A likely lad as well, I wouldn't wonder. Always has a smile and a friendly word—and he's not a bad singer and performer either! An old schooler, an endearing gentleman and his own best public relations officer. We sat backstage at London's Dominion Theatre sipping brandy. He was attempting to relax before going on stage, but his dressing room was a central point for his touring companions: Lynda Laurence popped by, Kim Weston wanted a word, Carolyn Crawford was in search of alcohol, and I was attempting an interview.

Let's talk history. A native Detroiter, born in October 1938, Marv Johnson had been recording since 1958, with Berry Gordy producing, and the tracks that spring to mind are his first 'My Baby-O' on Kudo; 'Come To Me' and 'Whisper', the latter pair eventually issued in January 1959 on Motown's Tamla label, the first official release for the operation. Local success and demand for this single, particularly in Detroit, prompted Berry Gordy to lease it to the national distribution arm of United Artists, who also insisted Marv fall under their wing as an exclusive signing.

CHINWAGGIN'

Marvin Earl Johnson would, of course, return to Motown—but not before he had left a legacy of music at UA.

'I'm Coming Home' followed the hit into the US top 100, but it was the catchy 'You Got What It Takes' that soared into the US top ten. Marv was a star, and still rising as the next 'I Love The Way You Love' peaked one rung higher at number nine. In 1960 two more hits followed, '(You've Got To) Move Two Mountains' and 'Happy Days', while over here at the same time he enjoyed a top five hit with 'You Got What It Takes' and a top forty title with 'I Love The Way You Love'. 'Merry-Go-Round' continued the run a year later.

He then retired from recording for a time before re-appearing on Motown's Gordy label with 'Why Do You Want To Let Me Go?'. Then 'I Miss You Baby (How I Miss You)' was issued and eventually became a British hit as the follow-up to 'I'll Pick A Rose For My Rose', a top ten hit in 1969. Prior to joining Motorcity Records a few months ago, it seems his last single could have been 'So Glad You Chose Me' in 1970, but Mr Johnson's not clear on that. British success ensured his popularity as a performer and he's been back and forth more times than he cares to remember. Well, that's his past, here's the current with flashbacks.

'By Hook Or By Crook' was his first Motorcity record in 1988. Strictly speaking, the title was issued on the Nightmare label, where a year earlier, he duetted with Carolyn Gill on 'Ain't Nothing Like The Real Thing'. His current single 'Run Like A Rabbit' was extracted for release from a series of recent recording sessions.

I was pleasantly surprised to learn that Marv still has the same enthusiasm for his career as he did when he took his first tentative steps. He's also grateful because, he said, the adrenalin that comes with the music business fights off the complacency which often sets in during a long career. "I've been entertaining for years and it's sustained me. It has helped me support my family— I'm now a grandfather—and it's something I love to do. But I believe your attitude with people in the business has a great deal to do with your longevity. The way you sing isn't the only thing involved. Your association with those around you has a great deal to do with whatever successes you have.

MARV JOHNSON

"In my case I try to get along with everyone, although I can't tolerate bullshitters. Don't get me wrong—I love people, but I have a sense that's been built in over the years and I can suss out if anyone's phoney. I like to be with real people."

This belief has stood him in good stead because he's still in the business to tell the tale. Through his involvement with Motorcity, his career has taken on yet another positive angle, as he explained. "The recording side has now been brought back into focus, but I was in a position where what I had recorded in the past was keeping me quite well. Having a hit record now isn't that important to me. What is important is my health, what people think of me and to remain in the business in one form or another, and whatever transpires in the face of these things, is OK with me."

Mind you, Marv was quick to point out that his career hasn't been without it's set-backs. Indeed, there are certain things, he said, that with foresight, he would have changed. "Well, if not changed them, then certainly bettered. But I guess on the whole I'm pretty satisfied with the way things have gone. Sure, I made a few mistakes but then... who hasn't?"

While he was releasing his first singles, Motown artists were few and far between. Probably Smokey Robinson and the Miracles were the only other singers he came into regular contact with, and together they encouraged Berry Gordy to keep his dream alive and expand his musical interests. Good days, Marv sighed. "I feel we have indeed played a major part in Motown and in a lot of cases I feel we don't have the type of respect that perhaps we should. Sometimes other people's efforts are a little more obvious for one reason or another. But I'm now satisfied knowing I am part of something that was wonderful. The much publicised family atmosphere did actually exist to a certain extent. However, it was more of a family situation to some than it was to others obviously. Diana Ross and the Supremes were blessed to have been favourites of Berry Gordy himself. There was a personal relationship between Diana and him, but there were so many others—Jr Walker, Four Tops, Velvelettes, Hattie Littles and so on—who played a huge part in launching what became one of the greatest companies in the world, but who received little credit."

CHINWAGGIN'

The singer's own relationship with the Gordy family was strained as he admitted. "We didn't get on too well in the latter years because there were tremendous egos, tremendous feelings of—I don't know how to explain it myself—but they weren't positive from Berry and with the family generally. I got along fine with Berry's nephew and Mrs Gordy Snr. She supported her son which was natural, but also she did try and understand my growth, and treat me like a decent human being and I appreciated that. Sadly, she's no longer with us...I didn't get on with Anna (Berry's sister) at all." But he omitted to tell me why!

Leaving the company he loved so much was a puzzling series of events, which he still hasn't come to terms with. Yet he smiled as he explained to me. "It was a funny thing. I was issued with a letter that said my contract had expired three years after it actually had. I didn't understand that because I'd have thought they wouldn't have wanted me around under those circumstances. I had been dismissed and didn't know. Being a man who wanted to support his family, I thought I'd be issued with a certain amount of stock or something in the company to establish a sort of secure position for us... to reap the benefits of what I had given in my younger life. But it didn't happen. Berry Gordy didn't choose to give me that stock, and it was difficult for me to understand, because he had made statements to that effect that Smokey and myself would be secure in this way."

With the interview rapidly coming to a close because Marv was due on stage, I threw a passing shot. Had he fallen prey to the many vices that show business had to offer? Bearing in mind, a half-full bottle of brandy was at his side. He laughed. "Yes, I've had them, but I've never particularly been heavily into drugs. Being an entertainer and being among my peers I've experimented in certain areas but I've never become a slave to anything".

Except music, perhaps!

During the early nineties Mr Johnson and I crossed paths literally. Martha Reeves was scorching on stage with 'Dancing In The Street' before a steamy, packed house in a Sussex holiday camp, when I spotted him at the nearby bar trying to buy a drink. He was getting nowhere, so I pushed my way through and took

MARV JOHNSON

control of the ordering. We were both on our way to see Johnny Bristol, so with drinks in hand, we traipsed backstage with Marv signing autographs on the way.

Barely six months after this, Marv Johnson was dead. A sudden brain haemorrhage on 15 May 1993 robbed us of an artist who was known to us as Mr Motown. Thankfully, he left us with a whole catalogue of timeless music, from United Artists to Motown through to Motorcity. Personally speaking, I was blessed to meet him when I did. I know he left a void in many people's lives.

GLORIA JONES
Dateline: May 1976

I t was just getting dark and the guest hadn't arrived. Things flashed through my mind: she doesn't know where to come, her mini had broken down; perhaps it was Thursday evening not Wednesday, or she's not coming at all. Before the second drink was poured, the doorbell rang and Gloria Jones, carrying bottles of wine and beer, stood smiling. She was ushered in so quickly her feet didn't touch the ground and on sitting down on the couch, one well-bandaged finger was pointed in my direction. The result, she moaned, of struggling out of her bath the previous day. Luckily, the injury wasn't so serious that she couldn't lift her drink or hold a cigarette.

"I changed outta my jeans to dress up for tonight" she explained

GLORIA JONES

with a laugh. "Don't let's make it too serious eh? But don't worry Cancer, you'll get something to write about."

I'd previously met Ms Jones socially with her boyfriend Marc Bolan; sometimes at Mortons, other times in a restaurant off Manchester Square. Her personal track record is pretty impressive—with Pam Sawyer she composed blinding tracks at Motown, where she also released a solo album, and, of course, there's others who will remember her for an almost obscure single that is high on the Northern Soul agenda.

Whatever the name Gloria Jones conjures up, she's now in London, having recently issued her new single 'Get It On' on the EMI label which, she admitted, wouldn't be accepted by certain people because it represents little of her upbringing and previous releases. "It was recorded because it'd be a song people would recognise. Northern Soul is where I'm going and I hope it appeals to the people there. Y'know, if it wasn't for them I'd still be singing in church. I want to be accepted over here, so I thought a well known tune was the obvious choice. Also, isn't it true that the faster the record, the better it is to dance to? In some reviews they say it's as fast as Concorde..so is youth. That's where I'm going. I'm working for the young and I'll give them what they want."

The single was the first from her pending album, which she claims is "very up-to-date. And there's some songs I've written. We've gotten Ollie Brown, Hubert Herb, Ray Parker and the Sisters Love as backers. They're also on the single...and you know I had a hand in their 'Learning To Trust My Man' cut. What a group, they're just dynamite."

Let's go back to day one (thank you Eddie Kendricks), I insisted. So sit back, enjoy.

"I was a minister's daughter... he was a fantastic father. I studied classical piano for ten years and picked up my voice from my mother's side. The gospel group I later kicked around with, I first met in church. Like Frank Wilson...we all had the gospel feel so a group seemed natural. I loved gospel. Still do. It's my upbringing. I knew I wanted to move with the group but I was afraid I'd harm my father's congregation. He said that it wouldn't, said I'd got talent and should use it. He gave me all the encouragement I needed and I'll never forget that.

CHINWAGGIN'

"I was a babe when I heard Frankie Laine's 'When I Lost My Baby' and the funny thing was, mother always said I used to run to find my doll. I suppose I thought someone had lifted it and I'd lost it for good! Seriously though, I always wanted to be a school teacher, if only 'cos I love working with young people. In fact, I went to college for three years and studied psychology.

"My first visit to London was with a couple of students and we stayed in places like The Cumberland and that. It was fun and I loved it. But the first place I really fell for was Amsterdam during our tour of the continent. What amazes me here is that you see people from all over the world. Take Heathrow, it's strictly cosmopolitan baby. There ain't another airport like it in the world. Fantastic experience when you walk through the barriers.

"Anyway, the gospel group had people like Blinky Williams (later signed to Motown), Edna Wright (The Honey Cone) and Billy Preston. We did session work, demos, gigs, and mostly had fun. People like Darlene Love would come along to see us...Must tell you this...later on I worked with her on Phil Spector's Christmas album, on the 'Silent Night' track, I think. And talking about that, I was also on a couple of tracks on 'Dylan's Gospel/ Brothers And Sisters Of Los Angeles' album. Lots joined in that, of the old crowd that is, and I've worked with Barry White, and Gene Page. That was with Brenda and Patrice Holloway... and before Motown of course. I've lost track now. Yeah, the group... one day we were called in to do some demo work and, guess what, 'Heartbeat' was the result. And I never realised I'd be remembered for that song. It's amazing."

With her arms in the air, she excitedly continued. "Up north, the kids come to me and say 'not *that* Gloria Jones' or 'Gloria Jones on "Heartbeat"?' I'm told it was so big on the northern circuit. Another song they loved was 'Tainted Love'. Can you believe that? I'm so knocked out by it all. In fact, everyone I've met on the northern scene I love—they're so good to me, making me feel warm and welcome."

Diana Ross played in the background. "Play 'Love Hangover', will you?" she instructed. "Went to see her show, really knocked me out, but I had some problems finding the ladies room. I was so desperate I thought about muscling in on the gents."

Returning to Gloria's demo days—estimated at ten years ago—

GLORIA JONES

she worked and played alongside artists struggling for recognition, like, Merry Clayton, Clydie King, Sherlie Matthews, while mixing with Susaye Green, Bobby Womack, Glen Campbell (who worked on sessions with Womack), Oma Drake, and others. "Los Angeles was the music capital in those days, and where there were young people, clubs and gigs, you'd find us. When one of the crowd was booked on a gig, we'd all go along and help out… usually ending up on stage for a jam. We had fun; yeah, they were good days for me."

It was following the release of 'Heartbeat' that she met two people who later became her closest friends, Brenda and Patrice Holloway. They teamed up as session singers who were constantly in demand, earning them the title 'The Little Hearts Of Los Angeles'. And it was during one of these sessions that a certain lady spied Gloria playing at the piano. "Why don't you do something with that tune?" she asked the singer. That question changed Gloria's life because the lady was Pam Sawyer. Before the dust settled, Gloria and Pam worked as freelancers for Motown until 1972 when they put their signatures to an in-house contract.

"The biggest thrill of my life was when we wrote 'If I Were Your Woman' for Gladys Knight and it was nominated for a Grammy. I wrote the music, Pam the lyrics—usually the songs are combined feelings at the time 'cos basically we work together. I was working in Las Vegas at that time with Wayne Newton and all of a sudden, nice things started to happen. But, must tell you about this writing thing. I've always been into the theatre and when writing with Pam, I was also performing. Really, in my heart of hearts, I didn't wanna be a writer full time." For the record, she appeared in 'Othello', 'Hair', worked with Jack Good, and appeared in other shows, which she can't now recall.

"I'd be touring around with Pam in Detroit, and I was getting more interested in the theatrical world but it meant having to be on Broadway, in New York, places like that before I could really get anywhere. In fact, I was in New York when Pam called me and said to go to Detroit. So I did, and I suppose, that's where I got into writing seriously. The theatre has never left me—I'd love to go back one day. I always thought I'd make a better Carole Burnett than she herself."

CHINWAGGIN'

Judging by Ms Jones' sense of humour, combined with her somewhat frivolous attitude, she could well achieve that goal! Being a Libran, she's typical of her birthsign, possessing that natural desire to be diplomatic and co-operative in a quest for peace and harmony. Yet, she's an idealist, with romantic and sentimental tendencies—her writing achievements are testament to that. For example, take 'When Your Love Hand Comes Down' and 'Your Love Was Worth Waiting For' written with Pam Sawyer and recorded by Jimmy and David Ruffin. Or, 'My Mistake (Was To Love You)', 'Where Do You Go (Baby)', 'Just Seven Numbers', 'Million To One', 'I Ain't Going Nowhere', 'I Ain't That Easy To Lose'; perhaps others written for Jr Walker, Eddie Kendricks, the Jackson 5 and Yvonne Fair. Yes, the list is quite incredible.

Refilling our glasses, Gloria once again took up the story. "Pam and I decided we must meet different people in the music business. You know what I mean—get to know them, make some contacts. Well, I was then Gloria Jones the singer, and singer-songwriters weren't the done thing then. So, at this party, I was introduced to some important folk and told them my name was Leverne Ware. I later wrote under that name (Sawyer/Ware). Then, singer-songwriters came into their own, for Carole King got accepted as both, and the door seemed to open. So, I changed back to Gloria Jones..singer-songwriter!"

The days at Motown were happy for her, then her life changed once more, as she explained. "After producing and writing for so many artists there, I found I wanted to do an album myself...as a performer again. I wanted to prove to myself that I could do it." So she released the 'Share My Love' album, arranged by Paul Riser and written almost entirely by herself. "It took so long and now it's three years old. At the time, I was really pleased with the result. It didn't happen all at once though because I was travelling about, so a track was cut a month, and so on. Listening to it now, it's really not what I'm into, but it was an emotional experience for me and I associated certain happenings with certain cuts. Motown treated me well. I can't say anything against them. All that happened was my contract ran out, so I came to London. And I'm happy again."

It was now past midnight, and Gloria was due home two hours

ago. Panic set it. Shoes were quickly returned to feet, glasses drained, vinyl returned to sleeves, cigarettes out and she hastily made for the front door to jump into her waiting car.

From that interview, Glo and I became close friends. We spent evenings together (sometimes with Marc) and talked for England. We gadded about London in her purple mini; travelled to Wigan, where she was always greeted enthusiastically, even though it meant long hours cooped up in a van. But we giggled our way up the motorways. We shared so much. Then tragedy struck when, on September 16th 1977, two days after her return to London from America where she'd been recording, Marc died in her mini. Glo was the driver. She suffered horrendous injuries and spent time in the Roehampton Hospital before recuperating in a London apartment. We mourned together, before she battled to face the future without her beloved Marc, and to secure a safe environment for their son, Rolan—born on 26th September 1975. She went through hell at the hands of Marc's family and the police, who insisted she be charged with manslaughter. (It was later discovered that two nuts on the mini's off-side wheel were faulty: she was blameless). Glo had little choice but to take her son to America, where in time she built up her life again. Time passed and we lost touch. But, in 2003, thanks to PR guru Debbie Bennett, we were reunited. Now we chat regularly, and plan to write a book about her music and her life with Marc and Rolan.

EVELYN KING

Dateline: November 1985

It was the afternoon the Queen was opening Parliament, so London traffic was in turmoil. Me? I was trying to get to The Montcalm Hotel to see Evelyn King (now minus the 'Champagne'). Compared to the Queen's activities, no big deal. But to me, it was.

Taking most people by surprise, 'Your Personal Touch', Ms King's latest outing, shot into the chart. Released by RCA Records it peaked in the top forty, her first placing since 1983 with 'Get Loose' which stalled in the top fifty. To support the single's release and her forthcoming album 'A Long Time Coming', the singer was in London on a hectic promotional trip.

Before getting into the interview, I must confess I was the one who introduced Evelyn to Chris Quinten, that one-time 'Coronation Street' personality. And their friendship suffered immense exploitation in the tabloids, which blew their relationship out of proportion. The subject is now long forgotten as far as the singer is concerned although she was, naturally, extremely annoyed at the way she was exploited. A case of the

EVELYN CHAMPAGNE KING

'scandal that wasn't', she said.

However, just lately our Ms King has had a mediocre time success-wise with singles. Two were lifted from her last 'So Romantic' album—the title track and 'Give Me One Reason', while America went with 'Til Midnight' and 'Out Of Control'. A confusing time. 'Give Me One Reason' is probably the nearest Evelyn has come to releasing a slow-tempoed single, although she's quick to point out. "On every one of my albums I've included ballads because I want people to know I can sing more than dance tracks. I don't get tired of singing beaty songs, but I'm looking at both a younger and older audience now. In fact, the youngsters are coming to me for tips now! That's how old I am!"

The singer had flown to London from Germany where: "I've been for four weeks touring, doing two shows a night, with no rest. Before Germany I was recording the album—and that wasn't even recorded in one place either. I moved from Philly to Los Angeles to New York. I don't appear to be able to do anything easily at the moment. Then I did a commercial for Budweiser, a nationwide thing—and there were no free samples either! It didn't bother me really because I don't drink the stuff. Then I thought how can I promote a product I've not tasted? But what the hell, it's money."

A downside of the German tour was the havoc it played on Evelyn's feet, particularly her corns. I remarked I wasn't surprised, bearing in mind her ten-foot heeled boots! She cracked up. "Look lady, I have been wearing heels since I saw my mother in spikes—I was five years old. You probably won't believe this, but when I wear sneakers or low-heeled shoes I fall over. I just cannot walk in flat shoes now—even my bedroom slippers have heels! But at the moment, my feet hurt real bad."

So, with her aching feet and brand new hairstyle, Evelyn confirmed she'd still like to live in London because she had fallen in love with the city some years earlier. "I like the clubs, and the way people get along. All the races, by and large, get on well together, and you don't see that in New York. Sure, you have your problems, we all have them. Y'know, when I heard about that poor woman getting killed last night—it's only down the road from here—I was ready to go home. Boy, I was really scared. But, the other thing about London is that I can walk freely

CHINWAGGIN'

where I want. Where I am in the States, a lot of people know me. They see me on a TV show or something and that's that. I can't go anywhere and I want to go places and be free, just like everyone else."

An ambition she's nurtured for some years is to become an actress. Not a fantasy either. She's had offers from the *'Fame'* people, the sit-com series starring Bill Cosby, and *'All My Children'*, a soap opera. "I want to do other things apart from singing. I can't be singing like I am now when I'm sixty, in a wheel chair and on crutches, can I? I'll probably retire when I'm fifty-seven because that's how long my record company has insured me."

From acting we moved to love, because Evelyn has a new man in her life. Lenny Green has made a big impact on her. "This will last a long time, I just know it," she glowed. "I am very fond and very proud of him. He loves me very much too, so I know I'm going to be happy. If you met him, you'd like him because he's in your business...a radio announcer, a media interviewer, who controls what we, the singers, do to a large extent. (Do we? Make a note to ask the editor.)

"Do you know, people have said to me 'Oh well, that's handy, he'll be working for you now.' That's garbage. I can do it on my own. I don't need his help. Sure, Lenny had heard of me and my records, because he used to interview me on his show regularly. And I always thought he was rather nice..." We then spent time discussing the joys of being in love which is a topic quite boring to someone who's not, so I won't print anymore.

Going to nightclubs is still one of Ms King's favourite pastimes, although, since her success, she's now restricted in her choice of venues. A nearby club is her second home. "It's called Dunhills, Lenny and I go there quite a lot. I love some of the London clubs, but I won't have time this trip to party. Oh, I buy most of my clothes in London too, with New York and New Jersey as close seconds. Some are made specially for me, but I always choose my styles because I like to be different."

Let's return to the music. Before starting work on her new album, the singer had trekked through a nationwide tour of American military bases—all those big, butch GIs! She had a lot of fun. "Those guys hadn't probably seen a woman in months and

EVELYN CHAMPAGNE KING

when I was on stage they were grabbing everywhere. They grabbed at my ankles—honest. I've never seen anything like it." Talking of the military (?), I asked whether she had secured herself a ticket to attend the Prince and Princess of Wales' reception at The White House. "No! No! I haven't. Do you know where I can get one? Diana's very nice isn't she, and he's obviously very fond of her. Did you see Charles went along to watch some breakdancers, then he tried to join in? I don't think it's a put on, because I reckon it's their way of showing they're interested in other people. I like the way Diana loves children—that's genuine enough...wonder where I can get a ticket from?"

I had to leave her with her challenge, with a promise we'd meet up next year. Meanwhile, just like the last time we met, she nicked my expensive ballpoint pen ... and the refills this time!

We did meet again in a London nightclub (where else!) and as far as I can recall, had a brilliant time. Evelyn's fans had tracked her down and, although they, naturally, wanted to spend time with her, were respectful of her private night out. Personally speaking, she sadly lost her baby daughter, Johnniea, in 1989, and is married to writer and musician, Freddie Fox. During the nineties, she released 'Girl Next Door' and 'I'll Keep A Light On', and has never stopped touring America and Europe.

KISS THE SKY

Dateline: April 1991

When two artists, who between them have enjoyed ten top twenty and ten top sixty hits, combine, the result has to be pretty good! And this has happened with Paul Hardcastle and Jaki Graham who, last year, released a re-make of the Jimi Hendrix classic 'Voodoo Chile'. The couple called themselves, appropriately enough Kiss The Sky, and watched the single climb the UK chart. Just recently they issued their second, the compulsive 'Living For You', with a naughty-but-nice slice of sampling from Minnie Riperton's 'Loving You' half-way through the song. Both artists, by the way, are signed to Paul's Fast Forward label and have been working solidly together under cover of his studio just outside London. And this is where I

KISS THE SKY

caught up with them.

It seems Jaki and Paul first met at a magazine launch, although he had been pursuing her—professionally, of course—for four years. "I spoke to Jaki's manager, Tony, and said that I had a few ideas if Jaki was interested," Paul said. "She was, and came down to the studio and we got one track 'Crazy' done. It turned out really well. Then I played her some First Light (Paul's previous group) stuff and she basically ravaged all the songs. We wanted to have a laugh, to have fun working together, then I came up with the name Kiss The Sky. We did some more tracks and it snowballed from there. So I thought why don't we release the product as a band."

At this point, last year, Jaki was signed to EMI and Paul to Chrysalis, but both felt they could go no further with their respective record companies, having suffered a series of yo-yo situations, and a distinct disinterest in their work, as Paul explained. "I felt I'd come as far as I could and I used my major company to my advantage, to earn enough money to start up my own operation. I'm not boasting but now I've got one of the best studios in England, full of all the equipment I'll ever need. Once I'd achieved this I managed to get out of the deal but they still asked for over-rides and things like that because they felt I would go away and have some more hits, leaving them with an egg-on-face type of thing."

As it was, Paul had released product under other names while signed to Chrysalis. "I won't say what they were, but you'll probably find that you have listened to them in one form or another!" Jaki too, wasn't without her problems, as she admitted rather grimly. "I had been bitching to Paul about what my management and record company were doing with me, or rather what they *weren't* doing with me. He'd got his own set-up and I really didn't want to go with another large company and face the same situations I'd left behind."

All well and good, thought I, but, wouldn't they miss the security that a major company had to offer? Paul immediately interjected. "*What* security? There's no security in a company saying 'Listen, we're gonna keep you off the scene for eighteen months until the right record comes along'. Now, say, if the first Kiss The Sky album doesn't do anything, we'll make another one

CHINWAGGIN'

and keep on until it does. With a major, if the first album doesn't make it, it's a case of 'see you later'. Then once you've been dropped by a large company, the future gets a little dodgy. The important thing is to have good distribution, and there's nothing wrong with, maybe, licensing a couple of things to majors, but I think you have to have control. I don't want to have to ask anyone if I can go into the studio to make a record."

And to back up his case, he cited the following example, albeit with a smile on his face. "I remember when I went to the A&R man and told him I wanted to record '19' (UK no 1 in May 1985). He asked me what it was about. I said 'the Vietnam War'. He asked how it would sound. I said *'na-na-na-nineteen'*. I've always remembered the look on his face...and the fight I had!"

Prior to teaming with Paul Hardcastle, Jaki, of course, worked with David Grant. However, she feels a lot happier and more relaxed with her new partner. "Paul has given me more scope. He's helping me to be more creative. I now feel part of a unit, being treated as an equal. I've always said to you that I'm comfortable with people and, as I started out with a band, it's nice to have someone's shoulder to lean on, and bounce ideas off. When I worked with David and Derek (Bramble) it was 'them and me'. Being naïve, I was probably manipulated and knew I was always in second place. But I figured they knew better than me, so who was I to put my ten penn'orth in." Paul took over. "It seemed to me that Jaki was kept in a cage a lot of the time. I thought she'd been involved in her work before but I really had to force suggestions out of her. Now, thankfully, she'll make positive contributions when we're recording. That inhibition has gone."

Talking of Derek Bramble, he's now working in America and Jaki said, using her work to help promote his career there. She continued. "He'd been playing my hits to publishers over there. I suppose he's right in trying to get well—or better—known singers to cover my songs, but what really upset me was I got the impression that when he was asked who the singer was on the songs, he just said 'some girl in England'. I thought 'well, thanks very much Derek'. Y'know what I'm saying, girl...this is the guy I used to say was family."

Being involved in a smaller, compact and tightly-run operation

KISS THE SKY

obviously suits both artists well, but particularly Paul who fondly remembered his times with Steve Walsh and their Total Control label, where Paul not only recorded but also delivered his discs to record stores! That part hasn't changed, he said, because he still travels to those same shops while conceding: "Music is so different nowadays. It's a lot more fashionable than in the days when Walshy began the label where we were all involved in every aspect of a single's life. If a single was dance it would be accepted, but, today, if it hasn't got the latest sample on it, it doesn't sound hip. Mind you, I'm not complaining because working on something of your own is better than someone else working on fifteen different records at the same time."

I then listened to a selection of tracks, some completed, that the two artists were working on, and have to say, was totally engrossed in the music. Paul is such a innovative craftsman while Jaki has mastered such a stylish interpretation of lyric against melody. Interestingly, the 'Kiss The Sky' CD was issued by Motown Records; the cover carried no pictures of the artists who were named only on the inside packaging. However, they were soon identified and the release was known as the 'Paul and Jaki' album. Sadly, it was the only one.

Steve Walsh, the larger-than-life club DJ/singer, died from a heart attack while undergoing surgery in 1988. He had broken a leg in a car accident while holidaying in Spain, and was returned home for the operation.

Paul continued to enjoy a lucrative career as a composer and artist. For example, he introduced a new hybrid of jazz and dance with the first 'Jazzmasters' project, featuring Helen Rogers on vocals. The album scooped the NARM Best Selling Jazz Recording Award and was one of the top selling independent jazz records of all time. 'Jazzmasters II' followed to repeat its predecessor's success, leaving Paul to release three albums 'Hardcastle I' and 'Hardcastle II', and the double set 'Cover To Cover'. The five albums sold in excess of one million copies and were later re-issued on his own company, Hardcastle Records, where 'Jazzmasters III' was also the debut release. He's composed television themes, including 'Top Of The Pops' and 'Watchdog'; musically contributed to the 'Spice World' movie,

CHINWAGGIN'

worked with S Club 7, and.... hell! We could be listening to his music right now and not know it!

PATTI LABELLE
Dateline: August 1986

Where on earth does one start? I mean, talking to Ms LaBelle about her life and career could take a month and fill a book or two. I've adored Ms Labelle for more years than I care to remember, so, hey, was I chuffed to have this golden opportunity! So, let's chat.

Riding on her second hit 'Oh People' from her landmark 'Winner In You' album, Patti's British success has been long overdue. This single followed her million-selling duet with Michael McDonald 'On My Own', a top two UK hit earlier this year. ('Oh People' peaked in the top thirty)

Did she jump for joy at her newly found fame? "No, and I don't want to sound ungrateful because I'm very happy it happened, but I've been doing this type of music for twenty-five years with the same intensity. I'm shocked at the single's success, and I'll get depressed when it doesn't happen again. However, I did have a secret smile to myself because you never know what's going to happen in this crazy business, do you?"

Ms LaBelle also hopes to work with Michael McDonald once more because—"I love him and always wanted to sing with him even when he was in the Doobie Brothers. I approached him—well, Burt Bacharach did then—and that was that. Choosing producers for 'Winner In You' was left to me. I didn't plan to use as many as I did, but they all had good songs and I couldn't resist any of them. But, Burt Bacharach is my favourite; he's so lovely, so cute."

To every self respecting music lover, Patti LaBelle ranks high in the world's list of soul singers, but now that her two latest singles have crossed over, was she worried about being tagged a pop singer (God forbid). "I want to be in the category of singer," she stressed firmly. "People can come to see me perform and put whatever caption on me they please. I can sing a lot of different music, and feel happy with it, and people can capitalise on that.

"If you're a black woman you sing R&B, that's the way this world is. Being called a pop singer seems strange to me, but as much as I'd like to change it, and these categorisations, it's not going to happen for a long, long time. I'm a singer, period. Once you get that crossover single there doesn't seem to be that boundary, and it's gratifying that singers like Tina Turner, Aretha Franklin and myself have finally crossed that bridge. It's not as hard now to do as it was for black women and men. Or should I say the move is a little easier! Everyone deserves the chance to succeed."

Born Patricia Holt on 4 October 1944 in West Philadelphia, Patti grew up in a multi-racial neighbourhood. Her parents divorced when she was twelve, so she lived with her mother. "I was a homely little girl with red hair that changed colour as I grew older. I was so shy my mother offered me money to go and play with the other kids! Needless to say, I wouldn't go—I used to stay in our house and sing in front of our mirror."

The songs the young Patti loved most at this time were 'My Funny Valentine' and 'The Party's Over', and she tried to model herself on singers like Gloria Lynne and Nina Simone. She was educated at the John Bartram High School, and sang in the Beulah Baptist Church choir. Whilst in her teens, she—with Cindy Birdsong—formed The Ordettes, which later included Sarah Dash and Nona Hendryx. The four girls became The Bluebelles in 1961, and a year later enjoyed a huge hit with the classic title 'I Sold My Heart To The Junkman'—the follow-up,

PATTI LaBELLE

she said, to 'You Better Move On'.

With the release of 'You'll Never Walk Alone', Patti LaBelle's name fronted the group. They toured continually—"Five shows a day, seven days a week"—and were lucky if they earned $1,000 a week. The girls supported The Rolling Stones on a European tour where their pianist was Elton John. When his flamboyant career took off, Patti, Sarah and Nona formed LaBelle, one of music's most scandalous all-black rock trios. Patti was the innovator of the sexy 'spacequeen' on stage, with costumes to match. "We wanted to have an image to encourage people to come and see three outrageous ladies," she said. "When the group Kiss copied us, we went into another direction, with feathers and so on. Honestly, when I look back on that period of my life, it's a good thing I have a sense of humour because we looked stupid in all those clothes, despite us being a bit ahead of our time."

The three ladies have remained good friends since the demise of LaBelle at Patti's instigation. "Nona wanted to go into rock, Sarah into disco, and I wanted to get involved in ballads. As I was lead singer, I was really afraid I'd be blamed for the split, and even turned to a shrink because I was so sure I wouldn't handle being a solo performer."

The outrageous side of her persona is mellowing, the star pointed out, yet she still insists on looking different to her contemporaries. She laughed, "I just like it! I spend a lot of time and money on my costumes and my hair, although that's now in the style of my album cover. I do my hair according to the way I feel. Y'know, I've always stood out in a crowd and if that wasn't due to my clothes, it was due to my big mouth!"

That statement led nicely into the Live Aid concert where Patti transformed the finale into her own. Despite rumours at the time, she did not have the only live microphone on that packed stage. "There were a lot of them," she protested. "If someone gives me a mike I'm gonna open my big mouth and sing. Some artists treat the mike as an enemy. It is my friend. God gave me a talent and I think it's selfish not to share that talent, don't you? I feel that if I don't share it, God will take it away from me. Sometimes I know I'm too loud, but I have good lungs, and in the Live Aid situation, I didn't take over. I just sang the loudest."

Actually, fellow artist Cyndi Lauper is quoted as saying

CHINWAGGIN'

"Singing with Patti is like being in heaven." An accolade indeed, I reckoned. Then Patti just laughed when I said she was identified on television as 'the lady in the hat'. "That wasn't a hat" she roared. "That was my hair! Well, not all of it was mine but some intermingled with hair-pieces! One of my styles actually has a name—trash can. For this, my hair is integrated with fake pieces, shaped differently and held together with pins and masses of hair spray. And it proves useful too because sometimes members of my audience gave me small gifts so I put them in my hair."

It's also been said Patti hid fried chicken in her hair, but I'm not sure I believe that. Yet, then again...

Another show was mentioned where the singer once again stood head and shoulders above the rest—'Motown Returns To The Apollo'. Here it appeared she was fighting for recognition against Diana Ross on 'I Want To Know What Love Is'. Once more she giggled. "Yes, it did look as if we were battling away there, but that's only because of the way the film was edited. It resulted in us fighting for the mike, which just didn't happen. Diana and I have always been friends, and the scene wasn't as ugly as it later appeared. The media turned things around into a way that they wanted to see it and I didn't like that because it wasn't the truth."

We moved on to a more pleasant topic—acting. She made her début in *'Working'* by Studs Terkel for PBS-TV, and starred in tributes to Eubie Blake and Duke Ellington, before being enticed to appear in a new production of *'Your Arm's Too Short To Box With God'* by Vinnette Carroll. As the show had been produced twice on Broadway, Patti was reluctant to accept the offer. However, Carroll re-vamped the production to create a role especially for Patti. So, for two years she toured America with the show, playing to packed houses. During September 1982, with Al Green as co-star, the show returned to Broadway for a third time, to break box office records.

In June '83, LaBelle left the production, and a year later made her film début in *'A Soldier's Story'*, the Pulitzer Prize winner by Charles Fuller. While concentrating on her acting career, Patti still honoured recording commitments that included duetting with Grover Washington Jr on 'The Best Is Yet To Come', and with Bobby Womack on 'Love Has Finally Come At Last'. Both were hits, alongside her solo work of 'If Only You Knew', 'I'm In

PATTI LABELLE

Love Again', 'New Attitude' and 'Stir It Up'—the former title being nominated for Best R&B Song 1985 and Patti, Best R&B Performer. "I should have been nominated in the pop category too. The people who choose the Grammy nominations, like the academy and people at the top of the industry, only accept maybe five or six blacks a year." A nomination for any category, I suggested, was better than none: she agreed.

Anyway, with the success of 'New Attitude', the media was in her corner, but, she chuckled, tended to enthuse about 'the new overnight sensation!' "Twenty-one years is hardly overnight! I've always been working and I've always done it the same. I'm outrageous, crazy, big and loud—nothing's changed.... Actually, I'm incredibly fortunate because I've had very good press in my life. Or course, negative things are said about me, but I look at myself and sometimes say 'yes, that's true' or, 'no, they're wrong this time.' I don't hate, or bear grudges against the person who gets things wrong, nor feel like smacking them. I'm too even-tempered...and just hope they get it right the next time round."

The singer is married to a former Philadelphian school principal, and has enjoyed wedded life since 1969. In June 1973 their son Zuri was born (the name is Swahili for 'beautiful'). Originally they didn't plan to start a family, as she explained: "I was touring a great deal and thought having a baby would slow up things. Zuri wasn't a planned child but I love him more than anything." The couple then adopted two boys, Stanley and Dodd (both in their twenties) and sponsored a child in Africa. "I love children and whatever I can do to help, I will. I don't think we do enough for underprivileged children and, honestly, don't think we do enough for each other in the Western world. A lot of times I see hostility, and it seems people don't want to make the effort to help each other.

"People are very greedy and wasteful; they waste food for instance. The South African situation is so horrible, so ugly, but I don't know what anyone can do to change it. It's not only a case of changing the country's government, it means changing a lot of governments in the world because it's all now too inhumane."

Spending time with her husband (who's also her manager) and her family is Patti's priority in life. She told me. "I spend a lot of time with them because I make time. My husband and I are a good match, and he's not a showbusiness husband either. Of course, we have our ups and downs just like everyone else. At one point we didn't like each other very much, so we thought about what we have and it wasn't difficult to make it work." It's interesting that one of her sons is quoted as saying: "There's nothing Hollywood about Patti. She cooks and we eat a lot, watch TV and play board games." Was this true about the cooking? "Anyone would think I was Italian. I excel in cappellini, vermicelli with clams, linguini, scampi and lots of different sauces. When I finish a tour the first thing I do is go shopping for groceries."

Then, her husband said of her: "I see a completely uninhibited person on stage. When I go backstage, that person is gone. Thank goodness I don't have to live with Patti LaBelle the performer!" That statement she agrees with: "Off stage I'm quiet and boring, very laid back, and even-tempered. I keep a balance between the performer and the person. In fact, if I hadn't been in this business I'd have been a housewife and mother. I had no real ambitions to do anything else whatsoever."

What a lady! In 2004 she released her 'Timeless Journey' album, which followed a career dominated by milestones. Like, scooping two 1998 Grammy Awards for 'Live-One Night Only' (Best Traditional R&B Vocal Performance), and 'Burnin' (Best R&B Vocal Performance). Prior to this, Patti won seven NAACP Image Awards, three Emmy nominations and a pair of American Music Awards. Earning an honorary doctorate degree from the Boston Berklee School of Music, winning a 'Soul Train' Lifetime Achievement Award, and a star on Hollywood's Walk Of Fame, she went on to author two books; her autobiography 'Don't Block The Blessings' and the cook book 'LaBelle Cuisine—Recipes To Sing About'. Starring in her own American television specials and series, she somehow found time to be the spokeswoman for the American Diabetic Association; later the National Cancer Institute. She also opened the foundation, The Patti LaBelle Medical Education Scholarship Fund. Yeah, quite a woman!

STACY LATTISAW
Dateline: November 1986

If predictions were my line, Motown's newest signing Stacy Lattisaw could, in time, become a serious threat to the likes of Teena Marie and Janet Jackson. She was, to all intents and purposes, quite a surprising addition to the Motown family, but with 'Nail It To The Wall' showing healthy signs of becoming a hit, it's paving the way for her stunning debut album 'Take Me All The Way'. So maybe Motown's knack of choosing winners is as strong today as it was in the sixties.

Before getting into the interview, a few facts and figures. The young singer was born in Washington DC and began singing at the tender age of six. At eleven years she appeared with Ramsey Lewis in the Fort Dupont Park, Washington, before thirty thousand people. Cotillion Records took a chance and signed her where her first album 'Young And In Love' was produced by the late Van McCoy, released in June 1979. Two more albums

CHINWAGGIN'

followed—'Let Me Be Your Angel' and 'With You', both produced by Narada Michael Walden. Single-wise Stacy Lattisaw enjoyed hits with 'Jump To The Beat', 'Dynamite' and 'Love On A Two Way Street'.

With success came the demand for live appearances, like being a support act for The Jacksons' 1981 US tour, spanning thirteen weeks. "The best part about it was meeting Michael." Stacy smiled. "I watched the show from the wings every night and every night I learned something new. I tried to copy the way he related to an audience. He gets so involved in every performance he did and the way he communicated with the public was something I wanted to do. And the audience liked the way he did it too. Yet, he was so quiet and shy offstage. It's incredible to believe he was one and same guy.....I love performing live because it tests your abilities. You have to give something to the audience to get something back, but when you do, you know you've earned it."

Joining Motown, she said, was the next significant move of her career. "We negotiated with different companies before deciding on Motown. And they didn't have a female singer like myself." It's the general feeling that she could fill the gap left by Teena Marie, whose talent to this day hasn't been realised or exploited. Stacy found the comparison a compliment but added this didn't form part of their negotiations.

Right, to the album which boasts several producers, like Kashif; Leon Sylvers; Steve Bari; Jellybean (responsible for the single) and Narada Michael Walden, of course. Not Stacy's decision, as she told me. "It was Motown's choice to work with the different producers. We wanted to produce an album of variety to show what I could do. There's a mixture of uptempo and ballads in there." Having worked with Narada Michael Walden during the somewhat crucial and successful stages of her early career, it seemed obvious he should contribute to the Motown project. "He sent me the song to my home and I liked it immediately. I told Motown about it and they wanted to do it. Michael and I have a special working relationship."

Taking two months to complete, 'Take Me All The Way' is a positive pot pourri of sounds: good, catchy and commercial songs. The album's title is the singer's favourite track, with 'You

STACY LATTISAW

Ain't Leavin'', 'Love Me Like The First Time' and 'A Little Bit Of Heaven' close runners. Her choice is spot-on, although I argued that 'Longshot' was the cream of the crop. A fabulous debut which is a credit to the young singer, her writers and producers. Both single and LP are moving fast in the States, she remarked. "People began wondering where I've been, so when the album came out I've had to catch up on the lost time."

Becoming part of the music business at such an early age, I wondered if Stacy felt she'd missed out on a normal childhood, like so many child stars. "I don't think so. I came out of school when I was fourteen, then I had a tutor from the 18th Grade, which was a little boring for me because I had no school friends around me. I also missed the school games, dances, boyfriends because I was always out of town...If I hadn't been a singer, I'm not too sure what I'd have done. Probably I'd have worked in an office, as a secretary. My mother insisted I take a secretarial course, just in case."

Yet being in this business does, she admitted, have immense problems, like, keeping in touch with friends. "They're not in the business I'm in. They're either at college or in other areas, which makes meeting up a lot harder. But I don't really think I've missed out on too much because this business has a lot of glamour, and it's exciting, although a lot of work is involved. Let's not lose sight of that."

Two years on, Ms Lattisaw and I spoke again. I noted a more confident artist, boasting a new image and outlook on life. Currently on release, was Stacy's second Motown album 'Personal Attention', and she was being whisked around the East and West Coast by her promotion team. I cornered her in her Washington DC home where our conversation found her pet parrot stealing some of the limelight when his claw caught in his cage. The screeching would have woken the dead!

If ever there was a marked change in an artist, then Stacy fits the description. 'Personal Attention' shows a maturer and assured singer performing tracks which all have single potential. Check out 'Let Me Take You Down', 'Find Another Love' and one of the album's highlights, 'Electronic Eyes'. Like Stacy's debut 'Take Me All The Way', this new album boasts a number of producers—Ron Kersey, Vincent Brantley, Jerry Knight and Aaron Zigman, and stablemate Brownmark with whom she penned 'He's Got A Hold On Me' and 'Changes'. This pair of titles also marked Stacy's début as a producer. "It took me a year and a half to complete 'He's Got A Hold On Me' because I was so busy. It's a personal song and, although I find I write best about myself and love, it's like releasing the secrets from a personal diary because everybody knows what you're thinking."

Teaming with Brownmark followed an introduction by Debbie Sandridge, the album's producer, as Stacy explained. "Brownmark is a friend of Debbie's and he had some material which we liked. He really is a very nice person and we got on well because he's about the same age as me at twenty-four." It was also Debbie's idea to team Stacy with Howard Hewett on 'Ain't No Mountain High Enough', which, I feel, is strong enough for single release. I know—not another bloody version, but, hey, listen to it!

It really is quite astounding how different Stacy sounds on this album; she looks so 'new' as well. The hesistant young vocals have been replaced by a deeper, almost sophisticated adult sound. She agreed. "I'm aware of my musical growth and I think this is probably the best album I've ever done. It is a very exciting time for me right now. I feel this album is more me because I enjoyed singing these songs. It was as if they were written with me in mind. I'm now at the stage where I have to believe in a song before I can sing it."

Once again, the album took so long to develop because of the assortment of producers involved, but she avoided falling into the trap of them saturating her voice. "Sure some take away artists' identities but I usually know what I want to do and get on with it. A lot of singers now work with several producers and the idea with me was to get the best out of me. Some people are amazed that such a strong voice comes from my small body. I'm only 5 foot 6 inches, and I don't know where it comes from. It's just there! I had early training though because my mother used to sing. In fact, the first questions that journalists always ask me are about my voice and being so young."

Choosing songs isn't a problem for her because ballads win every time. "I just love them!" she laughed. More seriously, she

STACY LATTISAW

added: "A singer can put so much more emotion and energy into a slow song, and I find them easier to sing. However, the public seem to expect me to release dance tracks as singles so I really have to go along with the tide."

Although her career takes up most of her quality time, Ms Lattisaw tried desperately to keep hold of her upbringing: that of a normal gal! "Huh!" she started. "It's so hard for me to be a regular person. If I go out I'm usually recognised. People just follow me around for autographs, although in Washington I'm left alone because they're used to me being there. But even that means I have to be on my best behaviour all the time. There are times though, when I want to be left alone, so I get in my car and drive—I just drive around enjoying my freedom.... I'm going out with someone in Washington and have known him a few months now. He travels with me because that's the only time I get to see him. Sometimes he can't travel with me because he's in school and it's hard for him to leave it, but usually we work something out. Being in this business artists have to be prepared to sacrifice personal lives and relationships, and I knew this when I started out."

Growing up in the entertainment business, Stacy has been aware of most of its highlights and downsides, but readily admits she was protected from, let's say, the more unsavoury aspects because her parents shielded her. "They've always travelled with me, and I think that was imperative with me being so young. There's so much related to the record business, but they've always been protective over things like drugs. Unless you're actually in the business you don't realise just what goes on behind the scenes. But I wouldn't be involved in anything else."

When Jheryl Busby, successor to Berry Gordy, took over the running of Motown, it appears he wasn't interested in Stacy's work. She did, however, release the "What You Need" album, and duetted with Johnny Gill, but her career stagnated. After Motown, she abandoned secular music. On the personal front, she married Kevin Jackson and has two children.

IAN LEVINE
Dateline: July 1989

Ian Levine with Chris Clark

Ask anyone what the two biggest musical influences were during the sixties, the answer will be: The Beatles and Motown. Sadly, The Beatles cannot be re-united, but the original excitement and magic of Motown can. And has been!

Motown today has become a mainstream R&B label with its musical heritage buried to make way for a new, changing roster of artists. The only way folk can hear those magical memories was to dust off well-worn singles or purchase a continuous flow of re-issues. That now has changed. The artists responsible for laying down Motown's musical foundation—some say, the company's finest years—can be heard again on record. However, this time their records don't carry the famous blue "M"...they carry the Nightmare logo, later to become Motorcity Records.

In 1959 in Detroit, Michigan, a black youngster's determination to produce music in a white man's world led to the opening of Tamla Motown. The youngster, Berry Gordy Jnr, born into a family of storekeepers, opened the first major black-owned and operated record company. From his run-down offices at 2648

IAN LEVINE

West Grand Boulevard on the rough side of Detroit, 'The Motown Sound' was brought to life by a handful of young enthusiastic artists and producers.

Twenty-seven years later, in 1986, a young white nightclub DJ and record mixer, Ian Levine opened Nightmare Records in Acton, London (The label name originates from The Andantes' 'Like A Nightmare').

Here's a short resumé of Ian's career to date... Larger than life, Levine ("My passion is food") is known for his hi-energy tracks, mixes and compositions. He is also a well-respected DJ but confines his turntable antics to the Heaven club these days. He first came into his own via his work with The Exciters. This was around 1976, the same year he discovered the Chicago sound with artists like Barbara Pennington, Evelyn Thomas and L J Johnson. Two years later his Chicago talent dominated the dance floor and later crossed over into the national charts with hits from Evelyn Thomas ('Weak Spot' and 'Doomsday') and L J Johnson ('Your Magic Put A Spell On Me'). In fact, both artists appeared on the same *Top of the Pops* programme and later—with Barbara Pennington—toured Britain as The Chicago Soul Revue.

With artists like Tyrone Ashley, Doris Jones, Carol Woods and James Wells, Levine enjoyed more success on both sides of the Atlantic. During 1976 the fast talker returned to DJ work for four years, following a run of contractual and financial problems, but his love of working in the studio got the better of him. Four years ago he decided to team up with Record Shack to spearhead the emerging hi-energy market, by turning this faster-than-speed music into hits, notably, 'So Many Men, So Little Time' by Miquel Brown, and Evelyn Thomas's 'High Energy'.

Satisfied he still had the magic, Ian once more turned his attention to expanding his artist roster with names like Earlene Bentley, Laura Pallas, Eastbound Expressway and Marsha Raven, and, with Record Shack, became a forerunner in hi-energy music which he calls 'the concept of light and shade'. Then, as often happens, a clash of ideas led to Ian leaving the Shack set-up. His loyal acts moved with him.

Initially he licensed his work to other companies—Steve Mancha and Hazell Dean to EMI; Sharon Dee Clark to Arista; Moonstone to Warner Brothers, and so on. Although this was a means to an end, licensing product wasn't an ideal situation for the ambitious Levine. So, late last year, he took his most ambitious step and opened up his own label, Nightmare. "I wanted to establish my own sound," he explained. "I had had no personal identity and this was bugging me. I had all this music inside me and it was going nowhere."

From his youth Ian's passion was Motown and its artists. The first artist he had the pleasure to meet was Kim Weston when he was fourteen. He was on a flight to Los Angeles with his parents, and a fellow traveller was Mickey Stevenson, then Kim's husband and head of Motown's A&R Department. Stevenson arranged for Levine to meet Kim and a friendship was sealed. This would stand Ian in good stead years later.

After building up a solid reputation for himself in the music business by, he said, spearheading Northern Soul, and working with the before mentioned artists, Levine was determined to bring Motown's glorious years alive again. This time, his way. The music he chose fits into three categories: to re-create the original Motown style with an eighties' arrangement, cover versions of original classics, and original material written in the sixties' style. By doing this, Levine says, the music won't be limited to any one market. "What will remain consistent though is the quality of songs and the outstanding vocals, both of which played a vital role in the original Motown sound. The music isn't geared to meet any fashion or dance-floor trend, it's geared to suit each individual artist and to fill the void for quality R&B. There's also a demand from people who want to hear the artists they grew up with and they're sick of buying endless re-issues. So I'm offering them something new. My first love is Motown, and I'm now in a position to do something about it. I believe in soul music, but Motown in particular, and to actually work with these great artists is a pleasure in itself."

When soul concert promoter Henry Sellers (also a dear friend of mine) brought Kim Weston to Britain eighteen years after Levine had first met her, the two agreed to work together. And so the Sixties joined the Eighties. Kim became one of the first artists to record for Nightmare and currently has three singles released—'Signal Your Attention', 'Who's Gonna Have The Last Laugh?' and a re-make of her Motown classic 'Helpless'.

IAN LEVINE

Joining her on Nightmare during the initial stages of recapturing the sixties were Mary Wells ('Don't Burn Your Bridges'); The Velvelettes ('Needle In A Haystack', 'Running Out Of Luck'); Marv Johnson ('By Hook Or By Crook', 'Ain't Nothing Like The Real Thing'—duet with Carolyn Gill); Jimmy Ruffin ('Wake Me Up When It's Over', 'On The Rebound'—duet with Brenda Holloway); Scherrie Payne ('Chasing Me Into Somebody Else's Arms', 'Pure Energy'); Mary Wilson ('Don't Get Mad, Get Even') and Steve Mancha ('Standing In Line', 'Hopelessly').

Once the word was out, Motown's acts flocked to Nightmare by various means. For example, Mary Wilson contacted Brenda Holloway, somebody else got in touch with others, and the little snowball rolled into an avalanche. The result is that a staggering number of artists are now signed to Nightmare Records. "My goal is to build another Motown here. It is our heritage and that sound has no musical equivalent in the history of music. Although I've never met Berry Gordy, I have met many of his writers and producers. And I firmly believe the magic of, say, Junior Walker or Mary Wells, shouldn't be lost forever. The crazy thing is Motown had all this wonderful talent and don't seem to want to do anything with it. Of course, there's nothing they can do to stop me working with these artists and, from the response I've had so far, I know the soul people want these acts on record again. Look, I'm not doing anyone any favours, believe me, because they want a deal as much as I want their singles."

In March 1989 ex-Motown acts assembled in one place—home on 2648 West Grand Boulevard, Detroit. They had gathered to honour Ian who was in America to announce that the 'Motown Sound' was back with a vengeance and that he, an Englishman, was in charge of the new project. "No-one's ever done something like this before. I honestly don't think it can fail. We'll capture the hearts of America. We're working with names people grew up with. Motown is the only music all of America loves."

Although he had hoped that a few artists and members of the media would support him in Detroit, he was stunned when journalists, photographers, radio and television crews fell over themselves to capture these precious reunion moments. The media crammed together on the lawn in front of Motown's home—now the Motown Museum, Hitsville USA—which carried

CHINWAGGIN'

a blue and white banner 'Welcome Home Motown Alumni' over the front window, while traffic was kept moving by police.

Neighbours and fans converged on the scene, not wanting to miss this historical occasion, which brought together artists who hadn't seen each other in over fifteen years but who had one common factor—they all wanted to record again. It was a trip down memory lane as Choker Campbell, Carolyn Crawford and Earl Van Dyke chatted to The Elgins, The Fantastic Four, Kim Weston and Marv Johnson. Memories were exchanged between Ivy Joe Hunter, Hattie Littles, Sylvia Moy, Ronnie McNeir, The Andantes, Rare Earth, The Velvelettes, The Vandellas, The Miracles, The Contours, Sammy Ward, Richard 'Popcorn' Wylie, Joe Stubbs, C.P. Spencer, and Martha and Lois Reeves.

Kerry Gordy, his wife Karen, Raynoma Singleton (Berry's former wife) and Motown Museum president Esther Gordy Edwards, represented the Gordy family. She said. "Anytime the Motown family gets together, it's just a lot of love and happiness and nostalgia. It's been thirty years and it's still a family". Not only did the Gordys support the public reunion but Ian stressed. "We've been pledged the support of the whole Gordy company now. I've even been wished good luck by Jheryl Busby, the brand new president of Motown. I can't really ask for more at this stage."

One of the more exciting attendants was Wanda Rogers of The Marvelettes, a tiny figure dressed in red and a pair of huge sunglasses. After a prolonged illness, Wanda, like so many, was reduced to tears of joy as she spoke of her delight at seeing so many old friends again. Probably The Contours' manager, Jack Ryan, summed up everyone's feelings. "When Motown left for Los Angeles, everyone left here was like a bastard child. It's nice someone thinks enough to come and assemble talent and take it into the eighties. We've been looking for someone who loves the music enough to do this."

Once the last flashbulb popped, the artists retreated into the Hitsville studio for a jam session, where Martha Reeves led the proceedings, which covered several Motown classics. "Martha originally refused to work with me but then she went to the reunion and changed her mind," Ian told me. "The Miracles too have resisted many offers to reform, but they're doing it for this

IAN LEVINE

project. And after six months of very hard work, I've got The Marvelettes back together again."

The week in Detroit was crammed with recording sessions at the United Sound Studios, and was the result of Ian's careful planning which had included writing and recording with partner Steven Wagner in 'Southlands', Levine's own studio. The artists earmarked for recording learned the songs before laying down their vocals. Many, of course, hadn't been in a studio since leaving Motown but, once faced with a microphone, the magic returned. Thirty-two tracks in all were completed in round-the-clock sessions. One recording achievement was the live session featuring Levi Stubbs on lead, Ronnie McNeir on piano, and members of Rare Earth on guitar, drums and sax. The song which featured the jamming artists was 'I Can't Help', which, when released, would benefit Detroit's homeless. The studio was buzzin' and the historic occasion was captured on film, as well as being broadcast live on American television.

As an aside, during his stay Ian was honoured by Detroit's City Council and the Michigan House of Representatives for his contribution to the betterment of life in the city.

Early in April, the Nightmare crew moved to Los Angeles for Phase II of the Motor-Town Reunion Project. Levine hosted a press conference at the Red Zone Studios where, once again a whole host of artists attended, like Syreeta, Scherrie Payne, Jean Terrell, Lynda Laurence, Mary Wells, Chris Clark, Frankie Gaye, Rose Banks, Barbara Randolph, Bobby Taylor, The Undisputed Truth, Sisters Love, Claudette Robinson, Leonard Caston, The Originals, Gladys Horton, Brenda Holloway, and others.

Once again, when the media formalities were over, sing-along sessions crept into the proceedings before the artists actually began recording proper. Bobby Taylor led the jam session, while Leonard Caston played piano. Frankie Gaye performed a chilling version of 'What's Going On', leaving Claudette to sing some Miracles' tracks and Mary Wells to perform 'My Guy'.

"The reunion was an emotional time for everyone," an excited Ian raved. "There were people in the studio who hadn't seen each other in years and when everyone got around the piano to jam, well, it was amazing."

The American trip gave inspiration and hope to many. Not only to the artists involved but to Detroit. When Motown moved away in the Seventies, the entertainment industry went with it. The nightly venues regularly used by those in the business, became empty and gradually closed down. The motor industry for which Detroit was also famous, ran into decline.

Today, Levine felt, the heart of the city is a dangerous place to visit, and the once grand buildings are slowly decaying through lack of city funds. Now, thanks to his determination to record the ex-Motowners, pride and money will hopefully be ploughed back into the community by people who care. "I feel like I'm on a mission to bring back music that should never have gone away. And to revive singing careers of artists who should never have stopped performing. This is THE Motown reunion. No-one's ever put all these people together since Motown was in Detroit. And I think it's kind of strange that it took an Englishman to do it."

In April 1992, Ian and I spoke again, as fans flocked to London's Wembley Arena and Birmingham's NEC to see the spectacular gala 'Giants Of Motown' featuring the Four Tops, The Temptations, Edwin Starr, Martha Reeves and the Vandellas, The Supremes and The Marvelettes. Some thirty thousand people have supported these dates, and many more attended the off-shoot tours. However, the 'Giants of Motown' also highlighted Motorcity's fifth birthday. The company, Ian explained, was partly financed from the money earned from Evelyn Thomas' 'High Energy' and: "I borrowed heavily from the bank and my mother, re-mortgaged my house to the tune of one and a half million, and all because I wanted to record these wonderful artists. And the more I worked with them the more I wanted to add to the label. I didn't set out to open Motorcity. I wanted to record artists from Motown. I formed the label because up to that time Nightmare had one hundred releases and out of that, twenty-eight were by ex-Motown acts. Kim was the very first artist I worked with. 'Signal Your Attention' was recorded in January 1987."

During those heady experimental days of the label, Ian's productions tended to be a continuation of the Hi-NRG sound—an electronic formula that worked but, as he pointed out, "The music had to change. Fans wrote to me, they wrote to you too, saying we love the artists, it's great to have them back, but we can't identify with the music. So I was really influenced by the fans to do something different. Y'see what they loved had dried up during the Seventies, so they had nothing to follow. Less so in the eighties. Motown had created a generation of fans for its music but Motown of the Eighties wasn't giving it to them. Sure we made mistakes at first, but I think we have eventually got it right."

Motorcity also had its fair share of criticism, or 'enemies' as Ian calls them, including the followers of Northern Soul. This surprised him. "They've never accepted the music. If it was released on some obscure Detroit label, say, it would have been a different story. Subsequently, we didn't get their support. However, the Motown fans have been our bread and butter...the hardcore fans who've bought all we've released because the artists meant something to them. We've got The Supremes, Martha Reeves and the Vandellas, The Miracles, David Ruffin, Earl Van Dyke. In fact, the lead singers or groups of some of the first artists to release product under the Tamla Motown label when it opened here in 1965...Brenda Holloway, Kim Weston...I could actually be repeating the original release running order here."

He's also the first to admit that Motorcity has been underfinanced, and money is always a problem with any independent label, especially when it's wasted. Er? Ian cited an example of this wastefulness—"Mary Wilson and Martha Reeves had advances and didn't honour their recording contracts. Between them it cost me $13,000 and this crippled me. I couldn't afford to lose that kind of money. When Mary was on the Joan Rivers show, she said she was looking for a deal. Well, she already had one. With me. She then recorded an album for some obscure label but I'm told there's problems there. If she'd done the job properly with me, she wouldn't be in this situation. I also heard the proposed single has been withdrawn as well." Martha's situation was different, he said. "She hurt me the most because out of all the artists I longed to record, she was the one... She also took every opportunity to embarrass me, but my respect for her prevents me from suing her over the unrecorded songs. I've just let it lie."

CHINWAGGIN'

These aren't the only ones to cause Ian grief; Syreeta and Johnny Bristol are at the 'irreconcilable differences' stage. Yet he said: "Who knows what will happen? I'm ever hopeful that differences can be fixed because the problems are largely creative. Like, Carolyn Crawford is known to lose her temper, but we laugh about it afterwards. She's such a great talent and has been wonderfully supportive.

"There is another side to the coin which makes Motorcity all worth while. I'm able to rely totally on Edwin Starr and Billy Griffin, and have their constant guidance and backing. Like, Edwin comes to London every two weeks or so with new songs. He never asks for a penny. He sings, produces, spends lots of time with other artists, helping out where he can. Marv Johnson too. Hattie Littles, The Elgins, J.J. Barnes, The Fantastic Four, Barbara Randolph are just a few who are so wonderful to work with. No problems at all, and they've stuck by me through thick and thin. Pat Lewis too, of course. Saundra Edwards—she's just flown in and we've cut fourteen songs. I mustn't forget Sylvia Moy, she helped me build the company. And the Vandellas are the sweetest people I know. And getting Gladys Horton back into the studio, well, that Marvelette magic returned as soon as she started to sing. The Supremes are a dream to work with, absolutely fabulous. Scherrie is a sweetheart. Sure, there are difficult moments but that's the business. They've stuck with Motorcity even though their fans may not have. And there's Frankie Gaye...."

Motorcity product was distributed by Charly Records, and when the deal was first forged, the future looked brighter than bright. From that relationship, Frances Nero enjoyed her first ever hit last year with 'Footsteps Following Me'. "Despite it being our first hit, it's well known there were contractual problems with Charly," Ian moaned. "I didn't receive any money for 'Footsteps' and neither did Frances. What makes me angry is that she had the opportunity to become a big star, but the follow-up 'Making My Daydream Real' got lost in litigation. No-one saw a copy. Motorcity and Charly were in dispute from May to September 1991; that's a long time and, naturally, the company suffered. Only two singles were issued—the Frances Nero title and Billy Griffin's 'Technicolor'. Charly then kept the rights to certain of these artists' tracks, but not exclusively so, as I can use them on albums."

Once the legalities were settled, Motorcity teamed up with the Total Record Company—a move that thrilled Ian. "I love them. They are wonderful people. They believe in what I'm doing and make constructive suggestions about artists and releases. We're currently in the dance chart with 'Snake Walk' by Beans Bowles."

Five years on, seven hundred and fifty songs later, Levine has become disillusioned with some aspects of the business and, surprisingly, some of the artists, particularly those motivated by money. "And I'm sure they're disillusioned with me because they imagined I could make them into millionaires, with million selling records. Believe me, I've done everything I can, I mean that. I can't make them rich, I only wish I could. I did promise that I could bring them back their fans, give them the chance they wouldn't otherwise have had, and I've done that. I set out with a dream in my soul, hope in my heart, but I had no idea the kind of shit I was letting myself in for. If I'm totally cynical about it, they burned me. So, things aren't the same now, they can't be. I just wish I could do more. Detroit is such a poor place, money is so short, and I can't guarantee financial stability. I am doing my best."

And that 'best' included co-promoting the 'Giants of Motown' tour which followed the Motorcity Tour in 1989. "Barry Collings got these artists together in the same way that I got them into the studio again. And now they've got Wembley! My God, some of them would have killed to get there. So, what I'm saying is, everybody's dream is becoming a reality. Fans have supported us, and with Barry Collings, we're now able to say 'thank you'. What Motorcity is doing is for prosperity, whether it's appreciated or not. I never expected to make any money from this, and that's not going to stop me now."

As time passed, Motorcity struggled. Finally, and with a heavy heart, Ian Levine stopped recording his artists. He'd hit one brick wall too many. Certain acts retaliated, either in print or verbally, because they believed they hadn't be paid their rightful dues. Some probably had a genuine point. Nonetheless, whoever or whatever was right, Levine's idea was unique and he made it work. As Kim Weston told me, perhaps he spread himself too thinly. Maybe he should have concentrated on just a few ex-Motowners; got them established, then signed more. Who knows?

Motorcity Records' material has been regularly licensed to various companies to release as re-packaged compilations. Ian continues to work as a composer/producer, while his most recent release is 'Reaching For The Best: The Northern Soul Of Blackpool Mecca'. The compilation representing the changing sound of the Mecca, was released mid-2004 by Sanctuary Records. Ian and I hope to write the history of Motorcity Records before I get much older.

HATTIE LITTLES
Dateline: 1991

It was a privilege talking to Ms Littles because not only is she something of a living legend in black music circles but she's survived the unpredictability of music's whims to record again. And this came about quite by chance...but more of that later.

Regrettably, Hattie Littles suffered from a lack of material while signed to Motown's Gordy label in the sixties, probably because she was one of Berry Gordy's 'strange' signings. The lady sang the blues—and the blues really didn't fit in with his commercial R&B sound at the time.

If our information is correct—and it took some time to sort it all out, believe me, Hattie actually issued two singles—'Back In My Baby's Arms Again'/'Is It Love?' and 'Your Love Is Wonderful'/'Here You Came' during 1963. But hidden away in the can are at least another handful of songs, including 'You Got Me Worried' and 'False Words', both written by Clarence Paul, while Marv Johnson penned another 'Wish That You Were Here'. One day, she says, these may be released but happily she did return to the studio after joining the Motorcity Records family, where she's just recorded her third single 'Waiting For The Day'.

The blues chanteuse was signed to Ian Levine's record company after Kim Weston saw her at her godmother's funeral. Kim passed on the word, and things moved quickly, culminating in Hattie visiting London which is where I spoke to her. Her first

CHINWAGGIN'

visit—"and it's snowed hard since I arrived," she told me. "Then when that stopped, it rained. I wanted to see so much of the city but all I've managed is Big Ben and the Queen's house. Oh, and London Bridge. I guess, once the weather clears I'll see a whole lot more. The rest of the time I've spent in the studio. So far we've recorded nine songs for my album 'The Right Direction'. I've actually done twenty tracks now both here and in the States."

Ms Littles spent a shortish stay at Motown, about three years in total she said. Her recording output might have been meagre but she spent much quality time touring, notably with Marvin Gaye and The Spinners on the Marvin Gaye Revue. "I was the opening act and toured on and off with them for quite some time. I think I did different gigs with The Spinners, then Jimmy Ruffin. We worked Cleveland together. I also toured with my cousin Choker Campbell—so I was busy most of the time."

She had nothing but fond memories of working with Marvin, whom she misses tremendously to this day. "Marvin Gaye spells g-o-s-p-e-l. He was the type of person you could talk to, who would listen. He'd never cram advice down your throat, but if you needed advice, he would try his very best to help you out. He was never critical, never used fancy words...never called you stupid or things like that. He always had time—and he was like that with everyone, not just me."

Staying under the Motown banner was a move she was content with at the time, despite the obvious drawbacks. "Yes, I was happy. Motown was a family—and I've repeated this phrase so many times. I don't know whether everyone actually liked each other or not, but I do know it was like coming home. Motown had a nice, homely feeling and I stayed because I had these feelings. I sang better with those feelings. Everything felt right...if I hadn't felt anything how could I expect anyone listening to me to feel anything!"

Hattie has, in fact, been singing since she was four years old. Her family wasn't musically inclined so she got her training and inspiration from the radio, listening to Howlin' Wolf, Billie Holiday, Bessie Smith and others. "I loved them all, the deep blues artists. And I later became inspired by B.B. King, all the heavyweights....'The Sky Is Crying' is the prettiest song I've ever heard. These artists meant the world to me, and I knew what

HATTIE LITTLES

I wanted—to sing the blues. The real thing, that is, the songs that curdle the cream in your coffee."

And as if to prove her point, a verse of soul wrenching lyrics filled the air as she wailed, "Ain't got nobody...."

Why did she leave Motown? "I don't really know how that happened," she laughed. "One day I was there, the next day I'd gone. But I didn't give up singing. I went back to the church and formed a gospel choir. And I was happy again."

So, being with the fledgling Motown: those innovative, heady and sometimes turbulent sixties, I wondered why, unlike some of her fellow artists she hadn't succumbed to the written word. I mentioned books by Mary Wilson and Raynoma Gordy Singleton, as examples. Once again Hattie laughed...jeez, it was a loud, ballsy sound! "Nobody would want to hear my story about Motown because I have no dirt to dig. I had no problem with anybody and certainly nothing bad to say about Berry Gordy because I don't feel that way. To be honest, I'm not inspired to write and certainly not interested in reading about slander. I feel it should all be left alone—nobody can change what happened, and those books made me feel sad. I'm not into hurting people...if you can't find anything good to say then say nothing. Then you won't feel guilty afterwards. That's the way I was brought up and that's what I believe. I'll never sell out. I actually walked past Ray's book, and also Mary's. I found me a crossword book instead."

I mentioned that in one of these books (I forget which one now) Hattie came across as not being too fond of Diana Ross. She instantly retaliated. "I was misquoted. I'll admit I was not in love with Diana Ross. I just stayed away from her. That's all I'm gonna say!" She then added—"Or you could say, I wouldn't buy a stamp to post a letter home about her, or, if I saw her in a storm I wouldn't give her my umbrella."

Having been in the music business for countless years, I wondered if there's anything Hattie would change. There was. "When I was at Motown I would have picked another single to sing! One that would have sold more than six copies!"

Anyway, to the present day when she told me her hiatus from the recording studio had affected her not at all. In fact, she was surprised at how easily she settled behind the microphone again, although admitted she thought the invitation from Ian Levine was a cruel hoax. "I really thought it was a joke. People do sick things and it took some persuading before I believed Ian's phone call to be real. I was so excited: I believe I cried all day. I was given another chance and I'm loving every minute."

Strangely enough, Hattie Littles' burning ambition is *not* to enjoy a hit single. "I want to sing the blues to the largest audience there is. A real-down-home blues. That would complete everything I have ever dreamed of during the last twenty-five years."

I don't know if Hattie's dream came true, but, unlike so many artists, she did remain loyal to Motown until she unexpectedly died from a heart attack in June 2000. Apart from her music, which thankfully is available on both Motown and Motorcity compilations, I'll never forget that laugh!

MELBA MOORE
Dateline: November 1982

What does the name Melba Moore mean to most people? Think about it and I'll bet your first answer is—a singer. Me too. But after spending a rather lengthy time with her just recently I was astonished to learn that singing is just one of her talents and as she listed her other achievements and capabilities I wondered how so much could come from such a wee lady—"Five foot and a half inch and a bit more, maybe less". Her words not mine.

True, Ms Moore is a singer and one of considerable note: she's also a stage and television actress. In fact, American viewers know her as a veteran of everything from variety shows to ground-breaking dramas. She made her Broadway debut in 'Hair' and received a Tony Award in 1970 for her starring role in 'Purlie'. In 1976 she won a Grammy nomination for her version of 'Lean On Me', and her portrayal of Harriet Tubman on ABC's 'The American Woman: Portraits Of Courage' received rave reviews.

Her recording career has seen her through deals with Buddah and Epic, leaving behind a trail of hit singles like 'This Is It', 'Pick Me Up And I'll Dance' and 'The Greatest Feeling'. Now,

CHINWAGGIN'

the lady is signed to EMI America, where her current single 'Love's Comin' At Ya' is doing business on the disco and national charts and, because of this, Melba popped into London for a short visit.

As well as the single, this trip gave her the opportunity to speak about her second and forthcoming album 'Side Of The Rainbow'—which is a cracker! She smiled in thanks when I said this, adding: "I've been on tour whilst doing this new album. I'm usually doing a lot of different things so what happens is that the backing track and rhythms, and sometimes the background vocals are done while I'm away. Then I'll come in and do my bit. If I'm singing background as well, the studio people will dub my voice onto that as well.

"Actually I used to be a background singer and love doing the 'oohs' and 'aahs'. These singers are extremely important to us, particularly on this album because there's not a lot of heavy orchestration, so the sound of their voices...well, let's put it this way, my producer and I are very picky that everything is right. We don't just take a bunch of background singers, we use different ones for different tracks."

Who chooses your material? "It's really a collective effort. Generally, I have the last say. Sometimes it happens we only have room for seven songs and that makes life awkward. This time we had that...I'll call it a 'challenge' with a couple of songs because we had more good tracks than we had room for. So we started arguing about what the guidelines were, found the priorities, and listened to each other's opinion."

Because Melba is such a petite lady one could well imagine her being pushed around in the studio, with no-one really taking much notice of her. It's not like that, but she was at pains to explain. "I have to carry a stick but obviously I can't beat everybody up! Seriously, I have to be diplomatic, and basically you have to have strong reasoning and I work with a group of people whose priorities are very much in line with each other. We have a specialised way in which we look at the same thing. For example, I might say: 'I love this song 'cos it shows off my voice,' and someone will turn round and reply: 'Yeah, but we can't sell it, so what you gonna do—listen to it in the shower?!' So I have to find a song that satisfies me artistically and that will

MELBA MOORE

satisfy them commercially.

"I would dictate to the people in the studio, if I thought I could get away with it! Because of my personality everybody just shoves me in a corner and I think there's reasons for this. You have to be aware that you are a woman, and primarily because we do a lot of things, especially when there's a group of men, we react to each other in a certain way—men and women— and that's why I usually slouch off in a corner. But then I have to remind myself not to let that happen. I can't push anyone around, not because I'm a woman, but because it's not the way I can get things done well. So I have to keep grabbing their clothes and say 'Look, I'm the singer, don't forget about me!' I really have to do that.

"Seriously though I have to be aware of my producers and for myself because with my new producers on the album they were a little intimidated by me being a star and that only got in the way. So I had to do a lot of play-acting to make sure that they saw me as I am, and that I was concerned about their point of view. I wanted them to be comfortable and be able to say what they thought without being afraid of hurting my feelings or being afraid of getting insulted. I aim to put everyone at ease in the studios, just like a social gathering, make the recording sessions a social event by just taking the stiffness out of it and that comes with being female."

Let me backtrack for a while. Melba Moore was born into a musical family and she reckons her parents were instrumental in pushing her into showbusiness. "My father said 'Mel, you always wanted to be different' and I don't really know why he said that 'cos he's an entertainer and so was my mother. So we—I have three brothers and a sister—were around music all the time. I wouldn't say my parents pushed me into the business, at least not knowingly, because they wanted us to have real jobs; what they considered to be security with paychecks at the end of the month. But nobody can guarantee that now anyway. They gave us a real fine education to make a life for us, but not in showbusiness. However, I really had to do it and I didn't even know why, it was just there. I taught in a school for a year before I went into the business because I didn't know myself. A job was a job, I thought.

CHINWAGGIN'

"I taught music because it was good to me. My parents probably directed me consciously more towards that until I had this terrible urge to be around music proper, and be around showbusiness people. I was just drawn and eventually it brought on a depression because I was so confused. I didn't know what to do and I just kept talking about it. My parents never realised I was that serious. It's a problem with youngsters today who don't realise they have this artistic mentality, but these drives can really send you insane if they're not channelled properly." Once Ms Moore was straightened out, she felt happier with her chosen career; able to cope with the strains of stage work and the demands of public life.

Let's return to her music—a woman working in a man's world—or at least that's what the male species likes to think, she said. "I've picked people to work with me, and they chose me, and I have to find ways of gently asserting myself continually because men do have the tendency to take over.... and I have this tendency to lay back even though it's not a real problem any more. But at the end of the day, I'm still a woman working in a man's world.... I don't like to think it's anything to do with my lack of height, but I know that people treat me the way I look.... I think I've always been treated like a child! It's not a disadvantage really; each of us has a personality, a visual personality that people respond to and what you have to do is understand that. If you don't, then it becomes a disadvantage or a stumbling block. I know this now. I have a gentle personality and that's OK. However, I still have to get the job done and to do this I don't have to become someone else but I have to work in a positive way.

"I suppose, when it comes to men I like them to be old fashioned. I like them to be gentle with me, opening doors, things like that. If it's not like that they'll tread on me! I spend the best part of my time just getting out of their way. I am a fragile sort of person but I have a strong spirit and that's all I need."

Do you see yourself as a sex object then? Well, that was the wrong question to ask as Melba collapsed in a heap. "*Me*??! You are kidding! No, I'm just the girl next door. If people think that, it's just the way my body looks and the way my mechanism works. It works best as a clean cut thing. And I think that where my mind and spirit is at now, supports that too."

As a rule Ms Moore endeavours to keep her personal life totally separate from her professional one, but she did open up—albeit very slightly. She's married with a young daughter. Her husband is a member of the management group that looks after her professional interests. She laughed as she remembered when they first met. "He actually asked me did I sing? In fact, I think he's asked me that more than once! He did ask me very seriously why I wanted to be in this business because originally he wasn't part of my management group. He was an entrepreneur; he's done a lot of things, and will do a lot of things because he's not one of those people who remain in one business and one area. He's just gregarious. And he wanted to know was I one of those show business people whom he doesn't have a lot of respect for. When I told him, it didn't seem to matter whether I had any talent or not.... Then he got involved with my career and I felt I should continue with it and should finish it wherever it takes me, because he agrees with why I feel I should do it. I feel the ability to bring with my little person very strong, positive energies and they didn't have to be confined to show business. It could have been any other area.

"We have a little girl but apart from saying I have a family I like to keep them out of the publicity; he likes that too. We're tremendously supportive of each other and I feel that he gets at least a chance to use some of his talent in what he's doing here, but eventually I think he'll really want to go ahead and do his own thing. This is a temporary partnership for now. We really have totally different areas that we function in, which again allows us to support each other, and still have our own lives physically and every other way, so that's really no problem for me, say, to be away from home. It's a good balance really. I do miss home, sure. Well, I do and I don't. I don't feel an aching. I miss things. But there's so much going on that I always have something to bring home with me."

One of her return plans was the possibility of a new television series titled 'The Melba Moore-Clifton Davis Show'. Negotiations were still in progress, she told me, before adding—"I really only said that to you to give you a bit of my background, and I don't know how important it is to this interview. What we're talking about is a comedy series, which will hopefully be based around the character in 'Purlie', the Broadway show. A southern bumpkin, that type of thing. We would create a kinda funny intellectual character because of my background in the south. Because my mother was on the road so much—like I am now—I was brought up by a woman who never learned to read or write, but who knew all about folklore and different customs. I had a very good education from one side and then there was the other side of me and that character comes naturally. It's difficult to put into words because I don't really know myself that way, but it's a strong part of me nevertheless. I've done very few things that I've compared to how much music I've done—yet those interests outside music have always overpowered everything. I've always marvelled at how easy acting is compared to some of the music I've done. Yet, music is very satisfying. I've got to have that challenge, but don't put it in the wrong perspective. Music isn't second in my list of priorities, but I think you have to understand that once you get the chance to do something that's important to you...like, before I had the chance to sing, I would have died if I couldn't sing. I had to do it. I had to have that channel and I'd hate it if it was cut off to me now. I was a trained singer and I've worked my life at it, while acting is something that's just parked out there and it got to me. So, by comparison to singing, acting is easy."

With a pretty hectic personal life and a career that encompasses most areas of entertainment, what did the future hold for her? "Hah! That's a question. I don't know, but what I will say is that with this new album it is the very beginning of a definite path that I feel now I'm able to take. This is a point in my life where I'm having a great deal of input and I know the direction my music is going; how it's exposed to the public and the image that has been created for me.

"If this album does what we hope it will do, it will unite my public—black and white, the theatre, television, a vehicle that crosses over everything."

'I'm Still Here' is Ms Moore's most current album, her first ever gospel recording. Prior to this release she wowed audiences with

MELBA MOORE

her two act, one-woman stage show 'Sweet Songs Of The Soul'. In 1996 she took over the role of Fantine in the Broadway musical 'Les Miserables', becoming the first black actress to step into the leading role. Six years earlier, her recording of 'Lift Every Voice And Sing' became the official African American National Anthem. A deeply spiritual lady, Melba is devoted to the rights of children as evidenced by her Melba Moore Foundation For Abused & Neglected Children.

ODYSSEY

Dateline: July 1982

A band that started its career with a direct stab at the top ten singles chart has gone from strength to strength with almost every release, enjoying both club and national status now. The membership is quite elusive; interviews are rather sparse and they don't lend themselves to scandalous headlines; in fact, they say, they don't really do anything that's exciting. A rather low-key, happy-go-lucky bunch that you'd pass in the streets without giving a second glance.

The name Odyssey is a household one, thanks to the succession of hit singles and albums. Now they're riding high on another—'Inside Out', a national monster, taken from their new album 'Happy Together'. Mind you, the single was drastically re-mixed, because the album track wasn't strong enough on its own. To be honest, I've never really thought too much about Odyssey. Sure I love their music, their distinctive style and ability to produce great, great sounds, but as for the trio itself, the people behind the hit machine, well, confess I didn't even know their names.

That has all changed as I was lucky enough to spend three evenings with Louise, Lillian and Billy as they ploughed their way through a string of club appearances to promote their current

ODYSSEY

single and album. And after three nights on the trot of early morning bedtimes, I felt like a walking zombie. Well, I was OK, as late morning sleeping is now a part of my lifestyle. But they couldn't enjoy that luxury as each day was crammed with something to do. Interviews, radio and TV spots, photo sessions and the like. Yet, the threesome carried on—smiling always, willing and friendly to the hundreds of punters who were fortunate enough to be at the clubs they visited. Yes indeed, Odyssey thrived with their public, and once the champagne, orange juice and Perrier was drunk, off they went to another club to do it all again. It would, they explained, have been impolite to rush in, lip synch to the single, and disappear without a word. The ladies in particular, enjoyed sitting, chatting and sipping with fans, while Billy was usually surrounded by eager girls who didn't want him to leave. All these extra-curricular moments, of course, shot their itinerary all to shit!

Louise Lopez is the more outgoing; her sister Lillian tended to be wary of those around her. But as she found her confidence, she soon realised there were some good people about and that the music business wasn't full of the sharks she's chanced to meet. As Louise is the older of the two, she calls the shots, by telling the others what to do, when and why. On stage the situation is quite different. Lillian is the one with the real distinctive voice, the red-hot gospel voice—one that cuts an edge.

Despite the massive success Odyssey have enjoyed to date— 'Native New Yorker' (1977), 'Use It Up And Wear It Out' and 'If You're Looking For A Way Out' (1980), 'Hang Together', 'Going Back To My Roots' and 'It Will Be Alright' (1981)—they are still the folk next door. Sounds corny, doesn't it? But that's the way it is with them. There's nothing 'fancy' about them; the girls are really more at home working behind the scenes than in the public eye. Whatever success does come their way, they thank God for it, although neither are particularly religiously inclined.

An incident which made me smile happened at The Norfolk pub in London. We were sitting, talking to the kids there and Louise wanted to go to the loo. I suggested she 'hold on' until we were ready to go. So she did. Thirty minutes later we were still chatting, waiting for the pub to close. Eventually, she could contain herself no longer. Once inside the ladies, she was

CHINWAGGIN'

confronted by a lady, absolutely in awe of Louise— *"Oh, you're one of Odyssey aren't you? We saw you at such and such...my husband is a great fan of yours...blah blah blah."* Louise just stood there, legs tightly crossed, busting a gut, carrying on the best she could, for a full five minutes. In the end I rescued her and by all accounts I was just in time! Silly, the things you remember innit?

At most of the club stints, I was on bag duty and, to be honest, was gratified to see the state they were in—Louise carried a chockablock bag with a busted zip which needed careful attention when being swung around, and Lillian carried a similar sort of disaster, inside which her make-up was housed in a plastic shopping bag! Just like us!

The Lopez gals grew up in Connecticut, although their parents hail from the Virgin Islands. The girls were originally known as the Lopez Sisters when their third sister, Carmen, was a member of the trio. This line-up, I was told, was relatively successful as they ended up appearing at Carnegie Hall in New York as the headline act in the 'New Faces Of 1968' concert.

"An agent heard us there," explained Louise, "and asked if we would like to go to Europe. We did play a lot of clubs throughout Europe and the Scandinavian countries." The touring lasted about five months and on their return to the States Carmen swapped entertainment for married life. That didn't deter the duo as they recruited Manila-born Tony Reynolds to become one of the rare two female/one male trios in the business, earning themselves a steady following in the New York area for several years.

In 1976 Louise and Lillian became affiliated with Chappel Music as writers (which is their main love) and there met Sandy Linzer, then producer of the Savannah Band, with August (Kid Creole) Darnell in the membership. 'Native New Yorker' was the result of that union and Odyssey became recording artists, with a gold disc for their efforts! Before recording their second album 'Hollywood Party Night', Tony Reynolds left the line-up to be replaced by their current member Billy McEachern—a native of Fayetteville, North Carolina, who was an experienced church and group singer prior to joining the girls.

As an aside here, the Odyssey ladies remind me of Sylvester's Two Tons of Fun, with Lillian portraying the red-hot mama that gospel music demands. She also possesses a sense of humour that is appreciated only by a handful, yet with her wit she neither hurts nor offends. Louise, on the other hand, tends to be the spokeswoman, being at the beck and call of journalists and amateur photographers.

I gathered the sisters lived in the same building now—one has the top flat, the other the bottom. "We get on fine, except for the phone bills," laughed Lillian. "I don't make any calls, she does. If it comes to that, I don't get any either. I just listen in on Louise's, so I don't see why I should pay half the bill!" In her half of the house, she has a reserved area for souvenirs collected from their travels. The shelves are now overflowing from her hoardings. "I'm thinking about moving to a larger place just to house all these items. I'm a compulsive collector and what thrills me the most is that I remember where each thing came from. When I'm home I spend the best part of my time lost in memories."

Both have outside business interests but I gathered their current obsession was painting. Louise used oils and Lillian water colours, as the latter told me. "Louise deals in oils because she's an aggressive person with paints. She likes to pile the colours on with a very vivid result. Water colours are that much softer but I find there's still a hidden depth. It's the calmer way of painting that I enjoy." Any chance of a public showing? "Oh God no... I'm not that good. The pictures I have done aren't that many and are personal to me. One day though when I get more confidence something will happen, but not now." Another of Lillian's crafts is her tapestry—"When I'm on the road I always take my sewing along. I relax like that. It's better than having a drink. I've got masses of stuff at home. We travel around so much, we're in different places all the time, and sewing seems to keep me in touch with home."

And there's more. As well as her other talents, Louise is a dress designer, favouring the old Ethiopian tradition, although not necessarily limited to East Africa. They both wear long, flowing gowns on and off stage, all designed by her, and this style has become their distinctive trademark. She also designs the jewellery—the Egyptian collars, Cleopatra armbands and Zulu necklaces. It beats me where she finds the time, particularly as their career now seems to be dominating every waking hour. She shrugs off my comment, claiming there's always time for the important things in life.

Back to the music. Lillian is the lady who sits at the piano to open her soul. Pull out 'If You're Looking For A Way Out' to see what I mean. "There were a lot of husbands walking out on a lot of wives when that song came out," she smiled. "It meant a lot of things to a lot of people. I guess it also broke up a lot of relationships 'cos it got to a lot of people which isn't good." Didn't she get tired of singing and listening to the same songs? "Sometimes it gets a real drag. But I haven't heard 'Way Out' for months and now when I hear it I feel good. I think I did a good job, even if I say so myself."

"What's that dear?" asked Louise, side-stepping her publicity work with a bunch of fans.

"Nothing, just blowin' my own trumpet. Promise I won't do it again."

Her expertise at the keyboards had nothing to do with childhood lessons, rather her mother's patience, as she told me. "Yes, my mother taught me. As a child I sat at the piano and it seemed to come so naturally. But, I'll tell you this, I could see this man, this person, standing next to me or near me. Every time I sat at the piano, this person would appear. I didn't say anything to anyone because I guess I was too scared to. I didn't really understand about spirits or the other world then, being a Catholic you're taught not to believe in these things. Anyhow, one day my mother and I were at the piano, and out of the blue she said to me 'do you see that person standing there?' Boy, did I feel happier when she said that! It was real spooky at the time but when I realised that it wasn't me who was cracking up, I felt so much better.

"I had mother's support and I suppose that it was through her encouragement that I persevered. I didn't go to no gospel churches or sing in choirs. Catholic churches don't have them. So I guess it all came naturally and for that I'm grateful."

Despite the fact that my 'official' interview was cancelled at the last minute due to press confusion, I was able to spend more time with Odyssey than most journalists during their three night promotional tour. A real bonus for me, and I can truthfully say, we had a lot of fun, met loads of people, but it was bloody hard work with long hours. I'm now off to my bed to sleep for a fortnight....

ODYSSEY

As far as I can remember, Lillian and Al Jackson toured Britain as Odyssey for several years. But other than that, I've lost touch with them. The trio last enjoyed a British hit in 1985 with '(Joy) I Know It' released by Mirror Records.

RAY PARKER JR
Dateline: June 1981

When Erskine Thompson (Ariola/Arista's promoter) phoned to ask if I'd be free on Bank Holiday Saturday to do an interview I told him where to go in no uncertain terms. However, my mind changed when he told me the subject was Ray Parker Jr, who was due in London for the weekend to do some annual shopping.

Before our lunch, Ray booked in time to talk with Robbie Vincent on his Radio London programme, and that is where I first set eyes on the star. The entrance to the radio station was locked, leaving me no option but to traipse though doors, along corridors in an eerie silence. Where was everybody on this cold, windy Saturday morning? Still in bed, if they've any sense. With Robbie's studio in sight—red light on—I waited in the newsroom. Twenty minutes later, Mr Parker Jr, his girlfriend

RAY PARKER JR

Debbie, the photographer, Frank, and Mr Vincent emerged. We moved to a nearby Italian restaurant, where the menu was varied and the waiters spoke little English. After much ado, my brandy and coke arrived, but Ray's pure orange juice took a miracle to appear. Due to the waiter's inability to understand the order, Ray tolerated squeezed oranges in various glasses, delivered at intervals. Why the fruit wasn't squeezed all together then poured into a jug was a problem we couldn't solve. I could have willingly strangled the sodding waiter for treating a guest to our country with such obvious disinterest.

However, the best was yet to come! Over Ray's sardines and mustard sauce, which were, incidentally, served complete with heads, tails and bones ("I reckon the only thing they did was kill them," the singer quipped), we talked music and he told me he had worked with so many artists that he had to be reminded of them. What he does remember is the fact that he's played on over five hundred gold albums and only received one—from Boz Scaggs. "More often than not, I'm not even credited on the sleeve! But hairdressers, studios, fashion designers are. That's just the way it goes; maybe they're more important than the musicians these days."

Ray's shopping trip involved buying boots as a priority. From London he planned to visit Paris to purchase jeans. You seem to have a passion for tasteful attire, I remarked, noticing the gold adorning his wrist and finger and the cut of his jacket. "I can't buy the clothes I want in the States. It's mostly off-the-peg stuff and if you want anything altered they look at you strangely. To have clothes made to measure takes weeks, and then they're usually not right. So I shop in Europe."

Tucking into the main course—under-cooked vegetables, scampi which was kicking and hamburgers dripping blood, served with so few french fries we had to share—Ray talked about Marvin Gaye, an artist he so enjoyed working with, having collaborated on several sessions, with 'I Want You' being the one actually released. "I haven't seen Marvin for over a year now."

"He's living in Brussels now after living here since last June," I volunteered.

"Oh yeah, that's right. Didn't he upset your Royal Family by cancelling a show? Boy, that was something."

CHINWAGGIN'

Subject change. Rick James. And the fact that he'd not as yet visited Britain, although there were rumours a tour was planned. Ray laughed as he spoke. "Rick! Now, he's fabulous. A little wild. I toured with him about a year and a half ago—it was real crazy. He got into a little trouble because he smoked dope on stage. Not only that—which was bad enough—but he handed joints out to the audience.... He doesn't do that anymore. He now hands out lines of coke! Y'know, Rick bases his show around Bootsy. In fact, he started out dressing like him, the whole bit... white suits, white guitar. He certainly can put an act together though—he's quite something on stage, believe me."

Is the UK ready for him? I asked

"I guess so, but you won't be the same again!"

Ray Parker Jr, a Detroit native, formed his first group, The Stingrays, at the age of six. And on reaching his teens, mastered the guitar and worked in Detroit's 20 Grand Club where he spent a couple of years working with a host of Motown acts, like Stevie Wonder and The Temptations. His house band included Michael Henderson and Hamilton Bohannon, and it was they who worked with Marvin before Ray was signed to Invictus—"with the incredible Holland-Dozier-Holland. They made some great records for their acts. Laura Lee, Glass House, Freda Payne—'Band Of Gold' just fabulous—I guess I played with them all. Invictus closed because of money problems. Holland-Dozier-Holland made a lot of money at Motown but there were law suits and that kind of thing floating around, so Invictus went out of business and sadly closed down. Very talented people though."

During 1977 Ray worked with Stevie Wonder when he toured America with the Rolling Stones. It was a great success, he said, but he returned to Los Angeles a frustrated man. The reason was he'd worked on hundreds of hit songs, had written top selling singles, yet he still didn't have his name in the public spotlight. "It wasn't all ego either," he joked. "There was only one thing I could do, I gambled and formed Raydio, and divided my time between the group and my session work." He penned 'Jack And Jill' for his new band in his home studio: a somewhat gimmicky sound he admits, but it did the trick just the same (The single was a top twenty UK hit in 1978). In the flurry of companies wanting to sign Raydio was Arista, who also offered him total artistic

RAY PARKER JR

freedom. It was an offer Ray couldn't refuse and they're still signed to this day.

Our meal ended with fresh fruit salad and *tinned* cherries—another uninspiring dish—which meant we could thankfully leave the restaurant to say our farewells. While in conversation, a guy walking along the street stopped before us to ask. "Aren't you Ray Parker Jr?"

"Yes, I am."

"It's a real pleasure to meet you sir, at last!" beamed the guy, shaking Ray's hand.

We trotted on, with Ray laughing—"He knew me! He knew me!"

"See I told you, you are famous after all!"

Within three years Ray was very famous indeed. 'Ghostbusters' was his greatest triumph as a single. Taken from the movie of the same name, this 1984 release was also a Grammy Winner in the Best Pop Instrumental Performance category. He enjoyed three further UK hits—'Girls Are More Fun', 'I Don't Think That Man Should Sleep Alone', 'Over You'—and through the nineties released albums like 'I Love You Like You Are', and a pair of 'greatest hits' compilations. He remains in constant demand as a session musician.

BONNIE POINTER

Dateline: November 1984

BONNIE POINTER

It took several attempts but finally the transatlantic phone wires connected me to Bonnie Pointer in Burbank, California, who, after a three year absence is back with her album 'The Price Is Right' and its first single 'Your Touch'.

We both agreed, however, that 'Johnny' was the better track—"I plan to get that out next. In fact, when we've finished this interview I'm going to phone my producer and tell him. Oh, hang on, Sharon, I want to turn my stove off...."

Here's the history lesson. The four Pointer sisters were raised by their minister father in Oakland, California. They sang in church choirs until Bonnie and her sister June began singing pop music in San Francisco nightspots. Before long, Anita and Ruth joined them and The Pointer Sisters were born. They became support singers for a number of acts, earning considerable acclaim on the way, before launching their own career with 'Yes We Can Can' in 1973. From that, they hardly looked back. Bonnie pointed out that one of their career highlights was being the first black act to perform at the Grand Ole Opry, and then being the first pop group to play at the Opera House in San Francisco.

As well as performing, Bonnie started composing her own songs and during this time co-wrote 'Fairytale', a country and western hit, and a Grammy winner for the sisters in 1974. Their crossover success was soon to come thanks to the semi-sellers 'Everybody Is A Star' and 'Fire' during 1979, which introduced the runaway hits—'Slowhand' and 'Should I Do It?' in 1981; 'Automatic' and 'Jump (For My Love)' in 1984. (Followed by 'I Need You' and 'I'm So Excited').

"I'm very happy about their success and happy for them. They deserve it and I hope it continues," Bonnie explained. "I don't regret not being with them now because I know my time will come. I'm a very patient person, so I can wait. It's like the Jermaine Jackson situation with The Jacksons, I suppose...and if 'Johnny' is the track to do it, I could well perform on stage with them as my backing group!" (It wasn't and they didn't.)

Bonnie confided she had to leave her sisters because the ideas she wanted to utilise couldn't be worked into the confines of the group. She added: "It wasn't the right combination to have at the time. I wanted to sing different songs, do other types of music that they didn't want to do. I also wanted to write more. Oh, there were so many different areas I needed to move into. So, it was best if I left to fulfil these things. We're still very close though, and of course, still see each other as often as we can."

Joining Berry Gordy's roster of artists to release two albums, was a move she was proud of, but one that resulted in no recognition. However, I hoped to raise the tone by mentioning the beautiful ballad 'Deep Inside My Soul' which, if there had been any interest shown in her Motown career, should have been subjected to a massive marketing campaign, because it was quite easily the best she had recorded whilst signed.

She explained that towards the end of her Motown stay she worked primarily with producer Jeffrey Bowen but the liaison was unsuccessful. What we did hear, however, was that she and Bowen had taken out a contract on Berry Gordy's life! Nothing more seemed to develop from this American source, I added, so what really happened? "It was pure fabrication. And I don't know how it all started. I was surprised when I read the press statement and let's face it, it's a pretty drastic statement to make. It's hard to explain...I was in a total state of shock...Berry Gordy is a wonderful person...."

Why didn't you just deny the charges I asked?

"There seemed little point, so I didn't bother. It was all fabrication and replying would have made things worse. I then got involved in legal hassles with Motown and couldn't work for three years. I really couldn't afford to be off for that time—but I did put it to good use. I took acting lessons and was offered a lot of scripts.

"Going into the movies isn't an easy step to take, but I feel for me it could be a natural progression. I enjoyed broadening my mind and studying daily. I really didn't want to become bored doing the same thing day in and day out, so I decided to make the time work for me. Now, I'm glad I did because I feel there are lots of areas I can get involved with, apart from singing.

"I also feel Motown wasn't promoting me properly. Like, I wanted to go on tour and Motown don't like their artists touring. They didn't seem to be bothered with me after a time and when I wanted to do something, they wouldn't let me.

"Despite what people thought at the time, I'm not married to

BONNIE POINTER

Jeffrey (Bowen). He's a real good friend of mine and I like working with him. I'm not married to anyone, although I'd like to be someday. When my work is done. It's not easy combining the two, but I suppose that depends on the person. I live alone with my dog Povlioni, and that's by choice. I actually like being by myself. I have a lot of friends, mostly in the music business because I can relate to them. We don't talk about the business all the time though. I get on with all types really—doctors, lawyers, even Indian chiefs!" I didn't pursue this.

Now to the album itself. 'The Price Is Right', a splendid selection of terrific songs, which, Ms Pointer explained, was a problem in itself because—"I realised that it would be a testing time for me, and I had nightmare after nightmare trying to decide what to record. I had to be very selective in getting things right, and it was so hard with over a hundred songs to choose from."

To help her, Bonnie recruited Jeffrey, Greg Perry and Brian Holland; together they sifted through music sheets. "We tried to pick songs people would relate to in the same way we did. Brian Holland's situation with Motown is of course, well...he was in the same boat as I, but now he has his own record company and is doing very well."

Greg Perry, who worked with The Honeycone, is married to Edna Wright, who wrote 'Under The Influence Of Love', which is included on Bonnie's album, while 'Premonition' features sisters Ruth and Anita as backing vocalists. Both are fabulous, but more significantly, mark a singing reunion after five years.

The personal, private Ms Pointer likes a quiet time when at home, reading, writing and painting. Says she. "When I'm away from the helter-skelter of the business I do need to have time to relax and do what I enjoy. Mind you, today isn't such a good day, because it's very windy, and California is covered in smog. It's like a blanket. San Francisco has fog like London, but here we have car exhaust fume based smog. I also exercise a lot, bike, use a few weights, run, jump rope and go to the movies. I like to laugh, although I do enjoy a series movie. Rodney Dangerfield is my favourite comedian...I like Joan Rivers too, but you have to be famous before she makes a joke about you. You know you've made it when she has a go at you."

For a lady who prefers her own company and a quiet life, how

CHINWAGGIN'

come the poses on her album sleeves hide few secrets, and indeed the jacket for 'Deep Inside My Soul' showed more than it should have. "You think those shots are risqué?" she roared down the phone; "Well, I'll tell you what happened. I got to the studio and the photographer gives me a swimsuit to put on. So I do. He makes the choice. I am a sensual woman, but even I was a bit embarrassed all the same. I didn't mean to shock anyone; it's just the way these things turned out. Say, you should see the posters of that album shot! I'm even thinking of doing a centrefold for Penthouse or Playboy.... no, I'm not serious. Honestly!"

A good time to close our chat. Actually, I was beginning to feel guilty because Bonnie Pointer was obviously hankering to eat her lunch of a ham, cheese and mushroom omelette, which had probably by now gone cold and stuck to her frying pan. So with no more questions under my belt, we gave British Telecom a rest and got on with our respective lives.

In 1994 Bonnie joined her sisters at a ceremony to unveil the group's star on the Hollywood Walk Of Fame, and two years later was reunited with them on stage. She also continues to perform as a soloist throughout America.

BARBARA RANDOLPH

Dateline: April 1989

Barbara Randolph's name has been missing from record sleeves for some time now, but thankfully that's all changed because she's recorded a track 'Joey' for the forthcoming movie *'Perfume'*, and has been in the Southlands studio over Shepherds Bush way to cut tracks for Nightmare Records—one being a new version of her Motown classic 'I Got A Feeling', first issued on the Soul label in September 1967. She followed this with 'Can I Get A Witness' during August 1968. Both singles carried the same flipside 'You Got Me Hurtin' All Over', but more about that later on.

The lady has also appeared in two movies—*'The Cactus Flower'* and *'Guess Who's Coming To Dinner'*, sang the title for a soap opera, and became a radio broadcaster. Yes, there's lots to tell and what follows is the result of a two-hour conversation held in London just recently.

Naturally, I couldn't wait to meet her, a Motown legend, and was flattered that she chose to share her professional life—told in a candid and positive fashion—with me, and ultimately, you the readers. She's quite a fragile lady; slightly built, quiet natured and extremely friendly. She also happens to be married to Eddie Singleton, a music business genius, and owner of Tarca International, his record company. However, let's start at the beginning.

Barbara Randolph-Singleton was born in Houston, Texas, and travelled to California when she was three, and has lived there ever since. She was an adopted child, and had one sister who died. Her adoptive mother also passed over, but Barbara was able to locate her real mother with the intention of building up a solid relationship with her, to compensate for the lost years.

Prior to signing with Motown, she recorded for RCA. "It was a nothing deal. I had a really brief situation with them. They sent a representative out from New York to California, and he signed up a few artists. Then he moved his whole family out and within a month they fired him and dropped all the artists! However, before that happened I recorded—you'll never believe this—something called 'Malaguena Salarosa'. I don't know how I got to do it, let alone who chose it! I was sixteen or seventeen at the time. So that was the end of my RCA career!"

She decided to abandon a future solo career to join an established group. "I travelled with the original Platters when Zola Taylor left. I recorded an album on Mercury with them, and then toured with them. I was about twenty years old then. I had two leads on that album, one was 'The House Of The Rising Sun' and the other was—oh, here we go again!—'Big Daddy, Tree Top Tall'. I have no idea where these titles came from. So that was like my second recording contract, and then...nothing."

In time Ms Randolph went to work with the touring band Steve Gibson and the Red Caps, and while working in San Juan she met a touring Motown show. Said she, "San Juan is like Vegas in as much as the hotels have a main room and a lounge. I was working in the lounge and The Supremes—Diane, Mary and Florence—were performing in the main room in this very fancy hotel. It was in 1967, I think. The group were just moving then, they were still little girls, but were big stars, even though they hadn't been around the world at that time. They finished their show then came to watch mine, and I think it was Berry Gordy's sister Esther who suggested I go to Detroit to record for Motown."

BARBARA RANDOLPH

This was during the period when Motown had a huge influx of female vocalists, as Barbara recalled and as the history books confirmed. "Brenda (Holloway) was there before I was, and I guess Kim (Weston) was also. She was involved with Mickey Stevenson at the time. To be quite frank with you, the first thing Berry Gordy wanted to assign me to—and I don't know if Esther had anything to do with it—was The Supremes. Even at this point Berry was thinking of replacing Florence in the group, but Miss Ross was averse to my replacing her. Although journalists have hinted that Berry fancied the majority of his female artists, we did not have any type of relationship. I rarely saw him because at that time he and Miss Ross were very close and she was very demanding, very possessive and seemed intent on having this man as her husband. I don't think anyone could have gotten too close to him even if they desired to do so."

Despite The Supremes being top group at the company, Barbara did get to work with their writers and producers, Holland, Dozier and Holland. According to her, any artist could record their product: "It's true. Anyone could produce you as well. As a matter of fact, Hal Davis, who ultimately became the one who produced The Jackson 5, was one of my original producers there. He decided on the tracks I would record. Hal was also from California, so I knew him first as a friend. So we cut one track and then the other. You see, when you signed to Motown, you signed with them for management also. So it was as if your entire livelihood depended on them, and you couldn't sign to an outside agency for work."

When 'I Got A Feeling' was recorded, The Supremes' presence was felt again. "My record hit the chart with a bang in the United States, then within a week, it was like everything stopped. The single went in with a bullet, then The Supremes had a single out and everything was geared towards that. Gladys Knight was there at the same time, and she couldn't get anything going. No female artist—Martha and the Vandellas were working in the clubs—could get a record out. No one at that time had a record promoted. They were just released and that was the end of them. I watched this happen with Brenda and Blinky (Williams) as well."

Then came 'Can I Get A Witness' which Barbara recorded after Marvin Gaye. This is what she told me. "Again it was the choice of the producer. The acts didn't have a lot of say in their songs. There were writers there on the staff and if they decided they wanted to produce an artist, they would get it approved, then go into the studios and record the material with you. The only problem with that was you were charged for the sessions! And this money comes out of your royalties. So, now you can see why I only released those three titles there. Today, the album comes first, but in those days it didn't. You did a forty-five and if that was a success you did an album. And I guess I thank God in a way because if I'd done an album I'd probably end up owing them $5 million!"

When Barbara received her first royalty statement, she said she actually was in debt to Motown for roughly $300,000 for those three songs! A smile covered her face. "I can't tell you how. They had a little bit that I had supposedly earned from sales, something like a couple of thousand dollars. And they had the 'you owe us' bit, and they subtract that from what you owe them. And it's still $300,000 or something. So it takes you a long time to catch up! I only imagine that other smaller acts that recorded albums were in debt to Motown for life. It was very difficult. Everyone was looking for a break...we were just kids after all. However, I did come from a show business background. My mother and aunt were actresses, and knew this was wrong. Also I had been singing and performing before signing with Motown, and my mother was very intelligent, but she tried not to interfere too much...even though she was kinda one of those interfering people! Nonetheless, she had the right instinct about this, but I signed anyway."

Being on Motown's management roster, Barbara, like other artists, had no choice but to rely on the department to secure live work for her. A situation she'd not been in previously. "Before Motown I'd go out as a single and work all over the United States. But once you've signed to them, you can't do that any longer. And if they don't give you work, then you're there without any income, and you're not making money off records. We were assigned to managers that we paid for, and that manager was in charge of getting you work. I had problems with the man who was managing me at the time. I had no trouble with Berry Gordy, but I had a lot of trouble with my manager and he wouldn't get me any work. Finally, I got work from Larry Maxwell, who was managing Marvin and Gladys. I just approached him, telling him the trouble I was having, and the company didn't seem to care, even though I'd done the major movie *Guess Who's Coming To Dinner*. He said he'd send me out with Marvin, and Marvin said it was OK.

"It was difficult working when I went out with Marvin because as you know, these was his troubled years. I was Tammi Terrell's on-stage replacement. This venue had booked Marvin and Tammi based on the popularity of their recordings, but Tammi was in the hospital, so I was sent in. The club didn't want Marvin as a solo artist, and I think I was chosen because I was capable of singing her part, and came the closest to her stature."

In fact, the two singers were great buddies after meeting in New Jersey because Tammi actually replaced Barbara in Steve Gibson and the Red Caps. She was, of course, devastated at Tammi's early death in March 1970. "I felt very saddened, as everybody did. It was a very shocking thing to happen to her at the pinnacle of her career. She was a very lively, zestful person and it made everybody wonder what is this all about. Tammi had paid her dues so to speak, she'd been out on the circuit, and finally gotten to Motown and she'd had success. I saw her all the way down to crutches, when her capabilities had just vanished. It was very disturbing to everyone. There are so many rumours about her death. The only thing anyone knows for sure is that she suffered from an inoperable brain tumour, which I imagine, in this day and age, they'd probably be able to do something about. But in those days...well. She had some very wild relationships with different guys, and she was a very emotional person. OK, so she lived on the wild side, but we all loved her. She was easy to love, and was a real personality.

"She always seemed to team up with someone that was in show business and had an ego. It was said she was first hit by a telephone and that injured her. Oh, many things were said, and I don't know if I believe any of it or not, but I'll tell you this. It's possible, very possible. Maybe certain people felt she was leading a reckless life, but nobody deserves that. Tammi was a sweet person, who came from a very respectable family. Her father was a preacher; she came from a religious background. When she

CHINWAGGIN'

started on the road, she was innocent. But an unbelievable change happened. She just loved and trusted the wrong people."

Replacing her friend as Marvin Gaye's partner on stage was another eye-opener for the lady because she never knew what to expect. "Working with him was hectic and nerve-racking. However, he was extremely likeable, easy going, with a very mellow personality. I personally never heard him raise his voice, or get into any type of loud situation with anyone. I had the greatest admiration for him; I admired him before I ever worked with him. But he was like that—everyone loved him. I met my husband at the time I was with Marvin. We were performing at the Coconut Grove, and it was Marvin's first really big main room engagement. We were there with a full forty-piece orchestra, the works. Ed was with Motown at the time, and came to see the show."

Not all her public engagements with Mr Gaye went smoothly, and Barbara cited one incident that she laughed about afterwards. "I was booked to appear at the Apollo with him, and it was one of the many occasions he didn't show up. I wound up appearing there alone which was really frightening, particularly if you know anything about the Apollo theatre! It's very scary—they throw hard-boiled eggs—and the audience is waiting to see Marvin! It was touchy, but in the end I guess they felt sorry for me. Usually the audiences don't feel sorry for anybody, usually they're very cold. But I made it through that, so I reckoned I could handle any situation from then on!"

Another aspect that caused the singer concern during her stay at Motown was the lack of publicity—a situation many ex-company acts have spoken to me about. For her own part, Barbara has no recollection of meeting the media, let alone conducting an interview. I asked her why she didn't question this? "Again, I felt as if Motown were building me into something at that time. They had their own publicity department that issued the pictures and articles, but there were very few interviews. I mean, articles would come out, but it would be their own publicity people providing the copy. And while you're with Motown you're still hoping that everything will turn out right. I wouldn't have even considered saying anything to anybody (about this situation). You're too involved in trying to straighten things out and make

BARBARA RANDOLPH

them work for you. And then.... you just walk away.

"Motown had the kind of environment that you did hang around a lot. You'd go up there on a daily basis and you'd listen to songs, to come up with something. Once contracts were signed, they moved very quickly, the work started. The word goes out—here's a new artist. People start looking into you, and the producers are there listening, the photographers start sizing you up, and everything gets very busy.

"I've got to tell you, it's quite a surprise to me to know that anybody has been following my career here. The United States is a very different place. Ed has often said: 'You're as well known as your last release'. I don't care if you've had ten gold records, it's just like they don't care after a while. They're very fickle, but the British are so loyal. England is attuned to the history of music unlike any other country in the world.... I never got anything at all connected to overseas sales. I'm sure the company did fairly well from the CD compilations. You never know. I might have earned a few bucks, and now that Motown's been sold it might be easier getting money out of them!"

During the early sixties Barbara befriended fellow artist Martha Reeves who, at the time, was another struggling for record releases. "I love Martha. When I was working in New York at the Apollo, Martha and the Vandellas were working at another club, a very nice nightclub, and I went to see them. She was really gracious to me. Sometimes there were some jealousies between artists and that sort of thing, but not with her. She was very nice. She's not really the difficult person people make out...she's been through so much. I'm afraid I haven't kept in touch with her... actually I haven't kept in touch with anyone."

In between the serious stuff, we shared many a joke. One in particular related to Mary Wilson's book 'Dreamgirl: My Life As A Supreme'. Barbara is mentioned in the novel (pages 69/70), but she's not really. Confused? "Yes, she has me in her book, uses the name Barbara Randolph and speaks of something, like how we went out in Detroit, and says she feels that I'm still there...I'm still a gospel singer there. What Mary wrote has never happened in my life! Someone showed me the book and said, 'You're in here, look at this'. And I'm reading it and saying 'who's this about'? She was speaking about someone else who was obviously very vivid in her mind, and somehow she put my name to that other person, and whoever that other person is, probably said 'Hey, that's me, but my name's not Barbara Randolph!' Still, she spelt the name right."

The singer's stay at Motown was relatively short, although she can't remember her contract's duration because there were options added to it. She does remember that: "It might have been longer than two years because I had to ask for a release. It took me a few months to get out, and it was like a blackmail attempt on my part, hoping to make them (the company) straighten up. If you're not going to give me work, if you're not going to record me then I want to be released. They mulled over it for a few months, then Ralph Seltzer (Motown's lawyer) finally said, 'You know, I'm sorry you feel that way about it.' He wrote me a nice letter, but you see, the other thing is, he gave other people trouble. Like I say, my family was sophisticated in many ways as far as this business was concerned. When my mother and aunt were actresses, it was in the days when blacks did very little outside of maids' roles and such. They were very progressive in the sense that they fought for rights in different areas. They were militant in their own way, they knew the law and they knew what to do. And so Motown couldn't really have given me any trouble...The rest of the kids, well, their families wouldn't have known what to do, but my family would have tied them up forever."

Many authors have given credence to the drug culture among Motown's musicians during the early years of the company. Barbara saw nothing. "I think there was more alcohol about during those days. Everybody was into that. Dope wasn't fashionable then. That was something that happened later on. Cocaine was the drug you heard about. Marvin might have dabbled with a little grass, but I never knew him to have the kind of drug problem he ultimately wound up with. You hear about these things later. Mainly the drinking was among the male groups and writers. It wasn't against the law. They'd be writing and there'd be a bottle of something around. When they were in the studios they would be drinking and recording, and nobody really thought anything about it but, as you know, a couple of them ended up with really major problems."

With her release finally secured, Barbara teamed up with Lee

BARBARA RANDOLPH

Hazelwood. A fruitless association because she felt he had different ideas about the record business which she didn't agree with. "Motown does spoil you in a way, because they take control, which is good and bad. Everything's mapped out for you, like, all your travelling is done for you. So then, when you go to someone like Lee Hazelwood, nothing is done and it's a big contrast. He assigned a producer to me and we did a couple of things. One was 'Miracle On 19th Street', or something. I wasn't really pleased with the production. Ed even went in and put background singers on because it was lacking something. Then the contract elapsed. I don't even think I called them five times during the time I was signed: they didn't call me either!

"I became very disenchanted with the music business. I'd been travelling for so long and suddenly I felt very tired and I just didn't want to sing any more. I wanted to be at home with a family, to hell with show business."

Barbara and Ed Singleton married in March 1970, and had a son, Darren, in 1973. When they met, Ed was in the process of divorcing Raynoma Gordy Singleton, who was also married to Berry. Both men credit Raynoma as being the biggest musical influence behind the company's success. "Motown started in her little apartment. She also plays fourteen instruments. The Motown Sound in essence stemmed from her—she even trained all the arrangers. She was the musician."

When the Randolph/Singleton marriage knot was tied, Barbara was a broadcaster for the American Forces Radio. "Someone called me and said they're looking for a young black woman on the station. I went and talked to them, and I was with them from 1969 until 1973. Guys used to write to me...I got a lot of mail because the servicemen were a long way from home. I used to send out postcards and so on, but once I got married and had my baby, the whole image changed and the radio bosses decided it was time for another presenter. I think they hired a guy to replace me!"

From radio airwaves, Barbara was persuaded by her husband to return to recording. Her first work was the title for a pilot TV show called '*Success*'. "It was very much an arm-twisting thing. I was happy to let him go ahead and do what he was doing because I became very comfortable at home and was content to watch everybody else pursue their careers. You get very complacent at home and he'd been out and about. Then I'd have the greatest time talking to him. But Ed kept on pushing me—anytime he was doing something, he'd ask me to do the songs. I guess I didn't feel like working! Then he said if you're going to do it, you'd better do it now. The meter's running. So I did."

She admitted it was pretty easy working with her husband, because, for one thing, she didn't crumble in embarrassment if she hit a bum note. However, those occasions were rare as I witnessed in Southlands studio, where, after studying the song she was due to record, followed by a hasty warm-up session, she finished her vocals in under two hours. The voice remains powerfully clear and distinguished; a couple of times a jazzy feel crept into the music, but nerves? Naw, she's a natural.

Finally, I mentioned that a little bird told me she was seen dancing with Gloria Jones in front of the Nightmare Records stand at Midem when 'I Got A Feeling' blasted out from the speakers. It doesn't take long to get back into the swing of things, does it?

Although Ms Randolph was correct when she said she hadn't released an album, it later came to light that she did record further tracks. She could easily have forgotten them or believed they didn't warrant a mention in the interview because they were incomplete. Not so, because during 2003 Spectrum Music, under the Tamla Motown logo, released 'Barbara Randolph: The Collection'. Containing 18 tracks, including 15 not previously available before, all bar one ('What's Easy For Two Is So Hard For One') were actually mixed and ready for release. Interestingly, other tracks include '(I'm A) Roadrunner', 'Chained', 'Baby Don't You Do It', 'The Look Of Love' and 'I'll Turn To Stone'. And, believe me, it's an absolute treasure. The only regret is that Barbara Randolph didn't live long enough to see it released. She unexpectedly died in July 2002. This tragedy obviously made my interview that more special.

MARTHA REEVES

Dateline: December 1985

Following our first meeting in London during 1969, Martha Reeves and I have kept in touch through the years. We rarely conducted interviews because our relationship was as friends rather than professionals. I've always respected that. We burned the phone wires, kept the postal system in profit, argued to the point of sulking (both being Cancerians), and when she toured the UK we re-energised our friendship, because that's what pals do. Growing up together meant we shared secrets, we gossiped through the night, and, when necessary, jointly rode the downsides of the business. Working together was never an option for us. Having said that, in 1985, for some reason that escapes me, we decided to try the journalist/artist lark. This is the result.

Conducting an interview over breakfast isn't such a strange

event these days. But when breakfast is at four in the morning after being up all day and night, well, that is something else. However, this unearthly hour was the only time Martha Reeves and I could talk, and believe me we tried hard to fit an alternative date in before she returned to Detroit. So, there we were at the Sunshine restaurant in London's West End having a natter over scrambled eggs. My friend was as candid as ever.

Ms Reeves has her professional life well under control and, unlike her contemporaries who gave way to despondency for failing to record outside Motown, Martha got off her butt and worked, and worked hard. Sure, a record from her is long overdue, but that's not her prime concern, she said, because at least she has enjoyed recording since she left Berry Gordy's company. "I have three agents in the States and they've now had me working constantly since I appeared on 'Motown 25'. I'm turning down dates now because they can't be fitted in. In fact, over the last three years, I've not had time for a *man*!"

Martha's presence on the very special 'Motown 25' was thanks to her friend Smokey Robinson, as she told me. "He called me up and said, 'It's Smokey'. I said 'Smokey who?' I wasn't thinking. Anyway, he told me about the concert and that he'd very much like me to appear. I was delighted to accept his invitation. In fact, I was pleased just to be a part of the show, to get on stage. After the show was over and we were all backstage, waiting to go on for the encore, I was asked to take Stevie (Wonder) on with me. I laughed and joked. I'd got my old job back! I used to look after him at Motown."

Returning to her roots isn't a move she'd shrug off, she smiled, but they would have to put the welcome mat out. "I would have gone back years ago.... Motown is my heritage. I mean, Berry Gordy taught me everything I know, and I remember when we were performing I used to look for him in the audience. I literally searched for him. When I found him, I worked even harder on that stage and when he wasn't there, I felt let down.

"He was concentrating on The Supremes and I wanted some of his attention as well. I began feeling like an outsider there and although Berry and I would talk, it wasn't the same somehow. It's funny because I long now to do some of the songs we have in the can. There must be at least three hundred somewhere in Motown

that we recorded. One of them, 'Spellbound', I actually heard on the radio recently. We did songs—we meaning the Vandellas and I—like 'Tracks Of My Tears' and so on. I think the tapes are either in Motown's library or in Abbey Road. Motown has got the publishing and I could continue my career, fill the gap, between 1970 and 1980 with these songs. I still make a good living, so don't get me wrong, and I thank God for that, and also that London and Europe still care for me."

Leaving Motown in the first place was a move she had to make. "I had reached the point where I felt I couldn't be proud of my achievements. I had my audiences, sure, but no back-up and I couldn't play the games that the artists did against each other. I couldn't criticise a new artist anymore than I could go against what they believed in. I was both physically and mentally stable and trusted my instincts. Now, I've been on my own since 1977 and I wouldn't need to be coaxed to return to Motown because I can stand up by myself!"

Bringing an original line-up of the Vandellas on this UK tour is an ambition she had nurtured for years. "I dream of bringing Rosalind and Annette with me, but they're into other things now. I'm not going to give up because I'm sure it can be worked out."

It was at this point in the conversation that Martha spoke of Sandra Tilley dying—two years ago. With sadness she explained:

CHINWAGGIN'

"Sandy had her own boutique and was doing OK. She died from a busted blood vessel on the operating table. Sandy had had a serious operation and had pulled through; she told me she was going to really live again. And she died. Although she had a lot of good friends, when she died we were the only people to attend the services. Duke (Fakir) sent his wife along. She didn't have a mother or father, and had no children either, only a husband. All she had was me and my sister Lois."

We, naturally, reminisced about Ms Tilley, and Martha for the first time confided that her early days at Motown weren't exactly what her publicity decreed. However, I promised not to print the truth, because she intended to document it herself. In fact, she had purchased a typewriter and had for several months now plotted her life as a Motown artist. She said she was aware of Mary Wilson's proposed book and the publicity surrounding that, and I think this may have prompted Martha to keep her secrets until she closes the final page on her manuscript. "I can speak for myself and am getting the chance to strike back as a journalist!" (In 1994 'Dancing In The Street/Confessions Of A Motown Diva' was published by Hyperion.)

Despite reports that Martha had recorded for Airwave Records, she confirmed, the information wasn't accurate. In fact, she's not sure whether the company still operates, as she elaborated: "They sent me a letter of a re-investment scheme, sent me a whole plan of their intentions, but my feelings about recording have changed over the year because I seemed to be waiting so long to get things together there. So, I suppose, I can't be signed to a company that doesn't exist anymore!"

On a more positive note, though, she is working on a television documentary with Rod Taylor. They had met in London during her last tour: "And the documentary is about Motown in the sixties with statements from people like Diana Ross, the Four Tops, Smokey, and I even got Joe from The Contours in. He's a cop in his spare time now. I still live in Detroit and speak to Esther Edwards frequently and through her we were able to tour the Hitsville building. All the original pictures, music sheets are still there. The first microphones, memos, all the first baby photos...they're all blended together. Stevie and The Supremes are all over the walls...and the Vandellas are there—once in a

MARTHA REEVES

while!"

And before breakfast was over, we talked about Marvin Gaye, or rather, Martha did. "I was *infatuated* with him. I was always looking at him, although I didn't want to be personal with him. He was a great talent and in the early days was a great inspiration to us...we got on well together."

Ms Reeves then returned to her hotel, and I hailed a cab home for a long sleep.

In November 1987 our paths crossed again thanks to promoter Henry Sellers, who had previously successfully combined three Motown acts to great touring acclaim—Martha Reeves and the Vandellas, Marv Johnson and The Velvelettes. I caught up with Martha in her temporary home in Bayswater one Saturday afternoon. When Henry first put the idea of 'The Sounds of Motown' tour to Martha, she attempted to secure the original Vandellas for the trip. "I told Rosalind and Annette that our music was still played regularly in Europe and that we should perform together for our fans. But they declined the offer. I feel at home in England. Always have, because my music has afforded me a place in people's hearts. I wanted to share that feeling with Rosalind and Annette. Before I come back next time I intend to have another go at persuading them because I feel that's what our fans would love." (Martha was later successful: the two Vandellas did tour with her.)

From touring we switched to recording, or rather, her lack of it. She was determined to return to the studio: "But I'm looking for a company which will give me the freedom to handle my own recordings. I didn't have that with Arista or MCA, so this time I am insistent on having creative input." As an aside, she said, Ian Levine had approached her to record for Nightmare Records. She felt the move wasn't right, yet later agreed to join her fellow ex-Motowners on his roster. Meanwhile, she had been approached by other interested parties, so upon her return to Detroit, planned to juggle the offers until she found the one that suited her best. However, she stressed, she wouldn't abandon her roots for disco/pop sounds. "I'm an R&B singer and I'm not suited to today's dance music. My music was actually premature dance and those songs have never been forgotten. Thanks to David Bowie and

CHINWAGGIN'

Mick Jagger, I'm hotter than ever in the States. The Beatles still sell records over there and so do we. It's quite incredible."

Her strong will has seen her through the traumas of her career, which she now totally controls. Surviving the musical fads and fancies by sticking to what she does best has stood her in good stead. And Martha credits her continued saleability to her upbringing and her faith in God. She's also fiercely loyal to her fans who have remained supportive during the years, and goes to great lengths to show she cares. For example, she invites them into her dressing room (often contravening theatre regulations), meets them before and after her performances, willingly signing items placed before her while talking and posing for photos. A trooper indeed; unlike some.

My cab was waiting outside her apartment as we talked about Mary Wilson's book. Martha was undecided about her feelings but did say: "I really don't appreciate being referred to as a fighter. I have never put my hands on any one of them. Sure, we used to have arguments with The Supremes, and we have had fights, but Mary should have referred to them as *debates*. Mind you, I know of other girls who have fought with them. I think also, Mary damaged The Supremes' mystique, but she didn't know enough about my private life to bring me down. All I can say is that no-one has snatched a microphone from my hands!"

Martha is constantly in demand on the American touring circuit, on television and radio specials. In fact, if any company requires information about Motown, they call her. She's one of the most popular and approachable of all company acts. And she's now spearheading the 'Dancing In The Streets' tour, following the sudden death of Edwin Starr. The two artists, with another (both Freda Payne and Mary Wilson have joined them) transformed the shows into their very personal Motown tributes. Martha was inducted into the Rock & Roll Hall of Fame in 1995. Her most recent album is 'Home To You' but her work is regularly featured on Motown compilations. In 2005, Martha became the first Motown superstar to take on a political role in the city of Detroit.

LIONEL RICHIE
Dateline: November 1982

CHINWAGGIN'

Tracking down the Commodores' Lionel Richie wasn't easy because with the release of his solo album, Motown had organised a gruelling schedule of radio and television spots for him. However, my luck was in. As he was taking a break from signing autographs at the WKYS station I had the opportunity to secure him for a whole thirty minutes. Something of a record, I was told, because his interviews usually last for a mere ten minutes, sometimes fifteen.

His album 'Lionel Richie' is currently on release in the States and hot on import here. 'Truly' is the first track to be lifted as a single; a powerhouse ballad in true Richie style.

Briefly then, the tracks include an R&B/pop flavoured 'It Serves You Right'; 'You Are' co-penned by his wife Brenda, who is also co-production assistant; 'You Mean More To Me'; 'My Love' on which Kenny Rogers sings second lead and backing vocals; 'Tell Me' with tennis star Jimmy Connors assisting on backing vocals; 'Wandering Stranger', and a short but dramatic spiritual ballad 'Just Put Some Love In Your Heart'.

Needless to say much American critical acclaim has been showered on Mr Richie, so it was an extremely happy man I chatted with. "It was a strange feeling doing this album and it was only when we were finishing it off that I realised there was only me on it because my picture was on the cover! It was different for me, for, you see, I was only used to submitting one song for a Commodores' album and when we thought about cutting something on me I realised I'd have to have nine or ten songs ready. Over the years, I've written eighty to a hundred songs and I still had those, so we had to decide which ones were the best. It was such a hard task that I decided to ask James Carmichael to help me. He's one of the Commodores really anyway. He writes and produces with us. I also felt he was the right person, and he really wanted to give it a go. The whole experience was fun: I really enjoyed myself."

He also explained that he wanted to use studio musicians and not the Commodores—anyway, they were tied up with other things—so he found Joe Walsh, with whom he'd wanted to work for a long time now, and Richie Zito. "I wanted to play around and not be part of a self-contained group. It makes things easier

LIONEL RICHIE

that way. Working with a group can become hard work because each of us knows what part we have to play in the recording and we rely on each other to play that part. I didn't want a cast of thousands either in the production. The challenge was to find musicians who were willing to sweat and pull off precisely what I was looking for. In fact, the piano I played was an old brown beat up one which turned out to be the piano Carole King used on 'Tapestry'."

Regarding the actual album content—or some of the tracks at least—he said. "I wanted to begin with a straight to the gut approach, so I chose 'It Serves You Right'. For me, R&B lyrics as well as country lyrics are the most direct in the world—they go straight from one person's mouth to another's ears. 'Wandering Stranger' is a song that sums up my inner feelings. It deals with my search and I think the search of a lot of people right now who are wandering around the streets without a clue as to what's going on."

Did he feel some of the songs he used on this album could usefully have gone to the Commodores, bearing in mind the recent dip in their career? "That's difficult to answer. Y'see, everyone in the group writes songs and a lot of them are used on our albums. I'm lucky if I get two of my compositions on an album now! There's six guys with a song each, so there isn't too much room for me anymore. If I said I was the group's writer, they'd kill me. I was never the writer of the Commodores, it was just that both of my songs became singles and were hits, and everyone assumed that the role was mine. I think a lot to do with the Commodores non-success is lack of communication and co-ordination, and getting six guys in a studio isn't easy when we're all doing different projects."

Some of Mr Richie's work outside the group included the Kenny Rogers project, and the title song for the movie *Endless Love* with Diana Ross. He told me about the latter. "The single came about by accident. Polygram called me and asked did I have a song for their new movie. I didn't have, so I went to see the movie, although I didn't really want anything else to do at that time. Then Polygram said all they wanted was an instrumental and I could do that on a weekend; that would have been easy—no problem. Next thing I know, I get told they want lyrics, and wanted me to sing them. So I agreed; still a weekend thing—no problem. Then I hear them say, 'We've got Diana Ross to sing it with you'—now I have a problem. This was turning into a bigger project by the minute but it turned out to be a wonderful weekend.

"One major aspect though had to be sorted out, namely, where the two of us would record the track. Y'see Diana was in Atlantic City doing some concerts, and I was in New York, and neither of us had the time to visit each other. So, we decided to meet in Nevada. She finished her concert at one in the morning and drove down, and I flew in. We started around three, three-thirty, and finished around six, six-thirty. Diana, once she showed, was a real professional. Diana Ross knows how to be Diana Ross. She kills a song.

"Let me tell you something. I was amazed at one thing that happened. She was singing her piece and once she'd done it and I didn't realise, she waited for me to come in with my bit. Oh my goodness, I thought *Diana Ross waiting on me!*" We thought about doing a follow-up, but 'Endless Love' can't really be followed. It was a great duet, but these aren't recordings that come by easily. Just think of all the wonderful duets there have been before, like, Marvin Gaye and Tammi Terrell, or Marvin and Diana, and so on. So it's pointless trying to outdo a good one, and a successful one. It has to be a project you come back to every now and again."

The conversation then turned to Benny Ashburn, the Commodores' manager and 'father' who died from a heart attack at the age of fifty-four. Naturally, Lionel and the group were totally devastated at losing such a close and treasured friend. Benny had worked with and stood by the group during the early days, he financed and supported them to the top. Without him the Commodores would have struggled, and Lionel was quick to admit this to be true. "We came through this thing together. After all the hard and terrible days of struggling to make a living we wanted to enjoy our success together, and with Benny to share it all, the acclaim, the Oscars and all the success with us. He was like a father to us. For the five years we were on a big scale, the group didn't live next door to each other. We couldn't call each other daily, so we'd all phone Benny and he told us what was going on and where to meet up; y'know, things like that. He was the middle man who kept us all together. Communication was very difficult at that time but Benny kept his family, for that was exactly what it was, together and happy."

Sadly, Lionel now has the unhappy task of finding a new manager—not a replacement because that would be impossible—but someone with a positive direction. "We need as much co-ordination as possible. Trying to find that and someone who cares is making it a really tense time right now. The Commodores are a package that took masterminding and as soon as I've finished here I'm returning to Tuskegee to see the rest of the guys to decide what to do. I suppose, I do feel responsible for the Commodores. We're like six crazy brothers; we've been too close for too long and the group is based on a lot of love. Nothing will change that. We have to make decisions together and make them work because it affects their lives and mine. Even with my work outside the group I am more concerned that I don't disrupt the Commodores organisation. It must remain intact. I've always been a Commodore and we must keep our heritage alive above all else. I can't expect the group to wait on me; it's hard to ask them to wait until I've finished my stuff before getting together. That's

CHINWAGGIN'

why we try to be involved in our individual projects at the same time."

So, a split with the Commodores is imminent then? "Ah, ever since 'Three Times A Lady' people have said I was leaving the group. Look, none of my own work was planned. Kenny Rogers, for example, approached me when I wasn't doing anything. And, believe me, I never realised 'Lady' would be as successful as it turned out to be. I don't think about things like that, I merely did a job that I enjoyed. And I never imagined 'Endless Love' would go as it did either. Don't get me wrong. I'm very happy it all happened. So much has happened in the last eight months or so. Life is very fast. 'Lady' was two years ago and more has happened to me since then than ever before. I just love it. The success I've been fortunate enough to enjoy with this new album is tremendous, but I experienced enough success with the Commodores to last me a lifetime. I'm past the glitter part and the money part of it, although money is always good, but I still get a bigger thrill out of recording and touring."

During 1981, Lionel Richie was the first artist in American chart history to simultaneously appear in the top ten as composer, performer and/or producer of three different records: 'Endless Love'; Kenny Rogers' 'I Don't Need You' (which Richie produced) and the Commodores' own 'Lady, You Bring Me Up'. He's won and collected American music awards, received an Oscar nomination, as well as being named the number one producer and publisher for the success of his own company, Brockham Publishing.

Did he have any trouble in controlling his ego? "Hah! I've been in this business for about fifteen years now, so my ego is the least of my problems. Everyone thinks I'm now enjoying instant success but that success has taken fifteen years. I'm overworked, naturally, but I've just been very, very lucky. I love performing. I love being in the studio. No-one can take that away from me. If I get tired on the road, the best place for me to go is in the studio. And we're not getting any younger! I suppose I am lucky because what I make my living doing is really my hobby.

"Paul McCartney, for example, certainly doesn't need any more money, yet he still records and tours. Man, he's almost the richest man in the world! It gets in the blood and I can't envisage ever

LIONEL RICHIE

giving up the business. Sharon, I must explain, I never thought I'd get this far. I don't really know how I got here in the first place. I'm just an extremely lucky man who thanks God for the success I've had and am still enjoying."

We talked exactly one year later, when Lionel had left the Commodores. "It's always nice to talk to someone I know," he said. Did I feel good, or what!!

Once more he was on the promotion trail; this time to celebrate the release of the 'Can't Slow Down' album and 'All Night Long (All Night)' single, both of which were soaring up the world-wide charts. "It's frightening. It's one thing to have a hit in the US and Britain, but for the record to take off all over the world, well, that's something very hard for me to believe. I suppose you could consider it as competing against 'Three Times A Lady', and that was frightening enough for us as it was."

On the single's list of credits, I noticed a Dr Lloyd Byron Greig—dialect coach—who I assumed was a professor of something or other. Lionel laughed. "He's a gynaecologist from Los Angeles, and a very dear friend of mine. He would come by and visit us and I started listening to his accent. We got talking a lot, and when I was in the studios working on the single, I kept phoning him up, saying talk to me. I wanted to do something different with this record, and when I found myself saying some of his phrases, I knew I wanted to use his accent on the record. So, I'd stop my musicians in the middle of a session to phone him. I must have worried him to death. I suppose in the end I talked to him for two days on the phone!"

Of 'Can't Slow Down', he confessed he'd steered away from overdosing on big, plushy ballads which are his trademark. "I always like to lighten things up now and again. I don't really like to fall into the trap of giving people what they expect, or come to expect, from me. I too like the lushy strings and the tearful ballads, but I wanted to do something special. I was also afraid of falling into the middle-of-the-road market with slow songs because that's not what I want to do right now."

He went on to point out that he's constantly being asked about duet work. "I'll duet again because it's something I like to do. But next time, I'll probably catch everyone off-guard. I already have some ideas, but would rather keep them to myself for the time being."

The tracks for the new album were specifically penned for the project and not taken from his vast back catalogue. "I was looking for more up-tempo songs this time that wouldn't sound like everyone else's. Michael Jackson seems to have that market sewn up for the next few years or so, and I wanted to create my own unique sound. I prefer to write new songs for new projects, although I'm sure I must have some good songs in store by now that I've forgotten about."

It seemed to me that 'All Night Long (All Night)' has done for Lionel what 'Masterblaster (Jammin')' did for Stevie Wonder, and this prompted him to tell me the following. "Stevie was performing in Radio City and in the middle of his show, he stopped everything. He told the audience that he wanted to play his current favourite song—and he played 'All Night Long' on tape! Right in the middle of his show! Man, can you believe that? That is the greatest honour anyone can give me. It's the ultimate compliment. Unfortunately I wasn't there to hear it, but I phoned Stevie afterwards and said he was real crazy to do that. It was the compliment of my life!" He also added that there wasn't a new album due from his colleague. "Only Stevie knows when it'll be ready. Y'see he doesn't have a co-producer or co-writers, and people like that, not like I do, and when you write, say, seventeen or eighteen songs for an album which you know can only hold eight or nine, it's difficult to decide which tracks to include. Now with me, it's a joint decision, but with Stevie he makes that decision. There's nobody around to encourage him to stick to a deadline."

Lionel's wife, Brenda, has become more involved in his professional life—credited as a writer and production assistant on the new album. "It's great," he enthused. "She really wants to be part of that side of my life, and she enjoys it too. I try not to let it affect our personal life, but it's difficult to live with Lionel Richie because I tend to put my mark on everything. Everyone who comes through our front door is aware of me, the artist, which can be pretty boring at times. We do have quiet nights, though. Brenda and I are fond of the movies, or we play tennis. We're both interested in sports."

LIONEL RICHIE

James Carmichael now worked for him exclusively because the Commodores decided they wanted to produce themselves. "There's five producers in the group, don't forget. So it wasn't James's decision. I reckoned that if you find something that's worked for eight or more years on hit records, why change it. So James works with me now. I don't know why the group made the decision they did because it seems so strange. The '13' album—which I like—is a good beginning for them. But they need an identity, a focal point. They need a face. When I was with them, I was the lead singer, and mine was the face of the group, like, say Mick Jagger and the Stones, or Michael Jackson and the Jacksons. I think Clyde should be promoted to be that face for them. He's a prominent singer and seems to be the strongest. The album as a whole is, I think, geared towards the US. It's not a set for outside, although I do think it's a very good beginning for them.

"I never wanted to leave the Commodores in the first place. It was stifling in the group, particularly when it got to the point where all of us wanted to write and produce. It was very competitive. I'd been a member of that group for fifteen years or so, and to leave wasn't the easiest of things for me to do. I don't have any plans, immediate plans, to perform with them again, although if it was for a very special occasion then of course I'd do it. I do miss them but we knew it wasn't going to work, particularly when the friction started."

I was fortunate to receive this phone call from Lionel because he's part-way through his first solo American tour which, he said, was tremendous fun. One aspect did attract his attention in a hurry—his audiences. "I just can't begin to tell you about those crowds. It's amazing. There's eight year olds, their mums and dads, grandmas, granddads; there's kids with red hair and orange hair, guys dressed in leather and chains. Rastafarians, all colours. Man, it's breathtaking. It's more like the United Nations than the United Nations—but I like it that way. And another thing, I never know who's going to sing the songs—me or them! I never get to finish a song that's for sure. People are crying, some are fainting, screaming and shouting. It's real weird; it's like I'm just the cheer leader. When we sing 'All Night Long' the stage is crowded because everyone gets up there with me!"

CHINWAGGIN'

His support musicians are talented professionals, some of whom lend their voices as back-up vocalists. They haven't as yet, he stated, worked in the studio with him, but they do have heavy credentials "and I've got them". he giggled, before listing them with pride. "There's Greg Phillinganes, he's the musical director and he played with Stevie on 'Talking Book' for example; then Henry Davis, he's bass guitarist and comes from LTD; Carlos Rios, guitarist, he's played on many Quincy Jones' sessions; drummer, Gerry Brown has played a lot with Stanley Clarke, and my percussionist is a lady, Sheila Escovedo. And she's wonderful. Finally, there's Randy Stern, the keyboardist, who's done sessions with Cameo...I must tell you about Sheila. She's just great with the audiences. She entices them and gets them going. We spoil her rotten, though, being the only woman in the band. My wife, Brenda, first saw her work and suggested to me that she'd be an asset to the band. I didn't have time to see her for myself because I was tied up in the studio. But now I'm just hooked. All the musicians are so good to work with. When we all go out on stage, we're all glad to be there. It's not working, it's a real pleasure. That makes the difference to the whole performance and it's a relief for me not to have to worry about how the musicians are doing, will they turn up on time, will they work OK, and things like that."

With a promise that he would bring his tour to Britain, the thirty-five minute phone call sadly ended.

Our next chat was in February 1986; 'Say You, Say Me' was his most recent hit single and he was working on his third album, as yet untitled. ('Dancing On The Ceiling') To date, his career had soared to unprecedented heights—nine UK hits, including his number one title 'Hello'—awards, honours, accolades and so on, far beyond his wildest dreams. Included in that list was being co-writer (with Michael Jackson) of USA For Africa's 'We Are The World' where all proceeds went towards famine relief in Africa. A host of fellow artists contributed to the single and followed in the footsteps of Britain's own 'Do They Know It's Christmas?', under the control of Bob Geldof. Lionel explained his feelings about the tragic plight. "I get letters from people telling me about losing their farms, people who are losing their way and can't

LIONEL RICHIE

quite figure out what to do about their lives, and people losing everything their families were built on. I look at a desperate world we're creating. We're wiping out the people who are the foundation of what America is about. The guys who don't have an IQ of 150, who never wanted to be anything but a shoemaker and now have no work. All you have to do is say 'America's in trouble' and they're the first ones who will fight your wars for you.

"But don't use them and abuse them. These are the people who lost their two sons in Vietnam. These are the people who, when there's a tax increase, will be hit by it. I don't mind growth and progress, but in this thing called change we're losing the most important thing there is—people."

His concern is, he says, invariably shown in his lyrics, insisting 'Say You, Say Me', the title track from the '*White Nights*' movie is a prime example. "You think I'm talking about a boy and a girl, but there's something else whispering at you under the surface. 'Say You, Say Me' could be a romance about white and black, American and Russian, Baryshnikov and Hines. It's about the awakening of the inner person to stand and be strong. It's about the '*White Nights*' movie, but if you never see the movie it'll still apply to the barriers that you run into in a love affair. The line 'behind the walls of doubt' applies to what we go through falling in and out of love or discovering a loved one. Yet it also deals with capitalism and communism, and civil rights, the complete spectrum of barriers. Why isn't the world the way it should be? Why can't people get along? Why can't we love each other? These are the questions it touches. I'm the songwriter, and it's my job to sprinkle the message, even if subliminally, on the airwaves."

The campus of Tuskegee Institute (founded by Booker T Washington in 1881) was where Lionel Richie grew up. His grandfather worked in the business office of the Institute, and today his grandmother, Adelaide Foster, still resides in the family house, over the road from the college's president's house. Now ninety-three years old, she was the first person to sit Lionel at the piano to teach him music. Education was also a dominant factor in the next generation of the Richie family because Lionel's mum was a high school principal, his dad a systems analyst for the

CHINWAGGIN'

Army.

Musically, Lionel was exposed to many varied forms. Tuskegee's radio station played country and western, and as the Institute was a black college, he became involved in gospel, soul and even African roots music. He readily accepts that those college days shaped him for the future, giving him his first break as a professional musician, although, he said. "I was the shyest guy in school and would curl up in a ball. A lady once said to me 'A guy who writes those kind of lyrics has got to be the world's greatest lover. The joke behind that is that I couldn't say the words to a girl face to face. I could write them down in a note and be halfway across the campus before she read it."

In an attempt to impress the ladies at college, he carried a saxophone under his arm! This ploy backfired when a group asked him to join them because they were looking for a sax player! He was forced to admit the reason behind the instrument carrying and that he couldn't actually play it! They invited him to join them anyway! Once enlisted into the group, his knowledge as an economics and accounting major was used to write a two hundred page game plan for success. The plan worked and the Commodores became a top international group. "After a while I had to say 'what have I gotten myself into?' I'm the guy who wanted to be a lawyer until the music bug bit me in about seventeen different places. I'm the shy guy who just wanted to sit over in the corner. You've gotten me out here, God. What in the world is going on?"

Even when he left the Commodores, Lionel still questioned his success, trying to bring it into perspective. "I'm still the guy who was too short to play basket ball, too slow to run track and too small to play football. I was not a ladies' man and the crowd I hung out with was not the in-crowd. So when people get all excited about me now, I start laughing and hope this other guy they're talking about hurries and shows up! I believe that a man who has lost or denied his past has lost his identity. I've tried to hold on to those roots in Tuskegee. I still own my student apartment there. Sure I fly coast to coast, fly around the world... but when I want to go home and reflect for a minute, I go in my car across town, get into my student apartment, close the door and say 'now God, this is where I came from'. And this gives me the incentive to figure out where I've gone and how far I would like to go. I sit in that room for hours at a time, making sure that when I leave that room, I have a sense of direction.

"Meeting people keeps me in touch with reality and this is reflected in my writing. When someone walks up to me and starts talking, he keeps me regular. And I write a story for him.... You spend your whole life saying 'I want to be famous'. But being famous is like being put in a little capsule that isolates you from being a normal human being. You're offered a delicious world with everything you could want, yet you're separated from normal people by limousines and bodyguards. So you have to struggle to get back to real human life."

To help with this aspect of his career, he goes to extraordinary lengths, as he told me. "Way past midnight, when it's so dark that I won't be recognised, I sneak out and people tell me the story of their lives. And from these stories come the songs. Other times I go out and walk along the beach at three in the morning. One night there was a moonlight and I saw what looked like a man huddled up like a bundle, sitting in the sand. I wondered what he could be all about. Then I heard a voice which said 'Lionel, I want to let you know how proud we are of what you've done.' I couldn't quite see his face, but the voice sounded educated. The man then stood up and came over to shake my hand. It turned out he was a bag man, but there was a dignity in his voice. It's a wonderful world we live in, but you have to be in communication with that kind of person to know it. You judge every man according to his own merit, and deal with the man and not the title. You judge a man because of what he offers in his work, and that is what I was taught. And that is how I live my life, and, basically, that is the foundation of what I am about."

In April 1987, Lionel was relaxing in his Mayfair Hotel suite, talking about everything. Several French film crews had taken root outside the door to his suite and people seemed evident everywhere, doing whatever they had to do. Outside the hotel itself, fans waited hoping to catch a glimpse of the superstar when he later left for the drive to Birmingham. Débuting in Birmingham: why? "I wanted to crank up the show so that by the time we get to London it will be ready...be ablaze. Also, I wanted to take the show to a small venue first, although performing in Birmingham scares me. You'd think I'd be confident as I've had plenty of years to practice. What makes the difference on stage is that I have a crowd of people saying, 'I love you'. It's not like a boxing match because I'm the only person on stage. European audiences have always come forward to tell you their feelings and of course they have always, always played my music.

"It's a strange thing but no matter how great you are in America, you never get the respect you get over here. You're only as big as your last hit single, yet in England artists who have been ice-cold in the States for years are always welcome. People like Chuck Berry, all those wonderful blues and soul performers come any time because you treat them as legendary. And that's a wonderful feeling, I can tell you."

People in the public eye are always open to undesirable attention—stalkers and so on. Lionel agreed but stressed he personally hadn't been faced with a potentially dangerous situation. "I am not bothered by threats, and even if I was I could never get into the position of not flying, or walking in the streets. Unfortunately, this problem is the nature of the world we live in. You see we have all been brought up with the idea that the bomb will go off at any minute. So I live my life one day at a time. There's only one safe bet in this world and that is death will always come as a surprise."

God forbid, but what if he only had a short time to live, what would be a priority? "Well, I'm doing what I like, and what I want to do. I'm visiting new cities, new countries all the time, and meeting different people every day. I couldn't want for more. I am really a people person. Life to me is not living with my buildings, my home, my car, but living with people, touching people and sharing with people. They can love you back, houses can't. So I suppose I am living my life as if today was my last day and I couldn't do anything any faster. I think what I love most about what I'm doing is I get to experience and live with the very rich and very poor and everything in between.

"What makes this business extremely difficult is there is no rehearsal time. I am actually learning about myself in public. Unfortunately, there's no school to learn how to handle fame. Like, it's hard enough getting married but at least you can work

LIONEL RICHIE

out the problems in private. I'm lucky though...the analyser, or the nervous side of me, usually comes out calmly in public which is what people want to see and expect from me."

At the time of our conversation, it was unclear just how many countries Lionel's tour was to cover—but he had been invited to appear in Russia, he said. It was something he wanted to do and wasn't put off by the country's government nor the restrictions placed on Russian people, as he explained. "If you take away the governments of the world, people are people and fans are fans. I agree, in isolated places of the world, people are oppressed, but people get around any obstacle. Like they listen to their records—R&B, rock and so on—and they go to discos or something similar on weekends, like everybody else. It's the ideas of the older generation that are making this oppression, but they're dying off now, leaving the newer generation to bring in what they want. I believe certain morals are good and I'm sure the governments are going to change, and that Russia, in particular, already has a brand new breed in there. They will get back into the race, into the competitive world. I mean, look at all the technology that exists now...this is a positive progression in itself.

"Music is bringing people together. Music is a medium and a strong force that has cut through areas when politicians, for example, can't. Attitudes and situations get changed with the least resistance. The key civil rights movement succeeded with non-violence and I'm convinced you can get through to anyone with music. A guy will listen to all kinds of music on his car radio. He leaves his house for his place of work, gets in the car and there's music. Even the biggest bigot in the world can be influenced in this way. Politicians listen to the radio via this means. I suppose it's like a form of brainwashing. And their kids bring music home. Their parents scream and shout the music is too loud, yet—whether they like it or not—they have been influenced by that music.

"I don't think anyone can say artists aren't politically motivated sometimes. There are so many causes we can write about...what is happening in society, etc. We can tell the truth through our music. That is the right of the business we're in. I don't know if the time will come when I'll get actively involved in politics because it can be a nasty and dangerous business. But I am at the moment in

CHINWAGGIN'

a position where I can tell it the way it is, leaving the chips to fall where they may."

Shit! Lionel's presence was needed for a filming session, and as much as I wanted to spend the afternoon with him, my time was over. If I was asked what impression Lionel Richie left me with, my answer would immediately be—he's a caring person who has a big heart. And that makes him rather special, don't you think?

Since this interview Lionel semi-retired from the business through illness and family bereavement. His album releases include: 'Time' (1998); 'Renaissance' (2001); 'Encore' (2002); 'The Definitive Collection' (2003), and 'Just For You' ("2004). With the release of this last album Lionel's career escalated once more as he embarked upon a world-wide tour to promote it. He sold out concerts in Britain during the autumn 2004. Personally speaking, his second marriage has ended in divorce. I know it's been said a million times before, but Lionel Richie is one of the industry's nice guys, and this is one of the reasons why I'm now writing a book about him, entitled 'Hello'.

SMOKEY ROBINSON
Dateline: October 1977

After a ten minute trot I actually reached London's Montcalm Hotel more-or-less on time to meet Motown's main man—Smokey Robinson. I caught my breath while fumbling to get my tape player working as Mr Robinson was spread-eagled across a couch in his plush hotel suite.

A placid, quiet spoken guy with twenty years in the music business to his credit. Singer, writer, producer, performer. And, of course, the vice-president of Motown Records.

His project of the moment is 'Big Time', which he's promoting in London, and as I was last on the interview list for the day, promised I wouldn't keep him long, as talking about the same subject must be tiring. "No, not really. Everybody's been so nice. I haven't been here in a long time and when I came it was with the attitude and expectation of doing this."

Was the trip primarily to promote his new project, Motown or himself? "Probably 'Big Time' but that does include myself and Motown—they're one and the same I guess. But as I say, I'm not tired of talking, everybody has been beautiful and nice. But that's typical of English people. I really look forward to coming here."

CHINWAGGIN'

Smokey has recorded the soundtrack to the movie 'Big Time' but that isn't where his involvement ends, as he quietly explained. "The movie is my project so that's why I did the soundtrack. I think that soundtracks are being done by more contemporary artists in this day and age than they were in the past. I also financed the entire film and have been involved since the writing of the script, right down to promoting the film. I've lived 'Big Time' since last June".

Being consumed by the movie project for so long, he said, meant he wasn't hands-on in his administrative position at Motown but—"My work does not bog me down, because of the fact that when my office was designed as vice-president of Motown Records I brought talent to the company. I signed them up, co-ordinated them with writers and producers, people like that, if I wasn't going to handle that part of their career myself. And today we must have fifteen people to do that so I have a little leeway... fortunately I have passed the years when I sat behind a desk. I'm free to do my own thing unless they come to me a say, 'Hey, Smoke, we've got this project we want you to be involved in,' then of course I will. Or I'll see something going down and I think I'll involve myself in this one because it's good...but apart from that I'm pretty free. I don't want to single myself out either because we still have three or four employees who were there from the beginning, as I was, and they have the same leeway."

From the reaction so far 'Big Time' looked set to give Smokey a much deserved hit. Obviously, with The Miracles he was constantly in the public eye, enjoying success and accolades befitting a group of such a high standing. However, it's true to say that as a soloist Mr Robinson has struggled for mainstream recognition. He commented that despite low record sales, he has been a regular performer in the States since 1975. "I left the group in 1972 and at that particular time in my life, I did think that I'd had it with doing dates. I didn't think I wanted to do any more touring. First of all, because I wasn't going to be with The Miracles and they were a big part of my satisfaction on the road, because I was with guys I loved and got along with perfectly well. Our backstage and offstage relationship has always been perfect and the only part that I hated about the whole thing—because I'd been doing it from '57 to '72—was the getting there, the travel, the hotels, the food in the restaurants and so on. It was driving me up the wall!

"Also I had two very young children, and I wanted to be their father, to be daddy, rather than being a celebrity that they saw every now and then. These are the many factors that made me decide that I had to stop at that time."

Despite all good intentions to find another direction in his life, the touring bug bit him again. "After being off the road for three years I'd had it with not doing live dates! I decided it's a very intricate part of me and when it came down to it I really loved doing them. As I say, I've been touring in the States since 1975 but not at the pace I used to do with The Miracles. I'm freer to do them at my own pace because now there's no-one else involved.... My act? I believe in pleasing the people who come to see me. So the first four or five numbers are formatted—just to get us started. After that we sing whatever the people want to hear. Whatever they yell out, we sing it, because that's why they come in the first place. It's a lot of fun. It involves the audience, and we get them to sing with us.... great fun!"

Touring with Smokey are his own group and a pair of backing vocalists. "Two beautiful ladies," he smiled. "They don't do steps or routines, anything like that. I have seven dynamite musicians; they're the guys who've been playing on my latest albums. They're called 'The Quiet Storm' now after the title of my album."

Somewhere in the recent past I'd read that Smokey intended to record his wife, Claudette (also an original Miracles member), but had heard nothing further. He confirmed the sessions had taken place. "We've finished four tunes. Actually it was three because one she never completed the vocal on. It became rather difficult because I was side-tracked with other things I had to do, 'Big Time' being one of them, and that was a twenty-six hour day thing! And, you know, it's very difficult on some nights to work with your wife! You know what I'm saying? Because in the studio I might critique her with something that I feel is a professional criticism—as I would do any artist—and maybe that night she don't wanna hear that. So, I think that in order to complete the project, we're gonna have to get another producer.

"We've also kicked around the idea of duetting, along the lines

CHINWAGGIN'

of Marvin and Diana. And I keep getting calls from people about the 'Deep In My Soul' album, saying 'well, you've petered out', 'you don't know how to write songs anymore' and so on. That album was a life-saver for me inasmuch as it says a lot to me because it should let people know, especially young writers, young producers, and people like that, that Motown is open and open-minded to good material. Any time they can come and record an album on me, who is somebody who has been doing their own stuff for years, and that alone should show people that we are definitely interested. Because of *'Big Time'* I couldn't have possibly done a quality studio album at that time."

Our paths next crossed in February 1986, when Smokey was promoting his 'Smoke Signals' album on which he was only the singer, not being involved in any of the production side at all. Sounds dreadful put like that, doesn't it? For this project, Smokey has handed creative control to Tony Peluso and Steve Barri. "They said they wanted to do this album in a manner where I just shut up. I didn't have any opinions either. I let them pick the tunes, I let them do everything. And here we have it. I think the concept of it was to freshen up my sound. And I think they did it more so than I would have done it myself, if I had done the entire album. They just wanted to take me and put me musically into what they felt is the mainstream of the music that's happening now...I'd just like to say that this album has been a different experience for me recording-wise."

Smokey might have handed over production control, but he retained his composing power by co-writing five tracks including 'Te Quiero Como Si No Hubiera Un Mañana'. "Usually wherever we play there's a large Chicano following. So I thought with my first Spanish single 'Aqui Contigo' ('Being With You') being so popular in person, why not record it? I think I'll probably include a Spanish or bilingual tune on all my albums from now on."

The album also holds 'Be Kind To A Growing Mind' (with The Temptations on vocal back-ups), his opinion on artists who promote sex on record and stage. "In the past few years the permissiveness of music itself and the people who create and play it has gone overboard. Everything is being said right out in front. There's no longer the little cliché phrases that may mean anything. They're just coming right out with it.... there are ways to say everything more-or-less acceptably and morally. It doesn't have to be explicit. The song is a very, very important issue to me. I think that by fellow artists hearing this from me, it will be more effective than all the wives, committees, parents and stuff like that in the world. The point I'm making in the song is that we have a lot of young minds out there. Morals are a joke, but I don't think it should be that way. Probably at least seventy-five per cent of the recording artists that are in the business feel the same as I do. But that doesn't mean that it's OK to say anything just because you have the freedom of speech and the freedom of writing.

"The last time I worked with The Temptations was at 'Motown At The Apollo'. I appreciated it very much, them singing on the song, because they feel the same way I do about it. And I wrote 'Hold On To Your Love' with Stevie Wonder. About a year ago, I wanted to work with him and I just happened to pop by his studio when he told me that he had this song that he wanted me to finish up. So, I finished the song for him and ended up recording it!"

The lack of big hit records (except, of course, his number one single 'Being With You' in 1981; 'Tears Of A Clown' with The Miracles in 1970) on this side of the Atlantic does, even now, bother Mr Robinson, particularly as he's a regular visitor to the American mainstream chart. Yet, he's one of those few elite acts who can still pack theatres, like stalwart artists Tina Turner and Aretha Franklin, whose careers have once more taken off after a lengthy lull. "I think it's wonderful because these veteran black performers are but a few of the ones that I think are just standard people. When they come back to the forefront record-wise, I'm very happy for them, and I feel lucky to be classed alongside them. If you last long enough to pass that point, you don't really need a hit record to really work."

From 'Shop Around' with The Miracles, Smokey knew his life would be far from normal. "I guess that was my first realisation of what it was really like to have a big hit. Now the business is so competitive, and there are so many people trying to do it because it looks so easy." He admitted he enjoyed a life many envied, not necessarily from his lavish lifestyle but because he enjoyed his

CHINWAGGIN'

work! "The best part of it is you're earning a living at it. I love to talk to people and love to see what they think, and what they think about me. I do believe that if I had to do it over again, I'd probably change half of my valleys. Those are really wonderful lessons for you to learn...if, in fact, you do learn a lesson from the hard knocks."

In January 1988, Smokey Robinson was in a reflective mood. He spoke of the early days of struggle and defeat, his precious memories reflecting his and Berry Gordy's determination to produce music for the world. Smokey acknowledged Motown was formed from Gordy's desire to release records that would have no barriers, race or otherwise. "We wanted to make music that would be acceptable in all circles and not just black records. All we did was put good songs on good tracks, songs that anybody could relate to. They weren't crying the blues, and R&B records usually had one theme that they pounded out over and over again. But we had solid songs that would fit any life situation, whether you were White, Oriental or Chicano. And that made the world of difference. The music wasn't copied from outside influences, except perhaps Fats Domino, The Coasters and Chuck Berry whose records had crossed over into the white market, but none of those artists were with companies that were black owned and operated. That's what made us unique and we came at the world with another black viewpoint."

The timing of the company's success was, he felt, synonymous with the fifties and sixties, and would probably not have occurred in such a big way in another decade. Certainly Smokey himself wouldn't have been as successful—"because I would be reluctant and more apprehensive about many things. Life teaches you so many things but at that point I was a virgin to life. I was fresh and young and didn't know anything about the crooks out there. There are certain aspects that are totally against you, but I wasn't thinking about them then. Now I know all these things, so perhaps I wouldn't have the same patience to wait until things developed."

He was quick to add this wasn't due to the loss of his competitive spirit, which is as strong today as it was then, but more his reluctance to build a record company from scratch in this modern climate. "I was just living my dream then, and few

SMOKEY ROBINSON

people get a chance to do that."

The 'Motown Sound' has been a debatable subject throughout the years, and has been claimed by Detroit as its very own music. Smokey believes the sound of the Sixties was attributable to the people who worked for the company and had nothing to do with the actual city. "I attribute the fact of Motown happening in Detroit to Berry Gordy. There are talented young people all over the world, and in every big metropolis that you can think of and we, as young people in Detroit, were fortunate that we had an outlet. And a man who was there saying 'I got this company, you got some talent, I'll give you a chance to put it out to the world.' If he had been in Minneapolis or Chicago it would have happened there. But maybe not in a place like Hollywood (Motown's current home) because there's too much hoopla about entertainment there. Berry too had the idea to call his music 'The Sound Of Young America' because that's what it was."

As he continued to reflect on Motown's past, Smokey insisted, despite public belief at the time, that the British invasion of the American charts affected the company's music not at all. "We had just as many number ones as they did during that sixties period. We just kept pounding them out. In fact, a couple of times we knocked them out of number one. But The Beatles were very refreshing inasmuch as they were a white group who said 'we grew up on black music'. They were in with black people." And to show their respect, the group recorded versions of Motown songs like 'Money', 'You've Really Got A Hold On Me' and 'Please Mr Postman'.

Other compositions have been re-recorded by countless acts since Motown's inception and the 'Sound' remains prominent in today's new material. "And when I talk to young artists, producers and writers today they all admit that influence. So I don't really have to listen for that Motown element in their music because I know it's there."

Comparing Motown of the eighties to its selling power of the sixties, he remarked that the company didn't have the same stable of artists now. "We do not have as many artists making hit records at the same time as we had back then. However, the records today are selling more in volume than they used to. We've graduated. We're an entertainment company now, whereas before we were a record company.

"Then during the seventies it was considered the 'thing to do' to record a politically flavoured single, although it wasn't an area I became involved in. Yet I respected and appreciated it. Marvin's 'What's Going On' is still the greatest album that's ever been recorded. I've never heard an album that touches it."

However, Mr Robinson did touch on a political viewpoint with his own 'Just My Soul Responding', even though, he insisted, the lyrics weren't deliberately pointed. "It says if I'm protesting all these things that have been laid on me just because of my ethnic thing or because the guy didn't want to go into the army to fight and be killed for something he didn't believe in, it's not because I'm a negative person, and it's not because I want to cause trouble. It's just my soul responding to the position I'm put in. The song was my political contribution. I wrote it at the beginning of the Vietnam war. Now it's passé. It's over, and black people were rioting all over America then. That's no longer news, and probably no-one will record those songs again. At the same time people were falling in love, and they still are. I could have written—like Holland, Dozier and Holland did—this song about 'Mickey's Monkey'. I could have written twenty songs about the monkey as follow-ups to that, but the monkey isn't done anymore. That's why I write about love, and in the year 2987, if it gets to that, people will still be falling in love."

Let's not forget that Smokey's songs of love sold volumes during Motown's heady days with vocalists like, Mary Wells, The Temptations and The Miracles singing his golden lyrics. The in-house competition was fierce, yet, somehow, he always figured highly in charting material. "Motown was a business and everyone connected with it knew that. That's how we grew up, so it was inbred in me, it's a part of me. But my idea goes even further than that because as a songwriter, I don't want to write records. I want to write songs, so that people will record them over and over again for years to come. So, yes, I want my stuff to be artistic, but I also want it to be commercial and I've never written a song without hoping it would sell.

"When we first started getting all those hit singles, people came from all over the world to record their acts in Detroit because they thought it was something in the air or something else. They

SMOKEY ROBINSON

thought they could just come to Detroit and record at a house or on a freeway and get the Motown Sound. But, little did they know...we recorded our acts everywhere!"

Into the nineties, Smokey's final Motown album, 'Love, Smokey', was followed by the SBK release 'Double Good Everything'. However, by 1999, he had returned home to record 'Intimate' and 'Food For The Spirit' (in 2004). Mr Robinson also wrote his autobiography 'Smokey', in which he confessed he had battled for years against cocaine addiction. He won the fight. And in 1988 he was inducted into the Rock & Roll Hall of Fame, which was one of his countless honours and awards received during his extraordinary career. Without any doubt, Smokey Robinson is a truly gifted man.

DIANA ROSS
Dateline: June 1992

Sitting on an over-soft sofa in a plushly decorated suite at The Dorchester Hotel, I spent a long while talking to a lady I'd last spoken to in 1981. This was the first time we had sat together for a one-to-one interview, even though we had touched each others lives during the past, when I assisted with background work for several of her projects.

DIANA ROSS

During this visit to London, I was the only journalist to be granted an interview—what a trip that was!

Dressed in casual black, immaculate day make-up emphasising her large, searching eyes and her hair wildly controlled, the megastar was at pains to ensure the interview was varied and informative. And, despite rumours to the contrary, Diana Ross was a relatable person, with not a trace of egotism while, of course, being overjoyed at the phenomenal success of 'When You Tell Me That You Love Me', a UK no 2 shortly before Christmas. The album from which the single was lifted has passed platinum and its title track, 'The Force Behind The Power', was also a top twenty hit.

Before getting to grips with this release, we talked of last year's Wembley dates where, once again, Diana presented her audiences with concerts that were unforgettable. Having attended one, I was astonished at the control she had over her public, none more so when eight thousand people rose to their feet to hold hands high and sing 'Reach Out And Touch (Somebody's Hand)'. She laughed. "Actually, in the last couple of years I don't really have to ask the audiences to hold hands anymore. It just kinda happens and it's a nice feeling when it does. As for control..." she paused, looking as if she's reading my mind because, when talking, we were in eye-contact for most of the time. "It's a funny thing about control. As soon as you let go of it, that's when you have it. The most important thing for me is to be there and my mind shouldn't be anywhere else except in that theatre with that audience."

For anyone who has seen Ms Ross on stage, that feeling of being overwhelmed is so apparent and I recall that, when she sauntered down the aisle on her way to the stage, I felt I wanted to stop her to say "Hi!" "*You could have*! I wouldn't have minded... but the security people probably wouldn't have understood. I've never had an audience who've wanted to harm me or tear at me, and I've been lucky in that respect. I don't think I provoke that kind of energy in my shows. The work on the stage is different for me...I don't know about other performers, because I find it's the most comfortable and most secure sort of place for me. It's something about the eyes, people being able to see me, and me being able to see them. That's a kind of connection, some kind of energy that happens. I actually feel as if I can throw myself, my

CHINWAGGIN'

vision and my voice all the way out in this whole space. It's something that's unexplainable. Maybe it's because of the number of years I've been on stage!

"The recording side of things is a bit different. What happens there is thought; the feelings behind the words which have to generate through the session. No, I have to admit it's the performing, the entertaining, the play, the being before an audience that's really comforting to me. I really hope never to give it up."

I suggested that there was a million light years' difference between the wild Wembley audiences and those she encountered at the recent Royal Variety Show. The star smiled and paused. "The people felt self-conscious, meaning they couldn't sit back and really be comfortable in their chairs and enjoy the show, because they felt they were a part of it, on stage in a way. All the lights were on, they're real conscious of it all. At Wembley, they're in the dark which I think gives some comfort. They can hold hands and nobody will really know it's you!"

Incidentally, Diana changes the content of her performances for British audiences, to include the favourites, 'I'm Still Waiting', her 1971 chart-topper being a prime example. "I don't do that in America, they don't know it at all there. And 'Chain Reaction' was such a big hit here and is still remembered. The record company likes to put it on B-sides. Over there in America, it did well, but not at the same pace as here."

Recently, thoughts had crossed the star's mind that perhaps the touring side of her life was one she should take easier. With ongoing family commitments she did feel time wasn't on her side to do everything. Yet, she urged, retirement was out of the question, she had other projects to do, so would change her working schedule. "I never studied music or anything. In fact, I never even thought I was going to be a performer. I have been given this gift and put in this very special place to do this work and to stand in front of people. So I feel I don't really want to throw it away. I think if, um, someday, somehow I get some messages that I don't need to work and do this anymore...well, I doubt it. I started singing not for—I hate to refer to it as *work*— because I enjoyed it. I was singing to entertain and I wasn't even making any money. So, maybe even when the day I'm not getting paid for it arrives, I'll continue to sing. Perhaps in a choir or something. The time may come when I'm not making records but I'll always sing...for an audience."

We pause for tea and mineral water, while Diana explains that she's really off schedule in London. "I didn't fly in until last night and I'm still on US time, so I'm rather disorientated." She put a sweetener in her tea. "No, I won't go to sleep, my eyes are fine, but I might not remember...it was funny. I was talking and thought what question did I just answer? What'd I just say?"

If 'Bohemian Rhapsody' hadn't been re-issued, it's fair to say 'When You Tell Me That You Love Me' would have reached number one. Diana was aware of the tragic circumstances surrounding this release of the Queen classic, and stressed she wasn't disappointed. These things happen for a reason. "I was just happy that the record was in the charts and I was a hit over again. I haven't left the hearts and minds of a lot of Europeans but sometimes at home people say, 'When're you going to have a new record out?' and I say, 'Uh? I have one out right now.' In some places it's not as wonderful as it is here...I've said this often, there's a loyalty here that I don't experience anywhere else. I feel a little loyalty in Japan, strangely enough, because they follow the records and stay with it. No matter what record I release it always seems to go to number one there. But the loyalty here is what really is so comforting to me. It is staggering, it really is. People of our age group have wonderful memories of the songs of the sixties and somehow once they become your fans and friends they kinda stay with you. They start to know about your personal life, what is she thinking now, how are the children? People actually stop me in the street and say 'how are the kids?' Just as if they'd seen me yesterday!"

Back to the music. Diana chose 'The Force Behind The Power' as a single. Stevie Wonder wrote it after years of badgering from her, as she explained. "He's such a special person, and I was really very pleased to have this song on the album. He calls his songs *gems*, a gift from God. People don't understand how hard it is to come up with the melody and the actual completion of the song, with all the thoughts he wants to say. Stevie read it to me when it was a germ of an idea and then it took a while to complete it because he was busy on another project. But I

CHINWAGGIN'

continued to pester him. After all, he's promised since he was young to write me a song and when I asked about it, he'd say, 'OK, it's coming,' and I never saw it! But, you know, he's busy with his own career and he does write songs for other people, then produces them, and that's the time consuming process. Unless a person really knows what the process is, coming up with a song idea, getting the lyrics written, then the music completed, finding the musicians, getting them into the studio, recording with people who have the same feeling or idea that you have is really quite a job. Years ago, we used to have a lot of songs on an album, sometimes twelve or more tracks. Today it really is a process trying to get eight to ten good songs."

Looking for the right material is an awesome task for her because she will only record songs she can identify with, as she told me. "Truthfully, I play them and if they make me feel good and are saying something, that they're the words I'd choose to use, I'll record them. Choosing songs for this album, Peter Asher and I found eight songs together. We sat down with the writers, some people had germs of ideas and we'd try to help them develop them. I had always wanted to work with James Carmichael—he was partners with Lionel all those years, then Lionel wanted to do something different—and James is such a talented producer. He's a very quiet guy, and I've always wanted to write with him. So he came by my house to try to write some songs together. Then out of trying that, he produced songs I'd already got. He's got a good feeling."

As her security man discreetly lurked in another room and Phil Symes, her PR executive, fended off the phone calls, Diana Ross and I continued our interview. The star was in London on a lightning trip following her all-consuming promotion for 'When You Tell Me That You Love Me' and 'The Force Behind The Power'. She hadn't planned to tour so quickly, she said, preferring to spend more time with her family, especially her two young sons. A difficult situation, I voiced. She agreed, while stressing: "It's not as difficult as it's going to be because as they get older they can't travel the way I do because, although they really like it, it's hard. The packing, the unpacking and all that. But I'd hate not to be able to come here, visit, and maybe do a concert. Yet, I realise, at some point I won't be able to do this, not at the pace that seems to be required. It's something about it having its own momentum because I really hadn't planned to tour like this...then you find yourself busy, busy and that wasn't the intent at all. These things start to accelerate somehow and learning to say 'no', well, you can't do that, can you?"

As success is once again greater for Diana in the UK and Europe than in her home country, would she consider gearing her future music to our market? She thought for a second. "Not a bad idea. I hadn't thought about it. But, yes, it's a good idea actually. I could find out the things that people over here would like to hear, rather than try to figure out what's going to work in America. Honestly, I don't know where I sell more records!"

Despite rumour-mongers in the industry, the star is still signed to EMI, her record company since 1964 when the single 'When The Lovelight Starts Shining Thru His Eyes' was released by The Supremes. "And," she insisted, "I'm happy to be with them. I had a contract with EMI so when I left RCA and re-signed with MCA, I signed with MCA for America and Canada. So when MCA and a financial venture purchased the new Motown, they asked if I would like to go over to the new Motown, and I made that kind of distinction that maybe I could be of service to the new company. It was nice to go back actually, in the capacity that I did. I have much more authority, and can be a spokesperson and somehow help out. So that's really how I got to go back to Motown. When my contract is up with EMI, or if I don't continue to work with them, Motown wants the next option on the rest of the world. For sure, I'll give it to them."

It was, I told her, a happy day for her fans when she returned—however loosely—to the Motown fold, and she now realises that any past attempts to shake off or play down her involvement with the company are useless. "I don't really want to shake off the Motown connection, although there was a time when I tried to remind people that I was with The Supremes for ten years and I've been on my own for the last *twenty* years. Doesn't time go..? but the records were so important, they really made their mark then, and that's what counts. Motown was a very important, very vital part of my career."

While on the subject, I wondered if her future plans included a reunion in the studio with Berry Gordy, particularly since his name and production company, West Grand Music, were associated with a recent Louis Price album on Motown last year. Diana didn't think so. "I'm sure he's retired...but what I'm thinking is he'll never give up his music. I don't know very much about this production company, but he may have started this for one of his sons, and that Louis Price is somebody he believed in and wanted to launch. But, basically, I don't think Berry's doing any business now."

However, she did confirm that the Motown founder was writing his own book and that she was happy about it. "I asked him to do this a long time ago because historically someone needs to put the facts down. There's so many books around at the moment that have re-written history and it's coming from a negative angle. People think the only time they can sell books is to say something bad about somebody, or to try to. I mean, Motown was really his dream.

"I was talking to a young girl today and she didn't know Berry started off as a songwriter, and that he's talented and plays piano and things like that. I don't think people know a lot about him and what he did. If he never speaks up we'll never know the wonderful things he did unless somebody like me tries to tell you. He opened the door and gave us an opportunity, and because of his genius and his dreams we're able to be here today. At least *I'm* here today...and I give him a lot of credit for that. I know that I had to do my part of the work and it was a team effort, but really Berry was responsible. He was my mentor and friend, and someone who really has made a difference to my life."

During the past few months, Ms Ross has emphasised more than once that the most important aspect and need in her life is her family. She had intended to keep her boys under wraps for a while longer, she sighed, but in the end found this impossible because they had started touring with her. Now she's faced with trying to maintain a healthy balance between her career and them. "I'm very proud of my children, so much so that I want to bring my family pictures out and show them to everybody. I don't know what I'd have done just having a career and not having them. However, I think it's real important to try to keep some balance in their lives. I was able to do that with my older girls and I'm hoping to do the same with the boys. Anytime you try to keep something like them away from the public that's the time when they want to get to it more. And then I worried that that wasn't a good thing either. So I tried to balance that while trying to protect them."

There were so many more questions but so little time. Diana was racing against the clock as she was due to choose a gown and cross London within fifteen minutes to be at a television studio. Following her appearance that evening, she planned an early dinner before returning home on Concorde the next day. Needless to say, it was a great thrill to talk to Diana Ross without interruption, and I felt I got to know her better. Despite being told she rarely agrees to autographs, I bargained with her. If she'd sign my book, she could have the CDs I'd bought her. A deal was struck!

So much has happened to Ms Ross since this interview that it would probably fill another book! But suffice to say, she's continued to enjoy career highlights and suffered personal downsides, including the sudden death of her ex-husband Arne Naess. In 2004, Diana took Britain by storm with a series of sell-out concerts; she's also writing her second autobiography, and plans to return to the studio this year. Meanwhile, her material is, of course, widely available via Motown and EMI Records. Diana Ross is a true icon of our time: she's worked hard to win that title and let no-one forget it!

PATRICE RUSHEN
Dateline: April 1987

It's been three years since her last album—but now she's back. 'Watch Out' is the title of the new album and single and, judging by response so far, both will be big sellers. Yes indeed, Patrice Rushen is back in a big way!

The album, incidentally, is all her own work except for three

PATRICE RUSHEN

tracks—'Somewhere', 'Anything Can Happen' and 'Long Time Comin''—and the project is a direct cross between dance and ballad—"because I do like songs I can get my teeth into, like a ballad. People listen to the lyrics more and, although it can be a little scary because artists put personal ideas into their writing, I believe it's the only way the listener can tell that the artist is sincere.

"Many times when I write the lyrics I have to check myself. There are just some things I can't put into words and besides, it takes so much out of me that I usually let someone else write the music. Writing is a very delicate operation and I wish more people were more concerned about the delicacy than the commerciality. Artists are pawns on a big chess board, but that is the business, I'm afraid."

She also believes the way artists are treated depends on how much success they enjoy, how much music they sell. "It doesn't matter even if the single is junk, so long as it sells. Yet having a hit gives an artist more chances to do things. There are so many barriers to be broken down anyway and sometimes that's real hard. Music is really a spiritual thing—a connection between your inner self and the projection of that in public. This makes artists a little bit different, I think, because it's a gift that needs to be developed. Sometimes it gets squashed when records don't sell."

Ms Rushen is newly signed to Arista Records following a lengthy stay with Elektra. She was urged to change companies by Arista boss, Clive Davis, although that wasn't her intention at the time. The lady explained what happened. "When I first met with Clive, it was as a producer. I wanted to find out if he was interested in me producing some of his artists. He turned the conversation around and we got talking about me signing to Arista as an artist. He's well respected in the business and Arista might be a small label but it does have a lot of influential artists signed. I only hope that I'll be one of those signings who will be one of the most innovative, with a certain amount of longevity."

Changing record companies is like, for you and me, finding a new job. Both scary moves. Patrice agreed. "I was with Elektra for seven years and before that with Fantasy for three, so signing this new deal was very frightening. Everybody has their own way of doing things and you have to learn them all over again. Also

CHINWAGGIN'

once the conversations are over and the promises are made, you have to be sure they're kept after your signature is on the contract. So, you just hope things go OK and go for it."

Clive Davis actually saw Patrice perform in 1980 when she was still signed to Elektra. "He said it doesn't matter how long it takes, so I guess he was impressed with me!"

Three years later, the album is released. "It took so long because, well, record companies do take time to schedule records, and since I am a new signing there were certain things they had to get just right. The actual album took me six to eight months to record and I finished it last year. Then Arista took over and, as I don't control the scheduling and that, I guess I just had to wait for my turn."

Apart from concentrating on her own career, Patrice has been involved in session work for other artists. For example, most recently she can be heard playing synthesisers on Vesta Williams' 'Once Bitten Twice Shy' and has scored the movie 'Hollywood Shuffle.' She met Vesta a few years ago when they did sessions together and: 'We kept running into each other and then I was called in to work on her single. Oh, we had a good time in the studio, I can tell you."

Hit singles are an important part of artists' careers but Ms Rushen said in her case they're now not as important as they were because: "I'm involved in so many aspects of music that I don't worry too much about hits. I worry about giving my best, and accurately projecting myself. As I mature I step back and let the music happen. I suppose it's very gratifying to have a hit, but more gratifying when that hit is based upon true feelings and personal satisfaction. It would be a nightmare for me to have a hit with a single I hated, and then have to sing the darned thing for the rest of my life. I believe records say a lot about an artist and I wouldn't be associated with something I wasn't at ease with. I won't settle for less than I am capable of doing."

Ms Rushen was born in Los Angeles. At three, she was enrolled in a special music preparation programme run at the U.S.C., where she studied until her teens, when a music teacher urged her to enter a competition at the 1972 Monterey Jazz Festival. Walking away with the first prize led to a deal with the jazz label, Prestige. "I wanted to be a studio musician and jazz is definitely

PATRICE RUSHEN

among the forms that studio musicians must understand. It requires the knowledge of extended harmonies, melodies and improvisation, all of which come into play in the studio."

A trio of albums later—'Traverse', 'Before The Dawn', 'Shout It Out'—proved Ms Rushen wasn't destined to be typecast as a jazz player. She expanded in other areas and headed up session work for the likes of Peabo Bryson, Prince and the late Minnie Riperton. As her reputation grew, she became known as the only woman to emerge from jazz and R&B as a self-contained recording artist, composing and producing her own work. She joined Elektra in 1978. "My main focus with my first album there was to get out of the jazz mould and I think I did that. In putting the songs together, I discovered I had a lot of vocals and no-one to sing them. People started coaxing me to sing them myself, so I figured what the heck and took the plunge!"

All in all Patrice recorded five albums during her stay, some of which won Grammy nominations. She also enjoyed crossover singles with 'Haven't You Heard' and 'Forget Me Nots', while her most commercial album was probably 'Straight From The Heart'. From the proceeds of these successes she built a twenty-four track studio in her home, which has obvious advantages, as she explained. "I can work as long as I want to, when I like...even in the middle of the night if I want. And I can take more time to record without worrying about a time limit and the money it's costing. I'm much more relaxed and find it a better working situation for me. I don't fool around either, otherwise I'd get nothing done and not meet my deadlines!" However, there was one huge disadvantage—"There's nobody to make the coffee, so I have to do it myself!"

If she hadn't ventured into the music business she would have been involved in some form of art, like dancing. "But," she admitted, "I'm not a great dancer by any means. I like movement, and after all movement is one of the inspirations for writing music. Maybe I've been a dancer in my past life or something. Yes, I'm serious about this. So many of the things that I do have come easily to me, even some things that are difficult to do, like getting into this business in the first place."

As a subject like this requires lengthy and serious discussions, we opted to leave it for another time. Suffice to say, we believed she has chosen her career wisely. She loves this business while admitting a few things irritate her beyond words: "But I try not to dwell on them too much, and to concentrate on things I do like. The politics and red tape drive me crazy, even down to the politics in getting records played on the radio and ascertaining chart positions.

"So, as I want to remain sane, I'll stick to what I'm best at—and that's music!"

In addition to Patrice's composing career, which included television and movie scores like 'Men In Black' and 'Waiting To Exhale', she produced Sheena Easton's 'The Nearness Of You' for the film 'Indecent Proposal' which, in turn, led to 'No Strings', an album of jazz standards in 1993. Considered as one of the world's top jazz pianists, Patrice has performed with philharmonic orchestras, and served as Composer in Residence with the Detroit Symphony orchestra, before composing symphonic works. Time permitting, she spearheads inner-city programmes for America's young.

DUSTY SPRINGFIELD
Dateline: July 1990

What's this lady doing in this book, you may ask yourself? Read on, because this much loved and respected singer was one of the forerunners in spreading the word—the Motown word, the soul word—although she's always claimed her promotion of the music was a modest contribution to its growth and popularity in Europe.

CHINWAGGIN'

So, here we were, sipping Diet Coke, lounging in The Churchill Hotel late one night, when Dusty Springfield—dressed in soft spring colours, with her large expressive, mascaraed eyes and long pink fingernails flashing to emphasise a point—was an absolute treasure as we sauntered down a musical memory lane.

Black music lovers will recall Ms Springfield's two critically acclaimed 1969/1970 albums 'Dusty In Memphis' and 'Brand New Me' (UK—'From Dusty...With Love'), her regular involvement with the racy, innovative Friday night music TV programme *Ready Steady Go*, hosting *The Sound Of Motown* and her participation in an American Motown Revue. And naturally some of these came into our conversation.

However, before getting into these "rather heady days," Dusty spoke of her current soul favourite, Luther Vandross. "He's a master at making the most of a song," she gushed. "Sometimes he decorates too much but that's Luther. If I wanted to do very soulful things now, I don't think I would. I have influences but I don't think I'd try to do that here. We have our own ways. I think bands like Soul II Soul are soulful, but in a different way; it's that wonderful mixture of sounds that I couldn't do. The closest I come to this is on my new album ('Reputation') where I sound free and happy on 'Send It To Me'. It has a slight wit to it and kinda slopes along: it's also very sparse. What you have is a Womack & Womack quality. It's simplicity and was a reaction to a lot of complicated stuff. I just wanted one song that was straight ahead."

It was over two decades ago when Dusty first flew her Motown crusading flag; she promoted the music in interviews, performed cover versions on television and stage, and recorded the company's tracks on albums. Why Motown? "It was so obviously better than a lot of things that were happening. They were really good songs done extremely rhythmically. It was the first time there had been that type of song structure. Some of them were sloppy but it was this sloppiness that made them attractive. I noted a lot of it was to do with the bass player, the drummer's licks, Holland, Dozier and Holland, and musicians like James Jamerson if you were lucky! That was the 'motor' of Motorcity. You could put anything on top of it and it would still sound like Motown. The artists were probably secondary, and certainly there

DUSTY SPRINGFIELD

were a lot of people who sang but who didn't last. Whether it was because they got worn out by the situation, I don't know. They were talented and certainly you could put all sorts of vocal people over an absolutely splendid bass line and have a hit."

Her love of this music inevitably got her into trouble, particularly with British musicians in the studios. "I was swiping things left, right and centre to record, wasn't I? It was pretty phenomenal to get that sound because the guys I had to work with—they were all sweethearts (she smiled)—but they were playing standard basses. I was actually the first person to ask them to play a Fender bass. I really was a stickler for just getting there, just as close as I could, and that's where my reputation came from because I kept saying 'no, that's not it' and so on."

Despite Dusty's close involvement with the artists, nobody asked her to join Motown, a move, she said, that wouldn't have been right at the time. "The climate wasn't right. I would have been intimidated because I was in awe of them and I don't sing well when I'm in awe. I usually sing better in England. A few white singers did try it and they didn't last...Chris Clark, Kiki Dee...I think Motown was right not to ask me. In retrospect, I'm glad they didn't because I might have accepted, and I wanted to stumble along on my own, make my own blunders."

Mid-way through the sixties, the singer flew to America to join a touring Motown Revue comprising some of the company's finest, like Martha and the Vandellas, The Supremes, The Temptations and Marvin Gaye, under the auspices of DJ Murray the K. "I remember it was the era of Beatlemania and Murray the K liked to consider himself the fifth Beatle. He thought I was from Liverpool and decided he'd got to have me! There were a couple of other white acts on the show, I think Jay and the Americans were there...Murray hedged his bets with a few white acts! I mostly hung out with The Ronettes who weren't on Motown, and shared a dressing room with them, which was an extraordinary experience! Y'know, it was like 104 degrees in this very, very small dressing room, and all our beehives were in there—three black beehives and one white one! It was collisions constantly!

"Next door were Martha and the Vandellas, and the other side The Supremes. I remember Mary Wilson was always reading

CHINWAGGIN'

Latin books and Diana Ross's mum helped me turn up my hems because I was always buying things that were too long. I had a lot of good times; very heady times being involved in that period. After all, what could be more stimulating than listening to the brass arrangements of The Temptations from the side of the stage? That was heaven to me. Mind you, I didn't like performing there or anything else, but I wanted to stand at the side of the stage and soak it all up so that I could use it. But I could never get anyone to do it! And this is where I got this priceless reputation of being difficult in the studios over here because I was always asking the musicians to do things they couldn't understand."

Apart from performing on this tour, Dusty became one of Martha's Vandellas. She laughed. "We started the show at ten in the morning and it went on until one/two the following morning. We only sang two or three songs each but it meant being in the theatre all the time, and there was always a Vandella missing! Since they were singing back-ups for Marvin Gaye from the wings, I used to do it. I never actually got to go on stage with them but I knew all the routines and knew exactly how to sound like a Vandella... and a Shirelle if it came to that. I know how to do that stuff to this day. I can still go off into my Shirley Alston impression. Whoever it was I wanted to be, I'd slavishly copy them because we hadn't caught on to them in this country so I could get away with it."

Her involvement with, and the influence from, black music showed dramatically in Dusty's recordings particularly on albums like 'A Girl Called Dusty' and 'Everything's Coming Up Dusty, so much so that she was nicknamed 'The White Negress' by a contemporary, a name that surely should have flattered her. "I certainly wasn't offended," she replied, trying to get her lighter to ignite, before adding: "I don't think it had any impact on me at all. It did, however, cause some resentment because it's not much fun having a glass of whisky thrown in your face by Nina Simone who called me a honky, and resented me being alive! She was having a few problems, which I thought I could solve by being nice. Huh. I was still as naïve as ever! I was on my crusade of being helpful to people who had problems and I was warned not to approach her but...I knew better, didn't I?"

Ms Springfield may have resisted joining Motown but she did

DUSTY SPRINGFIELD

sign with Atlantic Records to release the two previously mentioned albums. Ahmet Ertegun heard her 1965 single 'Some Of Your Lovin'' and begged her to record for Atlantic once she was contractually free. Dusty said the albums were largely recorded from fear as she remembered her first visits to the studios. "I got destroyed when someone said 'that's where Aretha stood' or 'stand there, that's where Percy Sledge sang 'When A Man Loves A Woman'.... I became paralysed by the ghosts of the studio! I knew that I could sing the songs well enough, but it brought pangs of insecurity... that I didn't deserve to be there. I just knew that Aretha's drummer was going to say, 'Ain't she a piece of shit.' It's the most deflating thing you can say to me that somebody I adore and worship actually stood there and probably delivered an effortless performance while I'm slogging away trying to get it right. They meant well but they didn't realise what they were doing. It's funny...I hated those sessions but the albums do say everything about the patience those guys had. They worked with me until they got it out of me.

"Probably the irony of those whole sessions was that I was so crippled with laryngitis they could only record me two or three words at a time. Yet, there are notes on the albums that I've never sung again, they're so stratospheric. They're so high. I'd be revving up and I'd just go for it. When I didn't make it I'd do it again until I did. It was rough."

Rough or not, I bet she loved every damned minute.

Dusty Springfield is Britain's finest white soul singer. She captivated the sixties; struggled through the seventies, but returned with gusto during the eighties. Her last album, 'A Very Fine Love,' in 1995 was typical of the familiar Springfield talent, and she was destined to reign once more, as the country's best-loved songstress. However, this was not to be. Dusty died from breast cancer in March 1999. Prior to her death, she was awarded the OBE, and eleven days following, was inducted into the Rock & Roll Hall of Fame. We lost a great lady.

EDWIN STARR
Dateline: October 1987

What would the music business do without this man? He constantly records mighty singles, is a blinding artist on stage, and makes himself available for charitable functions like no one else I know. He's also a dream to interview. Yeah, people like our Edwin are hard to find these days, but thankfully he belongs to us. He's one of the gang.

Just released is his 'What Makes Our Love Grow', written and produced by that we-can-do-no-wrong team, Stock, Aitken and Waterman. He met the trio at the recording session for the charity single 'Let It Be', as he told me. "I'd heard of them and they'd heard of me but we hadn't met before. We talked and it became apparent there was a possibility of doing something together. Two weeks later we were in the studio! They had already put the song together and I just went in to lend my voice to it."

With 'What Makes Our Love Grow' Edwin has secured a deal with 10 Records, which, he said, was a one-off situation at present. "If the record happens then I hope it's a long association. But, as you know, the fickle finger of fate can fall anywhere. If the record is the kind of number everyone hopes it will be, there'll be an album."

Signing with 10 seems to me to be a more solid relationship than his previous label flirtations but as he stated, "When you're in this business nothing is settled...you can't say you're gonna stay with a label from the first single. I'd love to stay with them, but they're in the business of selling records, and if mine doesn't sell, well, they could drop me. On the other hand, if it does sell, the association lives on. I don't see any underlying reason why the record shouldn't do well, and if I'm lucky enough to get a top forty single, I can push it into the top ten through my performances."

With his one ambition to secure a British chart-topping single, Edwin admitted the business had been too fickle to give him one. "There's too much variance in music as a whole. Who would have thought 'Pump Up The Volume' would have gone to the top? Especially when it's a non-existent group, and just a production record. When you have that kind of thing going to number one, how can you determine where records will go? This isn't a criticism, but an example of unpredictability.... pirate stations are (thankfully) making hits out of songs that don't get into the charts."

However, Edwin felt there was a marked improvement in music over the last five or ten years, although he said it was now technically perfect and not 'musician perfect'. "If you can type a letter at eighty words a minute you can cut a record. Everything is too neat, everything fits in too well. Before, those little mistakes on records made them more exciting, something special."

CHINWAGGIN'

As a recording artist, Mr Starr has always been more popular over here and in Europe than in America, which was a deliberate move on his part. "I've spent more time in the UK than the States. America is such a vast area to travel. For example, I can be popular on the West Coast, and then be nothing on the South Coast. Working in this country is easier in terms of distance and, of course, Europe is nearby. Certain artists like Julio Iglesias and Demis Roussos have Europe in their pocket, but as soon as they chased that American dream of money and higher royalty cheques, they found a whole different scene. It wasn't that easy, it's a big world out there. I had the opportunity to stay in the States—I wasn't chased out or anything like that—but I'm here out of choice and I prefer to live in this environment. Europe and the UK have been good to me...and others, like Frankie Beverly and Maze. They don't sell great quantities of records here, yet their shows are sold out. British loyalty is amazing.

"I've been working here for most of my life, and I feel blessed to have a British following. Going back to the fifties/sixties, when I returned to the States after touring here, I told artists like Jimmy Ruffin and JJ Barnes where I'd been and the reception I'd received, how I'd been treated. They didn't have a clue what I was talking about! I told them to get over here 'cos there's a whole new world here, new fans, people who know us. But they wouldn't. Subsequently, they never built up a solid British following, except maybe Jimmy Ruffin, who I believe now lives here."

It then wasn't surprising when Edwin said he's adopted Britain as his second home too, because: "it's the love of the British people that keeps me going. You can't fool the British people. You're true to your beliefs and causes. Sure, some Americans say you're stand-offish but that's because they don't know you, which is a shame. If they've not got the patience to find your qualities then that's their problem."

Another aspect of British living that appealed to him was the fact that, unlike America, we don't treat artists like unreachable stars or untouchable icons, which may or may not be a good thing. "I came to this country because I was tired of looking over my shoulder. The more I got out there, the more people wanted to take it away from me. The British don't treat us like stars which means when the time comes for the comedown it's not so far to fall!"

EDWIN STARR

Much of the singer's success is based around his live shows, which, by the way, I'm addicted to. Why is he so popular? "I care about my audiences. If you thought my show was good before, it's even better now. Y'see, I don't want my audience to walk away after a show saying it was a good concert. I want them to leave just as tired as we are on stage! I want them to be involved, to do what we do and enjoy themselves. Let me tell you, there's something I'd really like to do, but I need a hit record before I can, and that's hold a concert dance at the NEC in Birmingham. I'd take all the seats out, so that everyone can come and boogie. It would be a brilliant night.

"Get fed up singing the same songs? Never! I'll never get tired of them. When I see faces in the audience light up from the first bars of a song... no, those songs have been good to me, so I'll never drop them...I've always had the support of the Northern Soul Scene with songs like '25 Miles' and 'Agent Double O Soul', and it would be beautiful to combine that and this generation together. I do find my audiences are changing but, thankfully, the die-hard sixties people are still there. In fact, I thank the Lord for them."

Naturally, I tried to resist the temptation of mentioning Motown. But couldn't. As well as his solo work for the company, Mr Starr recorded an album with Blinky (Williams) in 1969 titled 'Just We Two'. It was a wonderful collection of songs that bombed. "Blinky and I were orphans because we weren't true Motown artists; weren't the flavour of the month. It was a blazing album and was a potential chart-topping album but we weren't Diana Ross and Marvin Gaye, so we didn't have the support needed for a hit." Edwin said nothing at the time about Motown's reluctance to promote the record because, he said, "There are two ways to do this job. You either say OK, make no waves and thank the Lord you're still getting your cheque every week. Or you make waves, knowing the only way is out after that.

"I had had a hand in my work before I joined Motown, but there I wasn't looked upon as anything other than a singer. I was part of the assembly line and had to take the songs that were offered to me. My manager got me out of there, which gave me a chance to get back into the swing of things. Then I had 'Contact' and 'Happy Radio', so I did the right thing."

CHINWAGGIN'

If Edwin hadn't followed his love of music, he said he'd have been a chef! "I was a very good chef before I started singing. Actually, I recently worked in a MacDonalds restaurant for one of their appeals. I raised £623 in one day. People who came in were amazed to see me behind the counter serving. They probably never believed I could do it. I served up milk shakes, burgers, fries, and then took their money."

Through all his years in the business Edwin has, naturally enough, a bank of memories, all of which are precious. However, he cites his recent Birmingham NEC appearance with Stevie Wonder as one of the most memorable. It was magical because I hadn't seen him in ten years. Luckily someone videoed it for me so I can treasure it. I try to meet my old friends when they come over, but sometimes I'm either not in the country or I'm working."

Talking of working, how long will he continue? "Well," he laughed. "I won't go on until I drop, that's for sure. As long as I feel comfortable I'll continue. I will know better than anyone when I can't go on. When I stop I'll probably become involved in developing new artists.... there are a lot of things I don't like about this business, slagging off and backstabbing are two in particular. I don't come face to face with it now because I don't put myself in a position to get into those things. I don't mix with music business people socially. My associations are local, like with the milkman, postman, and the car mechanic. Being with ordinary, non-pretentious people is my attempt to keep my feet on the ground. This business can affect you so much, like reading your own reviews: well, that's the worst thing you can do!"

In December 1992 Edwin was performing at the Southcoast World, Bognor Regis, East Sussex. The weekender event was 'The Giants of Motown', where night and day meant little, where Motown music was all you heard (even in the toilets!) and where the bars were open from daybreak. No wonder things got a little hazy, but when the fog lifted Edwin and I took time out for a natter, albeit briefly, the morning following his dynamic performance before a packed and sweaty audience. How did he sustain his high energy level on stage, non-stop from start to finish? "Touring is all I've got...this weekend, well, we had a fabulous time and had loads of compliments about the show.

EDWIN STARR

That's heart-warming to say the least 'cos the only legacy I have are my live shows."

However, it isn't cheap presenting a show like this: "Because the band costs a fortune and I'm not making a helluva lot of money either. I can't put on a show without them, but if I can get long-term commitments—like six, seven shows back to back—then I can make a bit. Agents aren't paying out fortunes for these types of tours. American acts still tend to talk silly money and often it's not worth agents bringing them in. I'd rather be working than price myself out of the market. I'm not silly about money, and at the moment I don't demand too much. You've got to build up interest and it's reached a point now where people come and see me through word of mouth. A hit record would help though."

And this is where his new single comes into the conversation. His version of The O'Jays' 1977 'Darlin' Darlin' Baby' which, he admitted, has already caused considerable interest. Television spots are underway, the airwaves have happily accepted it, so positive vibes all round. "I might have a hit this time, but if I don't, it's not the end of the world. I chose the song because I've always loved it, but with me being known for the belters, I wouldn't have considered recording it if I couldn't do it on stage. When it came off live, that convinced me. Now I do it at the end of the show...even after all the energy level this song with a slower beat works. I'm so proud of it."

Then, out of the blue, two names cropped up—those of Eddie Kendricks and Mary Wells, both recently deceased, leaving an irreplaceable void in black music history. Edwin shared the loss and spoke first of Eddie. "He was one fantastic guy. I had the pleasure of working with him and The Temptations, and he struck me as very introvert—he was very much into himself. Not in a conceited way though, he might have been timid of voice but that wasn't representative of the person. Maybe he should have been more assertive, and if he had he could have been a bigger star, I don't know. Sometimes the right combination of people makes things happen, and this was true with The Temptations. The chemistry that made that group, made things happen. I'm talking about the original group and their enthusiasm at the beginning, with Paul, Otis, Eddie, David and Melvin, that was the powerful combination. Don't get me wrong, the current group is a good

CHINWAGGIN'

one, but you can never, ever duplicate the original. Look, nobody can sing 'You're My Everything' the way Paul did."

Of course, Mr Starr wasn't with Motown at the same time as Mary Wells but their paths crossed constantly. Also, he grew up with the Womacks (Mary married Cecil and later Curtis) as they grew up in the same neighbourhood. "I always remembered how she was disheartened by the fact that she never got what she personally felt she should have done. It seemed to me she started to get what she wanted nearer the end of her career, more so than at the beginning, if you see what I mean. Like, she found her niche, her place in life. Prior to this it seemed that everything else had taken over her life. Both their passings are tragedies."

Prior to our interview, I'd actually spotted Edwin sauntering down one of the streets at Southcoast World, heading for the fish stall of all places. People stopped him for a chat, to sign autographs and simply wanted to be in his company. I smiled to myself, yes, that's Edwin's way! When mentioning this to him later and the fact, that he walked alone, wasn't he worried at his vulnerability? "Look, you don't need bodyguards, minders and all that razzmatazz over here. Maybe in America, sure, but not here. Fans respect us because they respect the music, and this is what some of these guys—those with the 'American artist attitude', which should be left at Heathrow—don't understand. How can I walk down a street, they say, be so vulnerable? Well, why not? Why not go out into an audience? People contact, that's what it's all about. I'm a people person, and it's certainly something that doesn't bother me and never has. That's the respect I'm shown, and I am so thankful. And I've never been threatened or hurt either!"

Yeah, that's Edwin Starr: one of us!

I was lucky enough to meet dear Edwin at most of his shows, and the last time we spoke wanted to start work on his autobiography. With his manager, Lilian Kyle's help, the book promised to be a frank and honest portrayal of his life and career. Tragically, the book was never started. Edwin died at the age of 61 from a heart attack in April 2003. We are still coming to terms with our loss.

THE SUPREMES
(FORMER LADIES OF)
LYNDA LAURENCE, SCHERRIE PAYNE, JEAN TERRELL
Dateline: February 1990

The Supremes (well, the ladies of...) had such an awful tour schedule that very few interviews were given, but when Scherrie Payne arranged for them all to be in one place at the same time, I jumped at the chance of meeting them. The venue was their dressing room, prior to them going on stage, and when I opened the door three stools stood along one wall, and one stool was opposite them. Guess whose?!

It was an immense pleasure seeing Jean, Lynda and Scherrie again, and during my stay there was plenty of laughter and masses of warm feelings. Also, they are fiercely loyal to each other; their respect and love bind them together because as Lynda said, they are in this new era of The Supremes together.

The trio were headlining the Motorcity tour and promoting their new single 'Crazy 'Bout The Guy', and you don't need me to

CHINWAGGIN'

mention that they're also music giants, former Motown stars and all genuine Supremes who reunited to keep the music alive. First question then—why?

Jean: "What happened was Scherrie and I along with Cindy (Birdsong) first got together. Then Cindy had commitments that she had to deal with, which she thought would conflict. So Lynda was available and..."

Lynda interrupted: "and I replaced Cindy again!"

Scherrie: "I want to say here that this was in 1986 when I was working with a record company called Supersonic International, and I'd done a single on the label. They were the ones who came up with the idea of putting us together. They contacted Jean and Cindy and that's how it started."

The trio subsequently recorded one single—'We're Back'—for the company, and provided vocal support for a version of 'Up The Ladder To The Roof'.

Lynda Laurence

LADIES OF THE SUPREMES

Scherrie: "That was Lynda, myself, Cindy and Jayne Edwards, the girl who was with the Bluebelles originally. The single wasn't released here, because I believe the company went under. But we didn't want this to stop us. Sometimes you think because the record is gone, there's no point in trying, so forget it. But we felt this group was too good to forget."

Jean: "When I told Cholly Atkins, one of the foremost choreographers at Motown, we were back together and who was featured in the group, he said, 'Oh yeah, that *is* the line-up'. He made me feel really good because he'd seen all the members of the group."

The ladies are unable to use the name, 'Supremes', which is why their first names precede it in advertising. Motown has approved this wording; a fact, they're happy with.

Scherrie: "With this situation we recognised, and so did Supersonic International when we first recorded for them, that we couldn't use the name, 'Supremes'. But we know we can say we're *formerly* of The Supremes, because we are."

During their nation-wide trek the audiences have proven time and again that they care little what name the ladies use, because the reaction has been the same, they say, emotionally fantastic. This has, of course, made them all the more determined to progress their act further.

Jean: "To be honest, we have to have a positive attitude about what we're doing. We're going to go on to project an even stronger image but I think that if 'Crazy 'Bout The Guy' does something for us...well, let's say we're buying time right now because we need a little more time to really do what we've set out to do, the way we've always wanted to. And when we do that, what you see tonight is going to be magnified by one hundred percent."

Lynda: "A hit record always helps. It's very important, but, on the other hand, we hope we have a group that's so well put together, experienced in what they're doing and continuing to work. A hit, however, enhances that work so much and..."

Scherrie: "And the money helps too! But more importantly, a hit gives the fans something to hold on to, something new to relate to, so they don't have to keep on relying on memories."

Jean: "We've covered our tracks to the point that we feel secure

Scherrie Payne

in ourselves about saying we were formerly of The Supremes. Legally we can't say we're The Supremes, even though everybody is saying it...and we can't stop people from saying it if they want. I don't think there's another group who can claim the name as much as we can."

She's right: think about it.

To recap now. Jean Terrell replaced Diana Ross: her first single with the trio was 'Up The Ladder To The Roof' when the membership was Mary Wilson and Cindy Birdsong. When Cindy departed, Lynda Laurence replaced her and Scherrie Payne stepped in when Jean left. After a 'retirement' of some years, I asked Jean how it felt to perform those familiar songs again— bearing in mind, her lead vocal mesmerised listeners to the new group line-up: 'Stoned Love' is a prime example. Was it still a responsibility to carry the group?

"This time it's not all on me, that's why I'm so happy everyone's sharing the leads on the old songs, like the ones Diana took lead on because at one time I used to crumble under the strain. Now that I've done them for so long I feel as much a part of them as she must have done when she originally recorded them. I'm certainly not taking anything away from what she's done."

This nicely led into a new publication about Ms Ross which, to all intents and purposes was non-complimentary, prompting—

Scherrie: "Diana Ross is a beautiful lady. You can't take away what she's done."

Jean: "I don't think negative things are so necessary. There's so much that's positive about Diana because if it wasn't for her we wouldn't be sitting here today. There's so many good things to write about her and I hope it'll be said one day. Mind, people only write good things when people are dead...and that's unfortunate."

Lynda: "The only way the record will be put straight is when she writes her own book. I was really in shock that she didn't come out with one before this one. I think if she had...well, she must have her reasons."

Someone said one time—probably a man—that if you put two women together you've got problems. Here we have three...is this true, I wondered?

Jean: "We all have personalities that gel, but we all like to have quiet moments."

Scherrie: "I think that comes from maturing..."

Lynda: "With being on the road as we are, and working together—even at home we have to rehearse—you just give a person respect. And if you're not feeling well or whatever, it's no problem."

Jean: "Each one of us has our own set of values and our own views on things, yet we've come together for a job. And some days things happen that cause us to want to sit there in a corner. I'm not the sort of person who'll be in a mood and not say it's happening to me. I don't like moods. I don't like to sit in a mood and stay there...if someone else can get me out of it I'm delighted because I'm not an entity here all by myself. There's nothing heavy here. When I have a problem, or mood or whatever, maybe that's to do with the feminine thing, or maybe somebody's rubbed me the wrong way, I still do the job. I'm still here, because we made a deal."

Lynda: "I can't begin to have a good show if Scherrie is having

CHINWAGGIN'

a bad one. That worries me. I want her to have a good time as well. We have to do it that way Sharon, we have to think in terms like that. Otherwise there's no point in continuing."

The ladies also have their own lives and careers to contend with. For example, Scherrie still records for Nightmare Records and, I teased Lynda, she'd been extremely busy over here under a different singing guise! An impostor, a fraudster, no less. "I heard about *her*! I sure didn't like it, to tell you the truth. But I decided to approach it from a different standpoint. First, I was angry, I really wanted to lash back and really prove who I was. But then I thought the burden of proof is on her. With this tour happening, nobody will be in any doubt as to who I am!"

When this month-long tour is finished, the trio return to America for an eight day rest, before zipping over to Japan for three weeks where they enjoy a huge following.

Showtime was called; as one, the ladies brushed themselves down and mentally prepared themselves to entertain their London audience who had packed the theatre. It was a terrific show and was one I subsequently saw, and thoroughly enjoyed, many times over.

The future of this trio was beset with problems from several quarters, but mostly about the legality of the membership which had the affront to associate itself with Motown's Supremes. The queen of litigation, Mary Wilson, was a forerunner in her plight to destroy what they stood for, while bogus groups, like The Sounds Of The Supremes, used the group's name freely and, it appeared, without attracting any legal threats. Its lead singer Kaaren Ragland stated she joined Motown's Supremes as Scherrie Payne's replacement in 1977, and later toured with Mary Wilson up to 1989.

Chris Williams, president of Lynda, Scherrie and Jean's fan club, had been involved in heated correspondence with Ms Ragland and "to this day she has not been able to substantiate her claims either by producing her contract with Motown Records or supplying any of the records she allegedly sung on. Need I say more?"

In 1993 Jean Terrell performed her last concert with The Former Ladies Of The Supremes (FLOS) to be replaced by Sundrey Tucker, an ex-member of The Third Generation—Stevie

LADIES OF THE SUPREMES

Wonder's backing group—and who, under the name Cindy Scott recorded the Northern Soul classic "I Love You Baby". She had also auditioned for The Supremes in the early seventies, but it was her sister, Lynda Laurence who joined them.

In May 1995, as the bogus Supremes situation got out of hand, Lynda had little choice but to vent her views: "I am tired of all the innuendo about who is and who isn't a Supreme. I had no idea when I joined the group in 1972 that I would have to define and actually prove who I am and what I have done in my career—after all, it is a matter of record and clearly documented. Anyone who is trying so hard to prove to be a member of The Supremes should simply check the facts. I am, of course, referring to the group, The Sounds of The Supremes. Clearly, the name says it all: the 'sound' which is quite definitely not their sound. The songs were recorded by The Supremes from 1961 to 1976 and it's therefore appalling that three women could simply decide to create something that they are not—namely the 'sound' of The Supremes when they have made no contribution to the real group whatsoever. I know that onstage they refer to individual members as having joined The Supremes in the late 1970s and early 80s but the real gall is when one of the individuals is quoted as an original member in an article I read. Frankly, if they are so duped by their own need to be who or what they are not, then I feel sorry for them. The individuals I'm referring to are Kaaren Ragland-Steele, Hollis Payseur and Angel Rogers. The latter I personally know...It is inconceivable that they can actually believe that they are (or ever were) Supremes just because some of them were employed by Mary Wilson as her back ups for a while.

"I am now and always will be one of only eight former members of Motown's Supremes. My group, which was formed in 1985 consists of Scherrie Payne, the last lead singer of The Supremes, and Sundray Tucker, who is not and never was a member of The Supremes (and never pretends that she was) and myself. Since Sherrie and I together with Mary Wilson are the only Supremes working today (not forgetting Diana of course) and Mary is not in our group, we needed a third lady to complete the trio.

"Our act is called Former Ladies of The Supremes."

Scherrie Payne added kudos to her colleague's words. "The Supremes gave their final farewell performance at The Theatre

CHINWAGGIN'

Royal, Drury Lane, London on 12 June 1977 marking the end of The Supremes—period. The final line-up was Mary Wilson, Susaye Green and myself as lead singer. During the concert Mary stated that this was to be her final appearance with The Supremes as she wished to pursue a solo career and that Susaye and I would be continuing as The Supremes with new member Joyce Vincent-Wilson (formerly of Tony Orlando & Dawn).

"However, several months later, Motown decided to retire the group and Mary duly embarked on her solo career, utilising the services of many others as background singers.

"After the farewell shows in England, Pedro Ferrer—The Supremes' manager and Mary's husband—discovered that there was one additional tour in South America that had to be contractually fulfilled. Susaye and I opted not to go and on the day Mary was due to leave, a lady named Deborah Sharpe auditioned and was selected. Cindy Birdsong was called to fill in as well. This was to be their only engagement. Even Deborah has stated that she knew this was simply a one-off experience to help Mary meet her contractual obligation, after which Mary would continue as a solo artist.

"Lynda, Sundray and I have never attempted to imply that we own the rights to the name The Supremes...there are only eight ladies who can rightfully claim to have been a member of the group—Mary Wilson, Florence Ballard, Diana Ross, Cindy Birdsong, Jean Terrell, Lynda Laurence, Susaye Green and myself...

"Of course, as promoters sometimes will do, an act is billed according to their own monetary interests, even though the contract may stipulate otherwise. I'm sure Mary was billed as The Supremes overseas where promoters thought it would go unnoticed in the USA. Mary was involved in litigation with Motown over the use of the name and was forbidden to use it as such until the case had been resolved. Mary eventually won a percentage of the name but could still only use variations of the name such as Mary Wilson Formerly of... or The Supremes' Mary Wilson....However, at no time was she ever permitted to use solely the name Supremes. It is worth noting that Mary sold her share of The Supremes' name back to Motown some years ago.

"The subject is touchy for me personally because Kaaren and

LADIES OF THE SUPREMES

Hollis happen to be friends of mine, but being a Supreme cannot be one of their assets because, much as they might care to believe otherwise, this simply is not the truth."

Although the last few paragraphs do not form part of my original interview, I've included them to—hopefully—put an end to the dispute regarding The Supremes' membership, and who has the right to use the name, and so on. Regrettably, as I write this, conflict still bubbles away—but the truth can't be re-written. Sundray Tucker left the group to be replaced by Freddi Poole.

Jean Terrell

SYLVESTER

Dateline: September 1982

I first met Sylvester James in 1978 when he came to London for a promotional tour based around '(You Make Me Feel) Mighty Real'. My first impression was one of a gentle giant—well, he does stand over six foot in bare feet. He was with his managers, Nancy Pitts and Harvey Fuqua (of The Moonglows, Marvin Gaye and Motown fame) and was in London for two sell-out performances at the Hammersmith Odeon, where the audiences were dominated by young males, packed in to see their hero, and his heavyweight back-up ladies, Martha Walsh and Izora Rhodes, known as The Two Tons Of Fun (later to become The Weather Girls). Together they produced a monster sound—literally—and as exciting a stage act as anyone would want to see. They battled for vocal dominance and shared ad-lib bitchy throwaways, but loved each other dearly. They were a team.

Sylvester let no-one down at Hammersmith. I remember that for one of his encores, he dressed up in his long evening gown and wore his tiara—"Every queen should wear a crown" he told them.

He was now in London once more, promoting another slice of

disco titled 'Do Ya Wanna Funk?', which promised to be a further hit under his belt. Unfortunately, his days with Martha and Izora were numbered.

When hosting interviews he always started by saying "Oh God, don't ask me how I got started or how old I am or about the Cockettes. Let's just say that I came from an upper-middle class black bourgeois family in Los Angeles, and that I left a boring nine-to-five job to move to San Francisco. Better yet, let's say I was the first test tube baby!"

I ignored him. The Cockettes was an outrageous unit that played on its own kind of sexuality. When they were born in the late sixties, Sylvester auditioned to join them. "I hadn't sung for years, but it felt good. The Cockettes were a gas. I loved them. I was already strange as far as the rest of the world was concerned, and I felt I had safety in numbers," he explained. "We did period pieces and we also did some preposterous glitter rock and roll."

Eventually he outgrew the group and chanced a solo career. "I still used sets and costumes, and my whole life was still a show. I would sing jazz and blues standards of the twenties and thirties, dance and roll my eyes." Working as a woman, he played two years at the Rickshaw Lounge in Chinatown. "I used to dress up like Billie Holiday, with the gardenias and all. I also lived in a 1930's apartment. I changed my name to Ruby Blue, drank gin and played piano on stage. I'd change from Billie to Bessie Smith or whoever, and I'd sing their songs. My show was titled 'Women Of The Blues'. I didn't try to impersonate them, instead I did my own renditions. My mother says I've always lived in my fantasies!"

His love of the theatre wasn't confined to song: he was a talented set designer with a flair for costume design. However, he remembered, sometimes this passion was misread. "What happened was that the theatrics got in the way of the music. I had to be 'on' all the time. People were more interested in my personal sexual orientation and my costumes than they were in my music. Sure I'm gay and I'm outrageous about it. But, I don't tell gay jokes and I don't sing gay songs. So, what if I'm outrageous—what about the music?"

To backtrack slightly, Sylvester started singing at eight years old and: "It was a confusing time for me travelling on the gospel circuit and being so young. I lost my childhood years and for this reason, I think, I turned more to fantasising. After I sang in church, I became very disillusioned with gospel and decided I never wanted to sing again." As a teenager he left home because his mother told him: "If you don't like what's going on in my house you can leave." Her son replied, "That's the most wonderful thing you've said to me, because I can escape from you." They're now good friends, I hasten to add.

In 1973 Blue Thumb Records signed Sylvester and he released three albums—'Lights Out San Francisco', 'Scratch My Flower' (it had a patch on the record cover which, when scratched, smelled of gardenias) and 'Bazaar'. From Blue Thumb, his current managers Pitts and Fuqua chanced to see him perform at The Palms Cafe, San Francisco, where he held his Sunday Workshops—"I would plan out my material before a live audience for free, work out things to see if they'd work or not."

This chance meeting led to a Fantasy Records recording contract. "The first album, 'Sylvester' pleased me completely. My other albums are forbidden to be played in my house. I've got them as mementoes but I don't enjoy listening to them. 'Sylvester' was the first time I'd done a commercial, well-produced album, and I've got the highest respect for Harvey Fuqua. He got the sound on record that I had in my head."

And to cut a long story short, during 1978 and 1979 Sylvester was the dancefloor favourite with the gay anthem 'Mighty Real'. His, or rather Harvey's, sophisticated type of dance music somewhat changed disco ideas. And not before time either.

Sylvester and I professionally met again in January 1985; contact in between times was on the phone or during his private visits to London. We had established a solid friend/soul ship, proven by his greeting as I walked into his Montcalm Hotel lounge. "There you are, bitch. I've been trying to get hold of you for ages dear, and you just don't wanna know. I was told you'd left the country 'cos your Marvin Gaye book's been published!"

Sylvester was true to his publicity; his tongue was quick, his humour as dryly wicked as always. Where had I been? Killing time downstairs in the hotel's bar, waiting to be summoned to his suite, following a phone call the previous evening to confirm the

SYLVESTER

interview.

Chrysalis's head of publicity, Bernadette Kilmartin was with us, and was celebrating working with Sylvester again after a seven year break. (She worked with him at Fantasy Records, licensed to EMI Records). "He's not as wild as he was in those days," she whispered to me. "We've matured together, but we still have time for a bit of fun!"

Looking a little heavy around the waistline, and wearing jeans, a thick sweater with his hair pulled back, Sylvester gushed he was in love again. He was an architect and they've been together for several months. He's a good looking guy I admitted, after seeing his pictures in the singer's wallet.

Any children? I asked.

"I'm not that clever, but we've got dogs."

His dress is more conservative, but he still has the desire to shock people, to be different and, of course, to give journalists a blistering story, full of juicy quotes. As he says, why is everyone getting uptight about Boy George, Marilyn and the rest? They're old-fashioned now, he smiled. "I was carrying on like that over ten years ago, and paving the way for today's so called shockers in music! Even my stage shows are toned down because you have so many wild people here already. I still love being glamorous, but it's also my work and a lot of the joy and the fun has been taken out of it because it is work.... Dressing up and being wild in all my costumes isn't that important to me now. I'm older and I've moved on from that stage in my life. Now I'm into chic clothes and objects, and...like people wear diamantes. Well, darling, I like diamonds. The real thing. Why wear something that's fake, when I can have the real thing?"

He confided that when he was younger, one of his favoured fantasies was to find a treasure chest crammed with wonderful and expensive bangles and diamonds. Like most fantasies, he said, he never found it, so he purchased his own chest and has been filling it with goodies ever since!

The ensuing conversation covered Diana Ross being busted for cocaine, which made *The Los Angeles Times* but no other paper, and how various people Sylvester had worked with (including Nancy Pitts, he sighed) had screwed him financially and were now having to pay the price with the American tax people.

CHINWAGGIN'

Actually, he announced, '(You Make Me Feel) Mighty Real' had made him a millionaire three times over, and yet during that time he was kept on a weekly salary. The tax forms he signed in good faith were never passed on to the taxman, neither were his cheques. He was still paying the price for this years later.

Retiring from the business at thirty-five was his ambition. At thirty-eight he's still working but the catch is, he said, he's doing it to do nothing. "I shall carry on working until I'm secure enough to do nothing at all. However, I still feel the pull of the greasepaint and roar of the crowd and reckon this will keep me going a while longer.

"Say, do you remember when I wore that evening dress for the finale at Hammersmith? With my tiara and all? Wasn't that something. That audience didn't know what to expect that night, that's for sure." I said I also recalled him arriving at Heathrow wearing that dreaded tiara. "I had nowhere else to put it dear. Didn't those photographers take a second look. I also carried a bunch of dead roses too. They died on the flight, and again I didn't know what to do with them, so I carried them like a bouquet! Ah, memory lane...

"I also told a journalist that I wanted to marry Prince Charles so's I could be queen of England. Oh, isn't Diana a lovely creature. I don't care that he married her. Mind you, at the time (1979) I ignored what the papers said about me. I don't read newspapers anyway, but so long as the people write something about me, that's alright. They capitalised on my so-called outrageousness, and now, these same people, listen to me and hopefully respect me more because they've read some interesting things about me. My priorities have changed. At the time of 'Mighty Real' I didn't want to sing disco, and I had no choice really when the record took off. I had to go along with it. Now, I'm lucky enough to be doing what I want and I'm singing still because it's fun."

The subject reverted to San Francisco, where he said he saw things and visited places he never knew existed. The gay lifestyle shocked but pleased him; he realised he could live freely, be true to himself. However, he was recently taken aback by the publication of Little Richard's book 'The Life And Times'. "Well, some of it made my hair curl! To read the explicit details

SYLVESTER

of some of his sexual activities, well, my dear...he's written it *all* down so clearly. He also says he opened up a lot of doors for singers like myself but to me that's a bit presumptuous. He did nothing new because all this outrageous stuff was going on in the twenties, like in Paris and places. Now, of course, Richard is in great demand; he's flavour of the year again because everyone wants to see this man who did all these explicit things."

And this was the subject I left on. It was midnight; Sylvester was due to fly to Italy in the morning while I was writing up the interview. We kissed farewell: I didn't realise it would be the last time I'd see him. Meanwhile, I made a mental note—get Little Richard's book in the morning. For research purposes of course!

Professionally-speaking, Sylvester's final British hit was 1983's 'Band Of Gold'. He continued to record and tour throughout the eighties until he fell victim to AIDS. Despite being wheel chair bound, Sylvester spent his last months supporting other AIDS victims in their fight for life. My dear friend left this world in December 1988; another soul lost to this most dreadful of diseases.

SYREETA
Dateline: July 1990

It was almost six years ago when we last chatted but when Syreeta and I spoke recently the years just flew by. Looking gorgeous in a stunning outfit, Syreeta—ex-wife of Stevie Wonder and the originator of some of Motown's finest music, including her duet with Billy Preston 'With You I'm Born again', and now recording for Motorcity Records—settled herself in while I cranked up the cassette player. We were in her Dominion Theatre dressing room and could hear other acts' voices in the distance.

First things first, I smiled, her love life. "Well," she started, "I'm no longer Mrs Robinson. I'm Mrs Torrence Mathis, as in Johnny Mathis, but no relation. And I'm very pleased about that. For once I have found the man that understands both sides of being in this business. He understands the side of being a performer and going into the studio and he understands me at home just as a wife. I know I'm very fortunate because it's so hard for a man to feel confident and strong when his wife is in the public eye."

Ironically, Syreeta has never struck me as the type of lady who could leave the stage to settle into a housewife's role, with the two lifestyles remaining separate. She insisted she could. "I have to be able to switch hats. The good thing about it is that my husband is a very elegant man. He treats himself like a king, therefore he is commanding, not demanding, but there's a commanding type of aura around him, so it's not very different being on stage and being with him. The thing is on stage I'm performing and doing a little showbusiness to each song. I'm interpreting the songs whereas with my husband I'm being *me*. At the same time I try to dress in a way and look in a way that's appealing to him because he is my man."

At our last meeting, the singer disguised the fact that her second marriage to Curtis Robinson was in such turmoil. "During that time I was actually very unhappy. Unfortunately, being married to Curtis...and he is a very good man but he wasn't the man I should have married, and that's with no disrespect to him. Sometimes we do things for the wrong reasons and unfortunately that's what Curtis and I did."

As soul fans know, Syreeta is respected for her writing talent which is equal to her vocal expertise. A distinguished career to date. When I mentioned this, she revealed: "I've just written a song called 'Searching For My Freedom' that, in my opinion, is probably one of the best things I've ever written. It deals with a person looking at their life and knowing or feeling their incompleteness and about how, when we get into those situations, we have to sit down for a moment and really search for the key to yourself. H-e-a-v-y!... But Stevie used to write about heavy things. He made the music work so that no-one felt heavy about what he was saying, and that's the way my song is. It's a beautiful ballad but it's very touching and moving, and it will bring tears to your eyes when you hear it because everyone that has heard it so far said it reminds them of their own life, but not in a sad way, more in a cleansing way. Each time life brings us certain pressures, we get relief afterwards. So this song is really more relief without the pressure, see?"

We changed the subject to Motown and Berry Gordy's recent sale of the company to the MCA conglomerate. Syreeta, who had spent all her recording career as a signed artist, was one of several artists to leave the roster. In typical frankness, she said. "When Mr Gordy sold Motown the new regime did not want the likes of 'With You I'm Born Again', or that type of format. They went for a younger market. I'm not that old by any means, but I'm not your teenybopper. So when he sold the company, we looked at each other and we knew it just wasn't a thing that would work. In retrospect it wasn't a bad thing because I don't want to be moulded into something that I'm not. I mean, I fought for my own identity and freedom for a number of years so I certainly don't want to be anywhere where they're going to put me in clothes that are slit from my toes up to my neck and where I'm wearing underclothes because it's fashionable; that's not me.

"Why should I be at a place where we can only give each other headaches? I'm too wise for that. So I've been writing, producing, doing commercials and taking time out just to enjoy my family and also to just think about some of the things that I want to do."

The build-up to Motown's sale is, perhaps, not generally known. So Syreeta provided the details. "During the last days of Motown there was a conflict constantly, mainly because of the fact that Mr Gordy was focused on trying to save a sinking ship and that was for a number of years before he actually sold the company. He put his own personal money into it to try and save it because he felt a responsibility to us, to all the artists who were there. He didn't want it to end up like it did but after a while he had no choice. Nobody wants to put their baby out. It's like a father giving his daughter away in marriage; he knows he still has the connection but there's something there that's a little uncomfortable."

In her time with the company, the singer was more fortunate than most artists because she enjoyed a special rapport with Berry Gordy and, thanks to this, was able to learn about the business side of her career. "I learned all the way up, and now have experience in a little bit of the business side because I used to sit in on Mr Gordy's meetings sometimes and learned how he manoeuvred things. Not to be an executive at Motown but just to know and understand the business side, and that was really thrilling. I was very fortunate that he would allow me to do that from time to time."

Happily, Syreeta has been able to turn her career around; she's recorded tracks for Motorcity Records, including a solo version of 'With You I'm Born Again' and the dance track 'If The Shoe Fits' which audiences lapped up during the tour last year. However, her next ambition is to don the hat of author, writing a

SYREETA

book about her life with Stevie Wonder, among other topics. "I know it's something I'm going to do, but it's something that has to be timed right. It's something I'll have to prepare people for. I mentioned it to Stevie and he went very quiet. I told him I felt we should do it together. He has to understand how the book is to come about and the things that I would like for the public to know. It's not just about these two people who came together, got married, got divorced and then...well, he's a superstar, and she's like sort of a star. There's a lot more to it because Stevie came up in this business as a child protegy. He was a child star and there's a lot to tell about living that type of life, and certain elements hanging over your life at such a young age sometimes leaves defects that we have to become adults before being able to fix and balance out."

In her much-respected candid approach to questions, Syreeta told me she was still fond of her ex-husband: "How could you not love Stevie?" But agreed he had one annoying side to him—time! "Stevie is so creative first of all, and secondly because he's blind he is totally on another clock. He knows no day and no night, so he maybe works when everyone else is sleeping. There's a silence in the earth that he feels and he's able to draw his creativity from that. So a lot of times, at three in the morning he's just getting to the studio!"

Syreeta has staying power; she's experienced in this unpredictable business. Indeed, for all the years I've known her, she's always managed to surprise her public. We exchanged phone numbers, promising a future of long, girly chats.

This was the last time we talked face-to-face. As time passed we lost touch, but during 2003 Lynda Laurence alerted me to the fact that Syreeta was suffering from bone cancer. She was hospitalised in Cedars Sinai, and the prognosis looked good. We held on to that thought. Sadly, it was not to be; Syreeta passed away in July 2004. Our beautiful songbird had died.

THE TEMPTATIONS
Dateline: May 1986

It was three very tired Temptations I met at lunchtime. In the plush surroundings of a top Kensington hotel, Otis Williams, Richard Street and Ali Woodson relaxed in track suits and sunglasses for one of a series of interviews to be conducted. In fact, Mr Street was so relaxed he nodded off, thus proving my interviews aren't as compelling as I thought!

"Take no notice, Sharon," laughed Otis. "He's always doing that. He'll wake up, feeling embarrassed in a moment." Sure nuff, he did.

The remaining group members, Melvin Franklin and Ron Tyson, were elsewhere engaged in radio interviews. Splitting the group like this ensured more promotional ground can be covered and one of the group's founder members always accompanied a newer one, securing a fine balance.

The Temptations had been partying all night at The Hippodrome, following their first performance in London in a long while.... "Yes, it's really that long," sighed Otis. "Ten years or so. Boy that's *too* long, but there have been reasons." Bopping at The Hippodrome, which, when it was the Talk Of The Town nightspot, was where the group did a week's stint "too many years ago", caused them to raise their eyebrows. Why? "It was shim night and nobody told us!" 'Shim' means all male, backs against the wall—and they're not my words either.

As The Temptations' history with Motown is well documented, we talked of other things, although initially I asked Otis whether The Temptations being a legend was too much of a responsibility now? "It's not so much being thought of as a legend, but being around in this business for so long. That's the achievement. I suppose the responsibly is there by keeping on top of things, like, on record and on stage, but it's our life and we're lucky to have this phenomenon in our life. The Temptations have been good to me. I'd certainly complain if my life had been spent working at Ford's foundries."

For their European concerts which are part of their 25th Anniversary tour, the group has included many an old and favourite tune, although that in itself causes problems, as Otis spelled out. "After twenty-five years of records it ain't that easy to choose what to sing. However, for our shows over here we have to take care to sing the right songs, especially those from the sixties. So, we've broken the act down into three sections. The Smokey Robinson one, Norman Whitfield's and today's."

And digging out songs they don't normally perform in the States has, of course, meant remembering old dance routines. Their choreographer is, I'm told, over seventy years old, yet jives like a teenager. "Most of the routines are done automatically now," Otis said. "We can't remember them all, just like that. But we're like computers... once we're programmed, that's it. It's all down to using the brain God gave you, and it's extraordinary the things you remember. That's why for the newer material we don't have gruelling routines. We have to catch our breath somewhere in the show because we certainly couldn't keep up the pace. Yet once the introduction of a particular song starts, my feet seem to know what to do. We certainly get a bit physical with 'My Girl' even now. That song, you know, bugs us. We daren't do a show without it. All over the world if there's one song our audience asks for, it's 'My Girl'. So, we have to throw our all into it."

Seeing The Temptations on stage last night was awesome. Their slickness of step remains; the unison in voice and movement can't be bettered and the pure excitement and thrill of seeing a group

CHINWAGGIN'

I've grown up with, hasn't faltered one bit. The sweat poured down their faces, soaked their shirts and jackets, so every now and then, one would sneak away for a date with a dry towel. The show's pace never let up either, until Melvin Franklin dipped into his boots for a deep-throated 'Old Man River' which could easily have lost the show for them, but didn't. The audience begged for more gospel, and more Melvin. So, I agreed, this choosing of repertoire actually involves more than a casual chat. Continued Otis: "Richard might want to do 'Please Return Your Love To Me' and I might want 'Since I Lost My Baby' included. Once everyone has thrown in their ideas and suggestions, we throw some out, balance the performance, and end up with enough songs for a ninety minute show with encore. It is very tiring, particularly with the dancing around, but so long as we pace ourselves we'll be alright."

We then talked about The Temptations' concerts with stablemates the Four Tops, a combination which originated from the Motown Revues in the sixties. When these dissolved, the acts went their separate ways until 'Motown 25' and their successful medley. "The response to that was overwhelming, so the Tops and our managers got talking, worked out the details for us to go on the road together. It's as simple as that. Originally, we were going out with Smokey Robinson, but," Otis smiled, "he didn't want to work that hard! Now, we and the Tops have dates through this year, into the next."

Something that has been niggling me for some time now is the 'Reunion' tour and album, with the introduction and speedy departure of original Temptations David Ruffin and Eddie Kendricks. There was a short silence when I raised the subject, then Otis obliged. "That was something we had to get out of our system, and it will never be repeated. I suppose you could say that when we went back to Motown the public wanted David and Eddie to be in the group. They were included for the 'Reunion' project only. We still see them periodically...I guess everything is OK between us, the relationship is cordial." He wouldn't be drawn further.

A hasty subject change was needed, so I opted to ask whether enjoying hit singles carried the same thrill now, especially as the group was knee-deep in charting repertoire during their heady,

THE TEMPTATIONS

successful years. Otis again. "We could never say hit records aren't important now. Getting that hit is still imperative regardless of how long we've been in the business and, believe me, we feel the same excitement as we did when we got our first hit. We've had our fair share of hits, I won't deny that, and we ain't through yet."

Talking of hits, 'I'm Fascinated' has been lifted from the group's current 'Touch Me' album as the new single, a track that's not included in their stage act. Otis said the choice of release is basically left to Motown's A&R department. "We cut it, say what we think would make a good single, then see what the A&R people come up with. We're more liberal now and trust Motown ultimately to make the right decisions. Obviously throughout the world different licensees have other plans for their markets, so everything is evaluated at the time." He stressed that even now, Motown and the group have a hand-in-glove situation. "All recording companies need an act they can work with and vice versa, and few acts actually get a company they click with.

CHINWAGGIN'

We've been lucky.

"I believe Motown helped make us what we are. We're two great forces. Without Motown during the sixties, The Temptations could have taken longer to achieve success, yet I think the combination was something that fate dictated. When compared to groups of today, I have to say, we worked harder, we were always working, so I can't say today's acts are cut with the same cloth, can I? Yet, that doesn't make them any less musicians or artists—it's all down to business value. I feel acts came along to Motown at the right time when the company introduced a unique idea into the business. Most acts nowadays don't get hit records because, well, let me put it this way—if you play good you get good dollars!"

Time was getting on, and although Richard Street had woken up, I felt they needed some space to prepare for their next journalist. I parted with the words they looked resplendent in their tuxedos last night—slick, smooth and handsome too. "Well, you're out of luck tonight, Sharon", they laughed. "Tonight, we're wearing hip-hugging, tight-fitting track suits on stage!"

"In that case fellers, I'll bring my camera long with it's zoom lens."

"Are you talking dirty now" the three laughed in unison,
"What? Me?!"

In December 1986, Otis Williams phoned me from Washington where the group were touring alone. They had recently teamed up with the Four Tops in Indiana, where they were joined by Mary Wilson with two backing vocalists. They didn't duet, Otis said, although hinted it might have been fun, bringing back old memories of working with Diana Ross and the Supremes.

The Temptations' American touring schedule has been non-stop for months, not that he was complaining. But they were forced to rest up for six weeks earlier this year because Otis underwent foot surgery. "It's a common complaint with dancers...and women who wear high heeled shoes" he moaned down the phone. "No, my complaint was nothing to do with the shoes. My feet are too big anyway! But I'm fine now. We're not chickens anymore: maybe season chickens!"

For some reason I can't recall, we spoke about Berry Gordy and

THE TEMPTATIONS

how he became so successful in music. "It's not magic for a start. He's got another kind of sensitivity that others don't have. Mr Gordy is a very talented man, and a good businessman too. When it comes to making things happen, he's there. I suppose he's a cut above the rest, one of a kind. And he's still very much involved in the day-to-day business of Motown. He's carved a niche in history for himself—like Napoleon did, for example."

As for The Temptations themselves, Otis reported they had branched out into other areas of the business. "We've done movies and commercials. We are starring with Peter Faulkner in his next film 'Happy New Year' and we were booked to appear in 'Rocky 4' but our schedule was very tight at the time so we couldn't do it. I'm not sure what the roles were but I hoped it wasn't opposite him in the boxing ring! We've also done some television shows like 'Love Boat' where we did a little acting, and with Lee Majors in 'The Fall Guy'."

Of himself, Otis said that if he hadn't chosen music as a career, he'd no idea where he'd have ended up. "I've only ever been a Temptation and I've been one for so long—I eat, sleep and breathe them...I grew up with them just like you have. Seriously, I might have gone into the arts, a commercial artist or into designing. I love clothes—I've got wardrobes full of them—and one of these days I want to open a clothes shop, or a boutique, of my own." He said he'd hoarded some of his stage clothes: "Although most are in the Motown museum now, and we've also given some to charities. But I've kept a few. I've also collected bits and pieces of memorabilia over the years, like concert programmes, a lot of pictures, plaques and statues, awards given to us. In fact, I must have an attic full by now."

And, on a personal note, he said when time permits he likes relaxing with a book, going to the movies and shopping... naturally! "I also shoot pool and I'm quite good, and I like all sports. I play basketball, baseball, the martial arts but I'm not belted, and I get involved in a few little training sessions. We also go to nightclubs because we like to get an idea of what's going on out there, so life is pretty full!"

Three years later I spoke to Richard Street, who was totally awake but suffering from a heavy cold—and I mean heavy! It was tempting (no pun intended) to wear a face mask, but I resisted.

The Temptations were part-way through a British tour in support of their new single 'All I Want From You' lifted from their recent 'Special' album. And it was this that Richard spoke about first. "For this album we used different producers and some were only in their twenties. That's the way the record company wanted us to go. The producers were fans of the group and maybe the result isn't exactly what people expected. If it had been left up to me, I think I'd have waited until all the tunes that moved me had come along before recording. But that would have meant waiting and we had a deadline to put the album out. It was a time-game really because we only have a certain amount of time to record because of our tight schedules.

"We didn't choose the songs as such. Y'see, it's the record company's money so they have a certain say in the recording. It's not like a Michael Jackson situation, where he pays for everything. So we do have to listen to the company. Songs are presented to us all the time, apart from those we write and produce, so we have a good selection. However, it's inevitable that we look back afterwards and say we wish we could have waited and done this one or that one...but there's always the next time around."

When MCA took over Motown, much speculation arose as to how it would affect the artists already on the roster. Richard said the group had, so far, noticed no changes, although they conceded the company family feeling had gone: "But the rapport and communication still remains. We can still talk to the president Jheryl Busby so that's good. Not many companies allow you to talk directly to the president without going through the secretary first. That's the nice part of the relationship. MCA told us they wanted us to stay when they made the changeover."

I felt The Temptations had suffered a lean period of late at the hands of Motown which brought back memories of their time at Atlantic Records. "Well, we didn't have a good time there," Richard admitted, "because we'd changed lead singers when we went over. The company was expecting Dennis Edwards and we had Louis Price. And the material was written for Dennis but, of course, it was too late. Although we don't have any definite lead singers, certain producers get someone in their mind, and when

THE TEMPTATIONS

they heard we were coming they had already prepared the songs. Subsequently, the album we cut wasn't in the right key and that changed the whole atmosphere right away. So, we were told as we weren't the original line-up—no Dennis Edwards—we weren't the group they wanted. So we went.

"In today's market promoters and agencies always take into consideration what you've done recently: a Grammy, a hit record and so on. If you are hot you can make more money, it's as simple as that. You can play larger venues, play to larger audiences and get paid more....We don't make money coming to England. It's a 'show and tell' visit. We want people to know we're still in the business, letting our fans know we're still around. We want to be well-known, not only in America, but everywhere. We're off to Japan at the end of the year, which is sort of a continuation of this tour.

"We're working all the time, and that's the way we like to do it. We've always been able to work at a medium range and we thank God for this...We probably spend ten months in every year touring and recording. It's a tremendous sacrifice, particularly if you have a wife or girlfriend because they have to be a very understanding person, knowing you won't be there all the time, and appreciate and respect you for what you do."

All the group are married, and all, he said, take a lot of crap because their lives are not the norm. "Our jobs are very demanding and we miss our home life, our wives and our kids. I have three children. I bring them on tour when they're not in school. They love coming out with us—the room service, going to the show, riding in a limo and plane. It's one big party to them.

"I'm happy at my job and I make a living at it, so when I feel it's taking its toll, making me tired and so on, I don't think about it. I think of all those other unfortunate people. Like, since I've been here I've seen some appalling things on TV about the homeless people in the world, and people who will never get the chance to do what they want to do. All the starving, over-population, people dying in the streets of India... well, you have to be thankful for what you have, and to be in this position, because not to be thankful is a sin. So, when I'm physically tired I remind myself that I could be in America with no job, or in a job I don't like. Life is very traumatic for everyone."

CHINWAGGIN'

On The Temptations' opening night in London, I said it was noticed that Melvin Franklin left the stage during the performance. Nothing was said at the time; was there a problem I asked Richard? Naturally, he respected Melvin's privacy and avoided any details, but did say Melvin underwent two major operations in 1988. "We almost lost him. They were life-threatening operations, and he's just now getting back. We don't let him do a whole show, he has to watch his heart rate. We're trying to nurse him through this, but Melvin wanted to do this tour. If the doctors had said, 'No way, wait for two years,' then that would have been the way it would have gone. He was told he could go onstage, if he felt like it. We read between the lines which is why he goes off stage, and we've tried to reduce his participation, taking some of the pressure away from him.

"Melvin *is* The Temptations. He and Otis have kept the group together through the good and bad times. Even when we were starting out, singing on street corners and in nightclubs, he kept it all together. I was with the group before it became The Temptations, then left to do other things before re-joining them.... Hey, that seems like only yesterday! Remember, you're only as old as you feel, or as young as the person you're with! I've a few years left in me yet, y'know."

News from America told of another Temptations outfit performing and pulling in the crowds. Richard confirmed this was Eddie Kendricks and either Dennis Edwards or David Ruffin. "As Otis and Melvin own the name 'The Temptations', they have to be billed as 'formerly of The Temptations'. I don't really feel anything about this; a man has to do what he has to do. I wish them all the luck in the world. I'm not prejudiced and don't hate anyone because of it. Look, they were part of The Temptations, so they're really entitled to use the name somewhere in the billing if they want. And they've both got families to support. They're not taking work from us. As long as we have a tenor, three leads and Melvin's big bass voice, that's the sign people identify with the real Temptations. Before talking to you, I hadn't given them a second thought." Trust me!

And with that, he had to depart. The other Temptations were waiting to leave their Holiday Inn for Nottingham. So, with his streaming cold, Richard Street stepped outside into the pouring

THE TEMPTATIONS

rain, where his car was waiting. The show must go on!

We grew up together, The Temptations and me. OK, so sadly there's only one original member flying the group flag now—and God knows the group has suffered more than its fair share of changes in singers—but the beautiful music lives on. Like the Four Tops, The Temptations have always toured, and for the past two years have visited the UK together for sold-out concerts. 'Legacy' is the group's most recent release in July 2004, with the membership of the mighty Otis Williams, and Ron Tyson, Terry Weeks, G.C. Cameron, Joe Herndon. Previous releases include 1991's 'For Lovers Only', 1998's 'Phoenix Rising', and 2001's 'Awesome', plus the DVD release, 'The Temptations Story'.

TINA TURNER

Dateline: December 1983

TINA TURNER

The mighty Tina Turner is destined to hit town very soon. I was able to catch the fiery lady between naps and cups of coffee in Germany, with a phone line that was as clear as a bell, interrupted only by the hiccups that Telecom loves so much.

Ms Turner was mid-way through a European tour. "I don't have the itinerary before me," she said, "so I can't tell you where we're due to go, but I do know dates in London are in."

This was the first time I'd spoken to Tina, and confessed that I was not an ardent fan as such, but a *worshipper*. Therefore every spoken word was treasured, and I do believe I had smug grin on my face when the conversation had ended. She appeared to be an interesting and friendly sort of lady, and certainly the shiver of anticipation I felt whilst dialling her number soon melted as the conversation progressed.

Briefly, Ms Turner moved from her native Nutbush, Tennessee, to St Louis where she met her future husband, Ike Turner. He was a member of The Kings Of Rhythm, and in time she joined him - creating one of the most exciting musical associations of the era: the Ike and Tina Turner Revue, whose stage act became an international success as fans flocked to see the electric performances that never failed to please. Ike and Tina joined Phil Spector to produce Tina on 'River Deep, Mountain High', followed closely by 'Proud Mary', although these titles by no means sum up their extraordinary recording career. In time Ike and Tina split up. The marriage was over, so was the musical partnership, while rumours of drug and physical abuse, and mental cruelty hit the headlines. This is now well documented.

To her most recent past now. Tina was asked by the British Electronic Foundation (BEF) to record a version of The Temptations' classic 'Ball Of Confusion'. Her interpretation brought a whole new meaning to the song as she aggressively turned the lyrics into a long-standing social comment that no-one could ignore. Released as a track on the Virgin Records' compilation 'Music Of Quality and Distinction', it made Tina a hot item once more, whereupon Capitol Records signed her.

She was now promoting her current hit for that company, the Al Green gem 'Let's Stay Together', and this is what she spoke about first. "I admire Al Green and this was one of his first

CHINWAGGIN'

singles I wanted to record. It's awfully difficult to decide *what* to record now, but I wanted a real classic, say, like Rod Stewart's 'Hot Legs'. I choose my own material and sometimes it's difficult to find the right stuff. I'm not a writer, so I do a lot of shopping around until I find what I want. The single is part of an album ('Private Dancer'), much of which is yet to be recorded. I've no clue at present what songs will be on it. When I return to the States though, I'll sit down and work some out with my producer. I am a visual artist and to a certain extent I have to record songs I can do on stage. Also what I record has to be in line with my age. For instance, I wouldn't sing teenage songs, or a song that doesn't fit my character. I have to sing songs that I could put to good effect...a good visual performance."

With touring being such an integral part of her career, I asked her feelings about travelling from hotel to hotel. "I love touring and travelling," she enthused. "Particularly in Europe, and seeing the difference in the lifestyles and traditions, particularly from the American way of life. If I'm at home, say, for a month or so, I'm ready again to tour. It is a lot of work, and very glamorous, but I never seem to get enough rest—that's the trouble. This time we're touring by bus, and it's more relaxing for me, and I can see a lot of the countryside as well. I'm really fed up with flying...like, you get on a plane and by the time you sit down, it's time to get off. Then you gotta get through customs, collect your baggage...it's all such a hassle. With a bus it's much easier.

"I'm always working! I have a band, and of course I like to keep them busy. This is my living and I'm really just not the type of person to sit back and do nothing. I get too restless too quickly."

Having been in the business for many years now, I started, how does she keep going on stage? Her act is fast, furious, visual, and just wickedly exciting. "I am a master of my work. I've been entertaining all my life. I am true to my profession and I do owe my audiences the best. They know I have my own style and this is what they come to see. I still enjoy what I do and it's my life now. It's a natural energy and once I get on stage I'm in a whole different world. I won't let up because it is me and I ain't gonna change now."

We veered away from her life for a second, as Tina asked after our Royal Family. Do you have a fondness for them? "Yes, I do.

TINA TURNER

You are lucky to have them. In fact, Charles is rather sweet. If I was thinking of getting married again, I'd rather have liked to marry him! I've always been fond of British men—they are so charming. And the British race have great brains. I've been around all races and all have good qualities.

"I'm having a wonderful time now, and don't want to look for another relationship. I didn't really know my possibilities when I was married, so I'm learning. I didn't really have the chance of doing anything before. I'm more confident now than I've ever been, and I have the opportunity of experimenting more."

Rumours are flitting around the music business that Tina Turner plans to release a new CD, which will be the long over-due follow-up to 'Twenty Four Seven'. She's currently in pre-production for a Merchant Ivory film set in India, due to be filmed in the autumn 2004. This follows her recording 'Great Spirits' for the Disney movie 'Brother Bear'. In 1983 Tina was starting out on a career that must have passed her wildest dreams (no pun intended!) She featured in the UK singles chart from 1983 to 2000, while her career as an actress included a co-starring role with Mel Gibson in 'Mad Max 3'. Her autobiography 'I, Tina' was the basis for the Disney movie 'What's Love Got To Do With It'. Throughout her career, and among the hundreds of honours given to her, Tina scooped six Grammy Awards, the 1999 MOBO Lifetime Achievement Award, and has a star on Hollywood's Hall Of Fame. Shortly before Ms Turner reached the grand age of sixty, she announced her intention to retire from the music business. She spends her time living in France and Switzerland with her boyfriend Erwin Bach. I once called her 'the eighth wonder of the world'. And I haven't changed my mind.

THE VELVELETTES

Dateline: August 1987

These ladies—Millie Gill-Arbour, Norma Barbee-Fairhurst, Carolyn Gill, Bertha Barbee-McNeil—known as The Velvelettes, were in London to tour, and for the first time in twenty years, to record a new single. Despite my loving their Motown singles, which were few, we've never spoken before. Well, that's not surprising really, because the group wasn't one that Motown promoted, so, as Millie smiled, their career lasted all of two years!

Way back in September 1964 The Velvelettes débuted on Motown's VIP label with the stunning 'Needle In A Haystack', followed three months later by an equally monstrous sound 'He Was Really Saying Something'. The sound wasn't that far removed from Martha's Vandellas and was created by their producer Norman Whitfield in the recording studio around 1962.

THE VELVELETTES

It was then the group recorded 'Should I Tell Them?', a song penned by Whitfield and Mickey Stevenson. This could, they say, be classed as their earliest work, and the beginnings of the style that was to become popular with soul fans. 'Should I Tell Them?' was the B-side of their first single. Some time prior to this release, Betty Kelly had been a Velvelette, but left to replace Annette Stirling in the Vandellas.

'Needle In A Haystack' reached the US top fifty and was their only big seller. 'Lonely Lonely Girl Am I' was issued in May 1965, and after a false start, a further classic 'A Bird In The Hand (Is Worth Two In The Bush)' (whatever that really means!) was released at the end of the year. Their last outing saw a label change to Soul when 'These Things Will Keep Me Loving You' had an August 1966 release. (In July 1971 this reached the UK top forty) Stevie Wonder played harmonica on their first three singles and the group recorded ample tracks for an album, but one wasn't forthcoming at the time.

Now, the girls have regular jobs and grown-up families, and we had the chance to chat while Carolyn Gill duetted with Marv Johnson in a downstairs studio in a Bayswater house. Norma acted as spokeswoman for the group as I asked what made them decide to re-form. "I got a phone call one evening from a DJ in the Washington area. He was a lover of The Velvelettes and asked over his radio show did anyone know me. He wanted me to get the others together. So I phoned them and we got together for the first time in twenty years. We acted like teenagers, I can tell you! We stayed up all night, it was wonderful."

They then performed at a festival which featured all types of music—spiritual, jazz, R&B, and so on. "We got the rock section," Norma laughed. "The Velvelettes represented sixties music. We got together for a couple of weekends and came up with a medley of songs that included both The Shirelles and The Supremes. It was about a fifteen minute show and we were scared to death."

By all accounts, the response was overwhelming, as she remembered: "It was a shot in the arm for us, and we got to thinking that maybe we could stay in the business. But we all had work and family commitments and reluctantly returned to our individual lives." Not for long because the next stop was an

CHINWAGGIN'

invitation to participate in a Motown Revue staged at the Fox Theatre, with Jr Walker, Martha Reeves and others. "We opened the show in front of six thousand people. It was fantastic because we'd not seen the other acts in years. People then sent us notes to stay together. Diana Ross sent us one too."

While in Detroit, they toured Motown's museum and visited Berry Gordy's mansion, although he wasn't available to meet them. However, the Detroit media descended upon them—"We were still newsworthy...it was astonishing."

The Velvelettes never realised their music had successfully travelled abroad and, when I explained it was well-known and respected by British soul people, they were surprised, yet, I suspect, silently delighted. This fact was, years later, hammered home to them when Henry Sellers phoned Carolyn asking them to perform on 'The Sounds Of Motown' tour. He then flew to the States to negotiate the deal and to sound them out about recording again. Norma takes up the story. "We were shocked British people remembered us. We thought The Velvelettes were long forgotten. We never knew we were known over here. In fact, Motown never told us we had released singles here."

Let's talk history. The Velvelettes were the first non-Detroit group to join Motown. "Our parents signed our contracts because we were all still at school, and the only money we made was on the road. We paid out on our recording sessions, wigs, gowns and so on. We were told if we got a hit after 'Needle In A Haystack', we'd really make money and we could record an album. We did the Dick Clark tours, when Diana Ross's mother was our chaperone." The girls' own parents also played an invaluable role in the group's early career by paying for their first stage costumes (which Norma called 'uniforms'). Motown purchased their second batch of stage dresses.

The group was actually born when they sang together at a fraternity party, and phoned Betty Kelly to join them for a subsequent talent show where they won $25. Berry Gordy's nephew approached them regarding a deal. "So we made arrangements to go to Detroit. We drove round and around but we couldn't find Hitsville, and when we finally found the place we were told auditions weren't being held that day. We were about to leave when Mickey Stevenson recognised Bertha and me. We

THE VELVELETTES

sang for him and he gave us the deal."

Stressing that they had written their own material—Norma had penned 'There He Goes', which was later credited to Stevenson instead—they had the upper hand because all read and wrote music, and were known for their four-part harmony. And it was the latter that spawned their name. As they were rehearsing one day someone said their vocals sounded as smooth as velvet, and as it was popular at the time to add 'ettes' to a name, they became The Velvelettes.

As they weren't Detroit-based, work passed them by, and as they were still at school, they could only work on weekends. It seemed Motown was unable, or couldn't be bothered to, arrange working schedules around their availability, yet, The Velvelettes were as popular as any company act, as Norma illustrated. "Berry Gordy would pit groups against each other at The Greystone Ballroom, where audiences would respond to the better group. We were put in against The Supremes—and won!"

As much as they credit Motown for giving them a recording break, the girls believe their work contributed to the foundation of the company. Yet, they weren't invited to participate on the 25th Anniversary Show, nor to the following Apollo spectacular. "Even to have sat in the audience would have been nice," the three said in unison. "And that hurts, particularly bearing in mind the support we've received now." It took Ian Levine to boost their confidence by inviting them to record for Motorcity Records, whereupon the one song they all wanted to re-record was 'Needle In A Haystack' because it would feature the original line-up.

Thankfully, The Velvelettes today are still enthusiastic about music and life because, for the first time, they have the feeling of being supported by the industry and public alike. I have to say, all the ladies are exceptionally likeable, each possessing a special charm and warmth. The years have been extremely kind to them, and, happily, their future career is based on business acumen rather than naïvety. Behind scenes, they're strong and active supporters in anti-drug organisations and regularly perform at charity functions, especially those related to scholarships and women's organisations.

"We like to project an image that sets a good example to teenagers. Even our lyrics are clean. Until all this happened, even

CHINWAGGIN'

our children didn't know we were singers. When they saw us perform at The Fox they were shocked—"Oh, look, mom's a singer."

I like these ladies: they're great fun to be with. They also have that hunger to succeed and please. In 1991 The Velvelettes celebrated their 30th anniversary. They continue to perform at prestigious US events and on the golden oldies circuit. Their music, thankfully, is regularly re-issued by Motown, including (at long last) their own album titled: 'The Velvelettes; The Motown Anthology', a glorious selection of musical memories. A UK tour is in the pipeline.

TATA VEGA
Dateline: April 1979

CHINWAGGIN'

She giggles and shrieks a lot and chatters away like a teenager on a first date. She has an answer for every question; she simmers in excitement without boiling over. She is Tata Vega, Motown's lady of soul and disco, who is enjoying the success of her third album 'Try My Love' which culled her current hit 'Get It Up For Love'. (Top sixty UK hit). It was great to talk to her again.

She was born in Queens, Long Island, New York in October 1951. Her real name is Carmen Rosa Vega, and because her father was in the airforce, she spent much of her younger years in places like Panama, Puerto Rico and Miami. At seventeen, Tata left Miami for Los Angeles, where, after a year of struggling as a street musician she won a place in a local production of 'Hair'. While there she met another struggler, Dobie Gray. When he left the production to form his own group, Pollution, Tata went with him.

After two years experiencing the somewhat harsh realities of show business, she retired because she'd met every shark, pusher and crook the world had to offer, and if that was showbusiness, she wanted no part of it. She explained further: "At the time all I wanted to do was sing my music, but I couldn't avoid the entanglement in management and recording contracts. I wasn't comfortable with that side of the business and I never felt I could trust anyone. I really enjoyed singing with Pollution, but the name seemed like a negative connotation during the time when people and myself were searching for something more positive."

A couple of years later, she changed her mind to form the group Earthquire. Whilst playing at one of The Troubadour's showcase nights, Berry Gordy caught her act and signed both Tata and the group to Motown. The deal was short lived, and the young singer was again left to her own devices. That is, until she cut some demo tracks with a composer friend who took them to Winston Monseque and Iris Gordy at Motown. Through their encouragement and Tata's mutual trust she agreed to return to recording.

It was early morning when we spoke: Tata was in Los Angeles wearing pyjamas and drinking coffee. She'd just got out of bed and her first words usually were, "'Good morning Lord', thank you for another day. Then I take a shower and eat." She laughed,

TATA VEGA

"No, I'm not into any particular religion. I don't go to church. I believe God is who He says He is. I also believe He gave me a gift. I've never had a singing lesson. He's my life whether I was a singer, nurse, cleaning woman. I talk about God when I'm asked, and I'm glad to talk about Him but I don't ram my beliefs down people's throats."

Are you married? "No, I'm not. I've got close friends. Special people who I go out with, but nothing with wedding bells. To be honest with you, I wouldn't go out with anyone if they weren't special to me. No-one's yet grown into the guy I'd like to marry. My career comes first but who knows, maybe in five years' time. I'm twenty-seven now.

"Sex is nice. I enjoy it. It's a very beautiful and precious thing that shouldn't be misused. I'm glad it's there. I don't do it that often as mine is solely reserved for the right guy. I don't want my 'pee-pee' spread around."

This led nicely into her current dance single 'Get It Up For Love'. "I really like disco but didn't think I'd be contributing to it. I'm hoping the single will take off in London as I want to visit. I've applied for a visa just in case....I don't want to be a superstar. I am a person. I want to meet people and get to know them. One of my goals is to be completely genuine. Honesty is the best. Everything I sing is honest, everything I do is honest. At least I hope so."

At this point, I complained at the impersonal way one has to use the phone to get to know an artist sufficiently to write a decent article. Likewise, it must be difficult for Tata to detect what influence she has on a journalist by talking into a mouthpiece. "I like all interviews and if some have to be on the phone, well, so be it. Since we last spoke I've had so many interviews and met so many people you'd never believe it. I agree, it's always hard to know what a person is thinking and the phones make it even worse, but if you're sitting close you can look into their eyes. The eyes tell whether you're thinking the same as you're sayin'. The complete giveaway."

Of the singer's pleasures—well, we've already discussed one earlier!—eating is top of the list. She giggled. "I eat everything. I am too fat, so I'm attempting to diet. I love Italian, Mexican, West Indian—that's spicy food from the Islands—curries. I love

CHINWAGGIN'

garlic too. And health foods. And if I want a drink in the evening, I'd rather buy a bottle of wine and bring it home. I don't go out much. I'm not a party person and don't go to nightclubs except when I'm singing in one, but that's not often. Anyway, there's not too many places a girl can go to over here."

It was clear from her début album 'Full Speed Ahead' that there was something extraordinary about her. She is everything one wanted from a singer—but never expected to hear. At times she sounds like Chaka Khan, combined with Natalie Cole or Aretha Franklin, with the sensitivity of Gladys Knight or Stevie Wonder. Indeed, when the latter heard her singing, he believed she sounded like him. Tata was beside herself—"Wow! what a rush, what a compliment!"

Ms Vega did visit London to promote 'Get It Up For Love' when we spent most days working and socialising. We cemented a friendship which has spanned two decades. In 1986 she was a featured vocalist on the soundtrack for 'The Color Purple' movie, and during the nineties released the 'Now I See' album. She continues to perform in America, works as a session singer and cuts gospel music. Future plans include a compilation of her Motown releases.

THE WEATHER GIRLS

Dateline: September 1983

Via the usual transatlantic phone system I was connected to sunny, gay San Francisco to talk to Martha Wash and Izora Armstead—The Weather Girls. We first met when they, known as The Two Tons Of Fun, worked with Sylvester as support singers. ('It's Raining Men' peaked in the UK top 80. Upon re-release it reached no 2 in March 1984)

CBS Records in London were in the throes of re-promoting the hi-energy single and it was paying off: the delicious slice of saucy disco was gaining momentum in the national listings.

The Two Tons Of Fun became The Weather Girls at the instigation of Paul Jabara for whom the girls have nothing but admiration. He had penned 'It's Raining Men' and originally wanted Diana Ross to record it, but she turned it down. Martha: "She had her muscles instead and we had the men! Paul got in

CHINWAGGIN'

touch with our manager, we liked the song and recorded it. It took about two and a half hours in all, and quite honestly, we forgot all about it." I was prompted to mention the promotional video where the girls, dressed in raincoats and umbrellas, plough their way through a number of dressed and scantily dressed males. Mary Poppins they ain't! "They were all professional dancers from New York, and all rather lovely," Izora explained. "Filming was hard work, it took five days in all, but in the end we were delighted with the result. Originally the video was banned by the media for being a little naughty, but a modified version has been produced just because Martha was laying on a bed—fully clothed!"

Martha: "And this guy jumps on me. He's dressed as well, and his legs are either side of my waist... I assume that's what got us banned. Anyhow, it wasn't suggestive at all."

Izora: "We tried to get as many of those guys as we could, because I'm trying to find Martha a husband...."

"I've got more good sense than to get married," she interrupted.

"And I've gotten a husband, he's our manager, so we're holding auditions to get Martha one!"

For those who don't recall, Izora and Martha were discovered by the 'mighty real' man Sylvester, and they subsequently sang with him during his disco explosion of the late seventies/early eighties. On stage, the girls wore colourfully outrageous costumes, sometimes complimented by flowing plumes of white. The more distasteful (or questionable) the outfits, the better they, Sylvester, and the audiences liked it. But, of course, this side of them is irrelevant when compared to the girls' talent and vocal chords. Martha Wash, for instance, studied opera which enables her to sing a range of three octaves. "I studied arias with a private teacher for a year and then went to choir classes. I also took piano lessons as a child but always played by ear. I took lessons with two different teachers and they both told me to stop wasting my money. In opera you sing from the diaphragm. I'm trying to sing strong over my strained voice. That's not good for my vocal chords really, but I can sing anything from a hard song to a very light soprano but it wreaks havoc on my throat sometimes."

Indeed, Martha's voice is powerfully soft and delicate, whereas Izora's is big, dirty and ballsy. She, by the way, has to her credit various scholarships to music schools, and when she releases her corsets, the audiences go berserk as the ground shakes and the heavens fall! "Growling doesn't hurt me because it comes naturally! You can always growl when you can't do anything else. Even when you are hoarse. I think it's a natural way of expressing the way you feel. I don't growl all the time, only on the special occasions when the stage is hot. When I get intensely into a song and there's a certain feeling. Like when I'm trying to get a point across."

And behind these powerful voices are mighty big ladies, weighing in at 200 pounds each. "Before I got married I could not get over one hundred pounds," said Izora. "I couldn't give a damn what I ate. You should see some of my old pictures. Somewhere between my first and seventh child I put on the extra weight. When I'm at home, I'm with my husband who's no help because he's constantly cooking and I'm constantly eating. And I can't refuse because it's just so good.... I play football, basketball, baseball, everything with my six boys. I move, and everything, and I feel good about myself. But...I am tired of sewing two coloured sheets together to make an outfit. If they'd only make two sheets that would look cute!"

Martha, on the other hand, jumped from 117 to over 200 pounds without knowing why. "I have to lose weight," she said, "because, first of all, I'm too tall for short, and too short for tall. I have tiny feet. I have problems with my leg. The doctors have told me to lose at least seventy-five pounds or so...I take off my shoes during a show. I can only wear high heels for so long, then the circulation gets bad in my legs. So I just take off my shoes. That became my trademark when we worked with Sylvester. He used to beg me, 'Please don't take off your shoes,' but I told him 'Honey, when my feet start hurting, I'm gonna take those girls off'!"

Martha and Izora no longer work with Sylvester; it was an amicable split. We chatted about the fun times they enjoyed together both on and off stage; the mutual respect and love, and that old fashioned good feeling of friendship. When Martha and Izora first joined Sylvester they fielded media questions about his sexuality; did it bother them? Izora told me she usually said, "I came up around gay people. They called them 'happy'. I don't like using the word, gay, homosexual or lesbian. I came up around people, period. So, no Sylvester's lifestyle doesn't bother me. He's happy, not us. That's his life."

On a more philosophical note, Martha added. "People should be happy for us. I like what I'm doing. They (who criticise her) are not taking care of me. They are not going to stand in judgement of what I've done. The Lord said go into the vineyard and work. And whatever you reap, the Lord will pay you. Not Izora. Not anybody else down here. So, what I'm waiting for is to get paid."

A combination of talent like that of Sylvester, Martha and Izora, often attracted criticism. One rumour I readily think of is the allegation that Sylvester treated his ladies in similar fashion to Diana Ross and her alleged treatment of The Supremes. Izora replied. "To me that's just a type of envy. We were a unit. There could have been truth in it and then there couldn't have. But I didn't look at it that way. I'm looking at what was making me happy. If I enjoyed singing in a unit with Sylvester, then it's because I wanted to. I'm the one who had to be happy when I went out on that stage. What's the use of singing how happy I am when I'm about to explode. If I kept constant turmoil around me, I couldn't relate that on stage. People were paying their hard-earned money to see a good show and not to look at my turmoils."

I'll say no more!

Following their split from Sylvester and as The Two Tons Of Fun, they recorded a pair of albums for Fantasy Records; nothing happened and the record deal expired. However, they were always touring and reckon they've played all of America, most of Europe and the countries in between. "We ain't had a moment's peace," they laughed. Now their new American single, and follow-up to 'It's Raining Men', titled 'I'm Gonna Wash That Man Right Outta My Hair' has been released. *Billboard* magazine wrote: 'It's a pop, rock and disco intersection that defies categorisation, except for its sense of humour.' The Weathers agreed!

We next met in April 1984 when 'It's Raining Men' had just vacated the top section of the UK singles chart. I arrived early at Marble Arch's Holiday Inn to see them, and was met by their

THE WEATHER GIRLS

manager who escorted me to an upstairs hotel suite where, once the hugs and kisses were done with, I settled in for an hour's chat.

The girls were, naturally enough, on fine form because 'It's Raining Men' had finally cracked the upper region of the national chart. Izora laughed. "We all knew it was a hit, didn't we? But we were beginning to wonder if we'd ever get in the chart here. All the company's determination paid off and so did ours. It's really strange. The single took off all over the world—America, Spain, the Continent—but England didn't seem to latch on to it for a long time. We're sure glad they came round to our way of thinking in the end. I'll tell you, sugar, we've packed and unpacked our bags so often to come here that when the time came for us to actually board a plane we weren't ready! It's great, really, and we can't thank everyone enough for their patience."

Martha: "We've done a lot of travelling since the record began breaking outside America. It's been a lot of fun but darned hard work. It is something we always hoped would happen one day... and now we have gold records on our walls!"

Much of the conversation was X-rated so is unprintable. They're not crude women, by any means, but Izora in particular has a dreadfully wicked tongue. But it was curbed to talk about 'Success', their current album, which contained a potpourri of sounds. Who chose the tracks? Izora: "As usual, not us. We never seem to be consulted on material. Everything is arranged before we go into the studio. We sing, then listen to the result—sometimes."

The duo hadn't changed much, although Martha had lost weight and Izora had married again. "Did you expect me to act like a star, sugar?" she retorted when I asked if a hit had changed her way of life. "I don't know how a star acts and should we ever get that far, I'll be too astonished to act differently. (I saw what Izora meant; she was still wearing bedroom slippers!) Seriously we've kept our fingers crossed to reach this far. However, if it all ended next week we'd just be grateful to have been there."

Typically, Sylvester came into the conversation. Martha had recently performed with him in San Francisco and indeed she and Jeanie Tracy had sung on his new album 'Call Me'. The Honey Productions and Fantasy Records' situation seemed to have been disastrous for all their signed artists, but all have managed to

CHINWAGGIN'

extricate themselves from their unhappy contracts. Izora, for one, walked away owning the name The Two Tons Of Fun.

I next spoke to Martha Wash in June 1988 when she was promoting The Weather Girls' new single 'Land Of The Believer', extracted from their third album, where they worked with Reggie Lucas and one of Arthur Baker's sidekicks, Richard Scher. The album, as yet untitled, presented a different side to Martha and Izora inasmuch that the aggressive funk which appealed to dancers has gone, a move due to the several producers involved in the project. Martha explained further. "And the reason we used different producers was because our A&R representative wanted to do it. He talked to us and said these people would be good for us. We went along with it because we liked the idea. In the end, we didn't choose any of the album tracks, we left it up to them. Certainly, the old sound as The Two Tons Of Fun has gone but that was a natural progression for us...I think we've matured musically, but 'Land Of The Believer' is pretty much our old funky dance sound. I guess you could say we're evolving. We have to look forward all the time and grow, but that's not to say we're turning our backs on our past work because we need those memories in our lives."

There was a strong rumour circulating the industry that The Weather Girls had split through some disagreement or other. Martha laughed this off. "Nobody gets on with their partner all the time but although Izora and I have been known to argue we certainly haven't split up, nor do we intend to." It's possible, I said, that this rumour stemmed from the fact that it's been two years since their last album 'Big Girls Don't Cry'. "I know it's been a long time. We had problems trying to get material for a new one and spent a long time pushing the last album over here. And for the last two years we've been touring America and Europe. So that may well have had something to do with you not knowing what was going on. We've actually toured Europe four times in two years, and they weren't short trips either. It was good to keep working but also very tiring. By not being in one place, it meant working on a new album had to be fitted in whenever we had a few days to spare."

The Weather Girls are extremely popular in Europe, more so

THE WEATHER GIRLS

than the rest of the world; therefore they are constantly in demand there. "We must have played about every town there was to play in Germany, Scandinavia and so on," a delighted Martha admitted. "We spent three months in Europe during the latter part of last year alone and that was one tour. We started off in Iceland and worked our way to Oslo, Stockholm, all through Germany, Holland, playing in big city theatres and small towns. It was very interesting for us because we'd never played Scandinavia before, although we had an idea we were popular there.

"The best part though was meeting the fans in these different countries and talking to them. They knew all our music, right back to The Two Tons Of Fun; it was incredible!"

Their recent American tour was a three-month stint with Eddie Murphy which Martha said, "was valuable exposure for us. A lot of people had heard our work but they'd never seen us live and with that tour they got the chance. I'll tell you, we've been busier now than we've ever been!"

Suggesting that The Weather Girls were enjoying more success of late than Sylvester, Martha was quick to defend him. "I think his going to another record company might have had something to do with it, because things may have changed on the European side. He has had some success with his last few songs, but he knows what's going on, he's aware of musical trends and the importance of keeping a public profile."

Time wasn't on our side, so to close we talked of her health, but more importantly, her dieting which will ultimately ease her foot complaint. "I've had to diet because I've gained so much weight and it felt very uncomfortable. I'm still young enough to lose weight easily...the older you are, the harder it is. My feet still bother me at times. Nothing can be done to cure the problem except an operation. I've looked into this very thoroughly, I can tell you, and the doctors want me to give up performing for over a year after an operation. I can't give up that time now because I need to perform to survive. Luckily, the condition doesn't worsen with age, so that's something."

We laughed, because prior to becoming a professional singer she was a hospital secretary. If she'd stayed there, she quipped, maybe she could have had her operation over and done with—and on the cheap!

CHINWAGGIN'

Ah, protested I, then there wouldn't have been The Weather Girls.

"I'm suffering the price of fame, Sharon!"

During the late eighties, Martha and Izora went their separate ways. An in-demand session singer, Martha did record her own work starting with her debut solo CD which produced three UK hits— 'Carry On', 'Give It To You' and 'Runaround'. She then teamed with Jocelyn Brown for two hits 'Keep On Jumpin'' and 'Something's Goin' On'. Her second album 'The Collection' followed in 1997 while three years later she collaborated with Small Voices Calling on their 'Sounds of a Better World' compilation to benefit a number of charities. Also in the late eighties, Izora moved to Frankfurt, Germany, where she formed a new Weather Girls with her daughter, Dynell Rhodes. In addition to their full touring schedules, they recorded numerous albums for WEA/Germany, such as 'Double Tons Of Fun' during 1994. In August 2004, Izora returned to America to undergo treatment for heart-related illnesses. Sadly, within a month the mighty Weather Girl died from heart failure in the San Leandro (California) Hospital near Oakland. I'll always remember with great fondness my time with Martha—and, of course, with the wonderful Mrs Izora Rhodes Armstead.

MARY WELLS
Dateline: January 1990

She was Motown's first lady, toured with The Beatles, among other high-ranking acts, and carved herself an immortal niche in popular music. She gave the world 'My Guy' in 1964. Other million selling records at Motown were 'The One Who Really Loves You', 'You Beat Me To The Punch', 'Your Old Stand-By', 'What's Easy For Two Is So Hard For One' and 'Two Lovers'.

However, the Mary Wells I met was depressed and fretful—a million miles detached from the soulful diva presented on record and stage. We were cramped in a small, unwelcoming dressing room in a Watford venue, which was more like a seedy supper club than the widely-promoted nighterie which boasted top name performances. Hell, I thought, Ms Wells is a star, and this is a deplorable situation to find her in. Her state of mind was,

CHINWAGGIN'

thankfully, comforted by her family who travelled with her.

Her musical director, Will Porter, sat on a stool in the corner of the room where she hung her stage clothes, while her husband Curtis Womack, sat on the toilet so that we wouldn't be disturbed while the tape ran. Their young daughter, Sugar, ran riot, as fans knocked at the door for autographs. It was chaotic!

However, through the shambles came the following and as I write it am amazed the tape managed to catch so much of my conversation with Motown's first queen of music.

The tour wasn't going that well, she told me. She had signed contracts indicating a joint headlining bill with Martha Reeves and the Vandellas. That had not happened. Also, there was animosity and jealousy between Martha and Mary. I didn't pursue this.

To the history lesson now. At the age of fifteen, Mary composed 'Bye Bye Baby' for Jackie Wilson who, at the time, worked with Berry Gordy, who later asked her to audition for his fledgling Motown record company. When she sang 'Bye Bye Baby', he insisted she record it. "I didn't think I'd ever be a recording artist because all I wanted was to be in the record business. I couldn't read or even play music but I had to sing that song." Following twenty-two takes, 'Bye Bye Baby' was released during 1961 to become an American hit, whereupon Gordy signed her—and the rest is history.

During her stay, she joined Marvin Gaye on record. Their 'Together' album spawned the hit single 'Once Upon A Time' in 1964. She readily admits to having great fun with Marvin—"and had a lot of success with the album because it went number one R&B and number one jazz as well."

From Motown Mary enjoyed a semi-successful career with 20th Century Fox and Atlantic Records, among others. More recently, she recorded 'Don't Burn Your Bridges' for Nightmare Records, followed by her new single on Motorcity titled 'You're The Answer To My Dreams'. This current tour is, she admitted, to bring public awareness to her revived recording career, but her new single wasn't included in her act. "I might as well tell you the truth," she sighed. "We're not paid a helluva lot of money to come over and do these shows. When I got here the band basically said that to do the rhythm parts they'd charge me £600. In America for £600 you can get a twenty-two piece band and

MARY WELLS

Diana Ross doing the backing vocals. So I said that I wasn't getting paid enough to do that.

"I've been so upset over everywhere I'm going...not getting equal billing and with everything being completely different when I got here." After gentle digging, it appears the misunderstanding, for want of a better word, had nothing to do with the British promoters but their American counterparts. The dates also left a great deal to be desired; the venues were supper club based, where audiences talked or noisily ate and drank through her performances. Soul fans were hard pushed to enjoy the shows. Miss Wells worked damned hard to keep her show pulsating. "It wasn't as if I was trying to win them over," she said in a husky voice. "Um, how can I put this...I've had top ten records over here, so I figured they would already be with me. I think a lot of it is, people didn't know how to react when I wanted to involve them in the show."

Prior to this tour, Ms Wells had been pulling in the crowds in America; her most recent performance attracted an audience of 89,000 in Denver, followed by a thousand-plus following at a beach festival. When she returns she'll be involved in political work which included performing at a benefit for Teddy Kennedy, whom she knows well, and collecting an award from Atlantic Records for her contribution towards black music. She's also been nominated, she said, for the 1991 prestigious Hall Of Fame. "The award is worth £15,000, but it's nothing to do with my royalties Atlantic owe me, it's a way of saying thank you. The company put in the trades that they're gonna give justice to their artists of the past, and I fall into that category.

"For the Hall Of Fame nomination—you can't be nominated unless you've had a twenty-five year recording history—well, I was nominated last year and that nomination is carried over to next year. Like, Sam Cooke didn't get in the first time round."

Another matter near to the singer's heart is getting paid her dues from Motown. Not the first artist to pursue this, I mentioned, and a determined Mary explained that she's hired one of America's most prominent (and expensive!) lawyers who feels confident she'll win the action. Ms Wells is not a vindictive woman, by any means, and this action hasn't been instigated from malice, but rather her receiving the royalties she believes are due to her.

CHINWAGGIN'

"Motown is gonna have to settle up the past. It should be around $10 million, it certainly shouldn't be any less than that. They owe me more than that really when you count up all the top ten records I had with them, and all the top ten albums.

"Up to a few years ago, when they fired this Japanese lady who was taking care of all the royalties—y'know, like whose records were the biggest and so on—she told me my 'Greatest Hits' album was outselling Michael Jackson and the Jackson 5, and not just in the States either."

Will Porter continued, "The album has never been out of stock. Tower Records say the album has been in their top ten, top twenty sellers for years. They order boxes and boxes of the record. You walk in there now and there are, like, twelve CDs also; in fact, everything that Motown ever issued. It's an enormous catalogue and heavier than those from artists of the last ten, fifteen years."

Mary, herself, has a fair idea of the product she's shifted because, she added. "In the sixties I used to look at the charts in Cashbox and Billboard for the different markets like Europe, New Zealand, er, Peru, and so on, and I'd see what we're about.... When I left Motown there was this female lawyer and at the time I gave her my only contract. I trusted her, she was an older lady, and she sold me out. She left; Motown have my contract and they put more years on it. I know Berry was gonna kill my career; he said, 'If you want out, settle for $30,000 and give up your rights.' I didn't mind doing that because I was having hit singles. When I left, one of the girl group members told me that he said, 'Whatever it takes, make sure of it. Nobody leaves Motown and makes it.'

"They did everything they could to stop the black DJs from playing my records. The only records I got played were on the pop stations. My sales went on both sides, that's what made me so...powerful. So when the records went top twenty pop without the R&B play to take them all the way up to the top ten, I was dead. So all this time I've been fighting against that set-up and it's not legal, and it's not in God's law for somebody to say, 'Hey, you, give yourself up.' It's my music. And what about the royalties from all the hits before 'My Guy'? Motown are still selling those records. Yes, I'm pretty sure I'll be successful with the action."

MARY WELLS

We deviated a second so that Mary could answer a question that's bugged me since seeing her perform on Motown's 25th anniversary gala—her gown, I suggested, did little to compliment her figure. Laughing, she explained she was carrying twins. "That's why I looked the way I did. My pregnancy had nothing to do with my short spot though...that's all the time that was allocated. I miscarried after the show. My grandmother had twenty-two kids including two sets of twins, one set of triplets, but they all died. That's where I got the twins from. My mom had a set but she couldn't carry hers either."

Still on the subject of the Wells family, during the last few years Mary had discovered the identity of her father, and was surprised to learn he was Sicilian. "He's more famous than 'The Sicilian', as in the movie. Some say he died in jail, some said he made a big score a couple of years ago and moved to Florida, where he changed his identity. It makes me feel better to know who I'm part of because I always wondered. My grandmother was ill and she was persuaded to tell all. I went into the bathroom, sat there for a long while all cut up because I always thought this other man was my father."

From one man to another, Marvin Gaye and her recording relationship with him. "He was really a gentleman, would do anything for you. I mean, to perfection. He was the ideal man for anybody...I miss him."

With that, Ms Wells' transport was waiting with her baggage already aboard. As she slowly walked into the outside darkness and cold, I went in the opposite direction into the smoky warmth of the theatre to catch Martha's show which had just started.

Despite great hopes, Mary's career with Motorcity Records ground to a halt. In September 1990 it was publicly announced that the singer was suffering from throat cancer. It seemed unlikely she'd perform again. When Mary was hospitalised she was unable to pay her medical bills. This led to former colleagues and peers contributing to a Mary Wells Distress Fund to cover the costs. The R&B Hall Of Fame also helped financially. Following two years of extensive radiation and chemotherapy treatment, Motown's first lady died peacefully in July 1992.

KIM WESTON

Dateline: August 1987

"I've talked more about Motown in the last four days than I have in the last four years," said Kim Weston in her Bayswater apartment. "I never realised just how important Motown was, and still is, over here. I was really surprised to be told that I'm known because of my records. It's quite incredible after all these years."

Ms Weston, ageless but tired, was in London to record her first single in years, having been signed to the Nightmare label where her debut single is 'Signal Your Attention'. "I first met Ian Levine, owner of the label when he was fourteen, and I knew he was interested in what I was doing then because he asked such a lot of questions! All these years later, I'm recording for Ian's label. It's a small world."

Whilst recording for Motown, Ms Weston recorded with Marvin Gaye—two singles ('What Good Am I Without You?' in 1964, and 'It Takes Two', 1966) and one album ('Take Two' in 1966). A second album titled 'Side By Side' was scheduled in 1964 but was withdrawn for some reason.

Prior to her work with Marvin, Kim issued her own material— 'It Should Have Been Me' and 'Just Loving You' in 1963:

KIM WESTON

'Looking For The Right Guy' a year later. Following the first duet, two further solos were issued—'A Little More Love' and 'I'm Still Loving You', all on the Tamla label. In 1965 she switched to Gordy where, in April, 'A Thrill A Moment' was released, followed by a song she never liked 'Take Me In Your Arms (Rock Me A Little While)' five months later. The evergreen 'Helpless' was released in February 1966. Kim's knowledge dried up as she laughed. "I don't remember everything I recorded because there was so much. I know there's still a lot of unreleased stuff I did with Marvin. I see one track has surfaced on Motown's last Marvin album ('Baby (Don't You Leave Me)' circa 1965 on 'Motown Remembers Marvin Gaye'). In fact, there's several thousands of dollars worth of unreleased material still there. One day I'm sure it'll be released."

Kim was married to Mickey Stevenson who was in charge of Motown's musicians, among other things, during the sixties. Kim elaborated. "He helped develop their in-house sound, what is called 'The Motown Sound' and this was a combination of many things. Most of the musicians were jazz players, and quite frankly, they didn't play any better than anyone else, but they had this magic." She added that her ex-husband was a very powerful figure in Berry Gordy's operation, yet she felt she, personally, wasn't treated fairly. The attitude was if Kim became a star Mickey would become even more powerful. "He worked with all the artists there and was probably directly responsible for the Motown sound. He actually got Holland, Dozier, Holland together after encouraging Eddie (Holland) to abandon his solo career. The producers were responsible for developing the musical style and it was the musicians' job to get the sound just right...people like Earl Van Dyke."

At this time Berry Gordy was immersed in the business side of his company, so Mickey Stevenson took care of the music on his behalf. However, everything was destined to change. Kim left Motown in November 1966. "I didn't leave on the best of terms either." Her discontentment stemmed from the company's method of releasing records. Regular product came only from artists making money. She enjoyed success, but her singles were months apart, or not at all. "I didn't make waves when I saw what was going on. Mickey was making good money at the time, so I didn't want to upset anyone. I kept quiet for his sake. When he left Motown to do his own thing, he was offered a great deal of money to stay, but moving was a logical thing for him to do. I felt I could accomplish more by staying with him. After all, he was the one who discovered me and was a guiding force behind my career at the time."

The singer also divulged that she toured as Marvin Gaye's co-star for three years before recording with him. She explained further. "He was like my big brother. The love I had for Marvin was not like the love of a lover. It was a genuine love. Sure, he was a little mischievous at times with me, but he loved me, yet it never went any further. We never fooled around, and I don't believe he fooled around with anyone. He was married to Anna (Berry's sister) and that was that—period....I only recorded with Marvin because Mary Wells was leaving, or there were rumours at the time that she was about to leave. If I hadn't left Motown, I'd have carried on with the duets with Marvin, so Tammi Terrell wouldn't have happened."

Like most sixties' artists, Kim—born and raised in Detroit's Paradise Valley (known as 'the Bottom' to the folk who live there)—sang in church from the age of three. As a teenager, she played piano and directed the church choir. She became a member of the popular gospel group The Wright Specials, founded and managed by Thomas Wright and tutored by James Cleveland. During this period of her life, Kim gained invaluable experience which stood her in good stead when she became a Motown artist.

From Motown she moved to Los Angeles and signed a deal with MGM, later People Records and Pride, which did little to progress her career. However, her love of music led her to the black community where she became an active worker, and during 1967 when America was in a state of upheaval as her race struggled for equality, Kim was a leading figure in the fight. She voiced her feelings by recording the Black National Anthem (written by James Weldon Jackson) called "Lift Every Voice And Sing". (a track on her MGM album "This Is America")

It was after a meeting with Jesse Jackson that Ms Weston helped form the Los Angeles branch of Operation Breadbasket. Part of her work there was forming the organisation's own choir

KIM WESTON

which was later selected to sing with the Los Angeles Symphony Orchestra. Singing, however, wasn't her only outlet for she produced and recorded a worldwide show for the Armed Forces Radio. Her average listening audience was about five hundred million! And, between engagements, she worked with luminaries like Billy Eckstine, Bill Cosby, Flip Wilson and Johnny Nash, and broke into national television by appearing on shows like 'The Tonight Show', 'David Frost', and 'Steve Allen'. Eckstine later became a close friend. "Billy showed me how to acquire the necessary humility that must be present in every artist who aspires to any degree of greatness. I also learned many of the technical fundamentals from him, like diction and intonation."

Her work for the black community was such that she was honoured in 1970 by US Congressman John Conyers Jr during a reception on Capital Hill. So, two years later, when she returned to Detroit to live, Kim was very much in demand. To cut a long story short, she said, she had her own programme 'The Good Citizens Award' on WCHB Radio, where food was distributed free on a weekly basis to people in dire need. She also created a further programme 'Rap With The Mayor's Office' enabling the community to phone various city officials about community problems. Then between 1975 and 1979 she produced and starred in local plays like "Little Red" and "Chattel", with her most memorable performance being Ms Rosa Parks in the musical "Selma".

Eleven years ago, with Mayor Coleman Young's support, the busy lady founded a Detroit Summer Youth Programme for financially disadvantaged youngsters with talent. These kids received professional tutoring and coaching in their particular artistic area. Kim opened this programme with fifty youngsters, but it became so successful that by 1983 five hundred had enrolled for the summer sessions. The programme continues to expand and when she returns to Detroit, she'll be preparing this summer's session. "Originally I just wanted a break all those years ago. I didn't really want to retire from the business entirely, but when I took my leave of absence in 1972, people insisted I get involved in so many things that my break ran into years!

"I get professional people to work with my kids in workshops, like Teddy Harris is in charge of the instrumental workshop. He was The Supremes' conductor. I have Clifford Fears who started the first Katherine Dunham School of Dance in Stockholm, and he's in charge of the dance workshop and choreographs for the whole programme. And the lady who started out at Motown and who makes most of my gowns, makes the costumes for the kids. Her name is Margaret Brown and she's in control of the costume design workshop."

So far, Martha Reeves' UK musical director was one of Kim's trainees; another works with The Drifters, while another is in charge of Stevie Wonder's backing group. So she must be doing something right! "I'm not concerned with any recognition," she insisted, "and that's what most of my associates kinda fault me for, because they think I should be getting more mileage out of my name. That's not why I'm doing it. I'm doing it because I saw a need to provide the help and facilities which we are making available. I could see that the young people were not being treated fairly."

Before I left the tired singer, she played me three songs she'd recorded with her own Detroit choir, formed from the youngsters on her programme. "They're aged from twelve upwards. I don't have a deal for them yet, but the songs do show, I think, just how talented they are." I might add, hearing Kim's voice against the gospel backdrop was a beautiful combination of a young and mature talent.

However, I asked, if her own career took off again, how would she juggle all her other commitments? "I can take three months out a year to work with my kids. Once I've finished a programme I usually take three months to recuperate before starting on other things. So there's time enough...if not, I'll make time, it's that simple."

In February 1990 I watched as Kim Weston walked out on stage towards the microphone, the audience rose as one to greet her, prompting a wide grin to appear on her face as she wiped sweaty palms down each side of her long, blue sparkling gown. Tonight she sang easily, in control except for a minute struggle to reach the high notes on one song before settling into her Motown classics. Then, she was off backstage where, after a quick rub down and change of clothes, we settled in as comfortably as

KIM WESTON

possible in a tiny, bare dressing room that was large enough to hold two chairs, a dressing table and a sink.

Kim has been with Ian Levine's record company since the opening and was with him at the recent Motown Reunion in America. "He and I were talking about him contacting ex-Motown artists and he asked me what did I think about some of the people he was talking about. I said if he could find them it was a good idea.

"For one thing, one of my godmothers, Beatrice Buck, is the president of the group called the Bellentine Belles that was started by Dinah Washington. She has written several productions, but what she's also done is she's found some of the ladies who worked in Paradise Valley which was an area in Detroit that was much like Vegas as far as entertainment for blacks was concerned in the 1930s. She's actually found some of the ladies who danced in the late thirties and early forties and she has them dancing now. So when Ian was talking about going back and finding these people—I knew what Ms Buck had done for these people—I told him to go ahead and remake history—Detroit history."

However, by encouraging him in this way, she didn't feel Levine's company would be a 'new' Motown. "There'll never be another Motown, but I think it could be the start of revitalising the sound and the feeling of the Motown days....It's my understanding that Mr Gordy is more interested in the motion picture industry, in much the same way as he used to be about the record business. I told somebody the other day that I hope he breaks through, maybe he'll give me a job...who knows! I don't know why he sold Motown either, before you ask. I've been gone so long—but my understanding is he did spend a lot of money trying to revive the company with someone else running it, but it just wasn't working."

I noticed that on this tour, whenever an artist has a problem they head straight for Ms Weston's dressing room: if she wasn't there, they'd wait. Apparently, she could sort anything. "They've nicknamed me 'Trouble'," she whispered, taking off her make up. "And I'd like to know what that really means...I think it might be because I do try to help if there's a problem. I think it's better to know if there's something wrong because it can be corrected before it gets serious. My own biggest problem is having to travel

CHINWAGGIN'

and do interviews. Just before the tour started I was in the studio recording until four in the morning. I was up all the next day, then I went somewhere about seventy miles from London for a one o'clock show the next morning. That meant I got back to London and in my bed at four in the morning, and I was up at seven. And this was before the tour *began*! That kind of thing throws you off balance, and yes, that's been the biggest problem for me."

To date, Kim has recorded a few excellent titles for Motorcity Records, so what would a hit single mean to her now. She chuckled, "Come on, I've been in this business off and on for a long time. I just haven't been performing on the road that much. What I think is a hit isn't necessarily right. The kind of music that I personally enjoy singing is difficult to judge because I'm a ballad singer, and ballads don't necessarily sell unless you have one that's particularly outstanding. However, having a hit would mean more money! I'd probably have to do more work though, which maybe I'm not too keen on doing...maybe I'll be able to ask more for less work. Um...what I'm saying is your salary automatically goes up with a hit record. So, instead of making a few dollars for a lot of gigs, you can make a lot of money for a few gigs."

Performing again doesn't bother her either; in fact, she said it was a welcome change. She's taken unpaid leave from her job to honour this tour commitment, but admitted she wouldn't have missed it for anything. Her cool image on stage isn't contrived either, she doesn't suffer from her nerves, but acknowledged: "There's a tension that—as the kids say—psyches you up before an audience. As far as being afraid, that kind of nervousness, I've been blessed not to suffer with that. I worry, though, when I'm not up to par, like this time because I'm having a few problems with my throat."

The extrovert on centre stage is actually an introvert offstage. To overcome this, Kim has attended classes to regain her personal confidence, although, at one point, she wasn't sure this was what she needed. "I guess it probably was. Y'see, when a person doesn't speak that much, something has to be done. I just wanted to be able to express myself better. That's one of the reasons I also went on the radio because I knew I'd have to talk. So when the job was offered to me, I convinced myself it was a good way

KIM WESTON

to practice. My mother was very quiet. In fact, there would be many days when we'd just say 'good morning' and that's all we'd really say until it was time for dinner!"

A knock on the dressing room door indicated it was time to pack her gowns: she usually wears two an evening—one for her performance, the other for the finale. Hell, there was a lot of luggage to carry—and we were three floors up! Twenty minutes later, after three trips up and down the stairs, it was safely stored on the awaiting coach.

In between gasping for breath, Kim Weston laughed—"That's showbusiness!"

I lost touch with Kim; then we found each other again. She later moved house—and country—but I understand she now resides in America. Most of her Motown material remains available on compilations, while her duets with Marvin Gaye are legendary. That aside, Kim Weston is a wonderful lady, who's so full of mischief, it is hard to believe she's one of soul music's most celebrated artists. She continues to perform, often with Brenda Holloway, at music functions and on television specials. Their most recent visit was in 2005. Kim is currently writing her autobiography.

BARRY WHITE
Dateline: February 1979

He's overweight, not particularly good looking and possesses a voice that can only be compared to a gravel pit. But, Barry White is a man of love, a man of music; not necessarily in that order either.

He has the power to make women feel like a million dollars, and he instils confidence and understanding into guys who seek his guidance. Yes, big Barry lives, breathes and eats love. His records ooze sex, which, he growls, is the ultimate experience between two people who are totally immersed in each other. Uh, huh, Barry knows exactly where he's at—but it was a devil of a long time coming. "I have been in the business for seventeen years and have only been recognised for my creative talent and forces for the last five and a half years. The twelve years prior to that were very rough, extremely hard, and I developed a sense of sincerity in trying to reach goals in music.

"One of the lowest points of my life was when I had to live in a motel for three months with my four children. We were all in one room. We had one bed; so some had to sleep on the floor. I had to sneak them into the motel too. I had no job, no money, no nothing because I refused to work a nine-to-five job while I was struggling. So I paid a high price for that stubbornness, for that loyalty to the business. You would have to go through that to know how low that really was. I didn't care who knew I was in that motel—the point was I was after something and it was a very low morale thing inside of me, and I had to smile over it and through it."

What was so special about his talents, when America always seems to have a superfluity of new artists? "I felt I had something creative to offer the world. It wasn't black music, it wasn't white, or Indian, German, Oriental—it was *music*. The way I hear it, the way I see it, and with a determination of refusing to stay down—oh, I was knocked down a lot of times—but every time I was knocked down I realised each time, that much more, I had to get back up.

"I am a minister of words and music. People have problems listening to what people say when they sing. Bob Dylan has been writing songs about the world for years, about things that are wrong, songs of love, but songs that no one really heard. You have to deal with a mental capacity to which that capacity is used to being with. For instance, sound and voice. I felt that since I was in the music business, and I was getting a chance to do it my way, let's try to sing some of it and let's try to talk some of it.

"Everything gets to talk on my records, the violins, the horns, guitars, drums, the background group—everybody gets a chance to say something. When I'm in the streets, or on tour, fans come up to meet me and say, 'Love Theme' was our wedding theme, or 'My, you'd be surprised, Barry, how much easier it is for my husband, or my boyfriend to talk to me.' I've heard that so many times. That's when I know I'm getting across to people because they are listening.

"Men are finding out that it's much easier to relate to women when they listen to Barry White telling them what they should do, and what they shouldn't be worried about. I find that men can't relate to women and that's a problem...a big, big problem."

He then switched the subject to his actual songwriting achievements. "I am a perfectionist. I'm a Virgo. I know when I go into the studio what I'm going for, and when I've got it, I leave. You can always do more to a song, but if you got on that trip, adding more and more you'll end up with a song that's got ninety different songs in it."

"For example?" I asked. "In '69 I wrote 'Sweetness Is My Weakness' after I met my wife. That song was written for her and I had it recorded twice since then by other artists. I decided to do it myself and it came out totally different than I ever expected it to from the way I originally wrote it. But, again, you have to be broadminded. In this business you have to know that things can change on the spur of the moment and you've got to be mentally balanced to change with it."

A change certainly came with his current single 'Just The Way You Are' as it isn't one of his compositions. "The only way I can record someone else's song is to love it," he explained. "I don't record songs that I don't like, whether or not I wrote them. 'Just The Way You Are' says it all. It says everything and it fits. If I had to write a song called 'Just The Way You Are' I would have been privileged to have written it, to have thought of the concept, to have thought of the melody and lyrics. I didn't write it, but when I heard it, it had no meaning to me whether it was number one or number ninety-one. Barry White cut it the way he hears it."

Big bad Barry was a regular in the UK singles chart from 1973 through to 2000. His career was quite remarkable, not only as an artist, but the innovator of Love Unlimited and the Love Unlimited Orchestra with whom he recorded and toured. His albums included 'Let The Music Play', 'Just Another Way To Say I Love You' and 'The Man'. However, after eight Barry White albums, four Love Unlimited albums, and four Love Unlimited Orchestra albums, constant touring and the pressures of music business, Barry decided to retire for a while. He returned in 1992, with a new A&M Records contract and his career began again. During 1999 he published his autobiography 'Insights On Life And Love', the same year as he scooped two Grammy Awards. The artist had suffered from chronic high blood pressure and hypertension for some time, and in September 2002 he was hospitalised with kidney failure which sadly led to his unexpected death on 4 July 2003 in West Hollywood.

VESTA WILLIAMS
Dateline: February 1987

I'm a totally nutty person. I even laugh at my own jokes" giggled one of our newest chart singers, Vesta Williams, who sounds so serious on record, but is entirely different when giving interviews.

Ms Williams had flown to London from Holland to promote her runaway hit 'Once Bitten Twice Shy' and her excellent 'Vesta' album. Both releases, she said, have made her dreams come true.

CHINWAGGIN'

"The success is the same in the States. It's a love or hate thing over there, and I'm glad to say they love me at the moment. I did a lot of touring before I hit the 'big' time—what a terrible expression that is—but it doesn't present any problems for me. I spent $1,000 on two costumes—one gold, and one gold and green—for this tour. So that's just one bag. Should the time arrive when I travel with, say, $9,000 worth of clothes, then I'll worry about lost luggage and extra staff....And I personally carry my face with me! My face, my make-up. When someone offers to take that bag from me, I scream: *'no! I've got my face in that, so don't touch it!'*"

Vesta has known no other life than music and admits to being just so-so at school. "I had certain skills which I pulled on. I am a great interpreter of words, which helped me write lyrics. But I was a very bad student in maths. My father was a DJ, and because I can use my mouth, I used to do guest-spots for him. That takes a certain type of personality and so on, which I had. So I was always being asked to introduce records. I loved it because it was so easy. You could say I was an early bloomer in terms of talent, and a late bloomer in terms of being an exhibitionist."

Despite trying to develop her schooling and her outside activities, the young girl actually found time to enjoy adolescent love—not once, but several times. She laughed. "I can't really remember a time when I wasn't in love, or when I didn't have a boyfriend. I went from one relationship to another...no space, no nothing. I guess I never wanted to be lonely. I'd leave one guy, then move to another. I never had time to go through all that broken heart shit, and suffer the way I should have done. One of my ex-boyfriends pleaded with me not to leave him, and when I did, he said he wanted me to be broken hearted for four years! Girl, he took to hiding in the bushes to catch me out and watch me. I often wondered if it was me he was actually in love with, or my money. Let me re-phrase that, or the money he thought I was going to make. No, I couldn't handle that."

At the young, but certainly not tender, age of fourteen, Vesta performed her first paying gig. She sang with her sisters, hoping to become the next Jackson 5, before wanting to be Tina Turner. "Later I played with my cousins in a band and we giggled a lot. I was staying with my grandmother and I travelled three hundred

VESTA WILLIAMS

miles on a round trip to gigs—and by myself. We never thought about being attacked or raped in those days. Hell, I was a big girl too. I wore make-up, and lots of it. I wore a padded bra. I padded everything I could find, so everyone presumed I was a lot older than I was—and a lot bigger!" She admitted though, that if trouble had brewed, her drummer cousin acted as bodyguard. To this end, she cited one incident. "He intervened at one in particular—I don't know whether I should tell you this or not. We performed at a party where there was...ladies of the night and their pimps. If a guy liked the look of a lady he tapped her on the shoulder. I kept getting tapped. But I didn't know what it meant. We had no idea of the type of party it was either, but, I can tell you, I was horrified later when we found out. Anyway, my cousin got me out of that situation, with a smile!"

Today, her security is in the form of a girlfriend, a karate expert, as she boasted. "When she gets her noon chucks out (wooden sticks with chains at either end) it's a frightening sight. I'm very thankful she's my friend, and not my enemy. Mind, I don't get bothered that much, but just in case, it's comforting to know she's around." Vesta also added that she had been raised on the rough road to music, so has become accustomed to most types of unsavoury situations. "Nothing really shocks me now, except sexual abuse, particularly with children. I don't think I saw anything really nasty because I was always protected from it. People over-dosing on drugs doesn't surprise me. I believe things like that happen through lack of parental guidance. When I see things happen to other people, I use that as experience. I've been in some precarious situations though, but I reckon if I can survive living in New York, I can survive anything."

The singer's current visit to London isn't her first. She replaced Randy Crawford when she toured with the Crusaders during 1984/85: an experience she thoroughly enjoyed. Vesta now has her own band for touring purposes and hinted that her show would surprise me. "I do impersonations! It does mean I have to twist my mouth around and look real stupid, but I can impersonate Tina Turner, a brilliant Phoebe Snow, and Sarah Vaughan, complete with her handkerchief, which doesn't do much. I also do Patti LaBelle and Michael McDonald's duet—and I do both voices! I've always been working out comedy

CHINWAGGIN'

routines. There's a lot of places in New York to study, although my humour tends to be off-the-cuff. Y'see, I don't think about what I'm going to say, so I really don't want to tamper with that in case I lose it."

However, having such a quick tongue, no matter how funny, does, she admitted, have its disadvantages: "Because I've upset people with my mouth. I've got a very vivid imagination, and see humour in everything. And some people get the butt of my jokes, but let me stress, I always take the mickey out of myself as well. Sometimes people get annoyed and ask 'what do you mean by that?' And I'm afraid I fob it off."

On a more earthy note, Vesta was married and is currently in the process of a divorce. She has a young daughter, whom she adores. The marriage broke down because she wasn't able to be the wife her husband had expected. "I'm unpredictable and I could never survive in a situation that was a routine to me. I become bored too easily. I consider myself to be well-balanced, but I believe I have a bad habit of making men feel insecure. Then they have a tendency to get nasty because I am so secure. I'm even thinking of writing a book about my sexual experiences. That would be something...nobody would talk to me then." Whilst on the subject, I wondered how she thought men saw her. Smiling, she answered. "They say I'm well stacked, and I take that to mean I've got more than most women. More than a handful, more than a mouthful..."

On that, I felt it was time to go. Throughout our interview, Ms Williams' humour had me in tears; therefore, holding down a serious chat was hastily abandoned. What struck me was the similarity between her tongue and that of Joan Rivers. She wasn't surprised I thought that. "You're not the first person to tell me that. No, I'm not insulted, far from it. I'm very flattered. Joan is the funniest person living, and I would love to do the sort of thing she's doing. What about me being the black Joan Rivers?"

I'm outta here!! Sitting at home, listening to my tape, I concluded she's a woman of principle and talks as she finds. Also, Vesta is a performer of note, and is, I believe, a real asset to the business.

During the nineties, she became known as 'Vesta', and issued three albums: 'Vesta 4U', 'Special' and 'Relationships'. 'Once Bitten, Twice Shy' was her only UK hit.

VIOLA WILLS
Dateline: April 1980

CHINWAGGIN'

I first met the subject of my interview at one of London's fashionable nighteries, and as the champagne flowed, she agreed to an interview. Viola Wills is a dance/disco artist who really doesn't give a damn about her current music because she feels she is being manipulated on the money-making machine which coughs up stereotyped dance sounds. Her heart lies in her self-satisfying and creative talent. So, one Sunday afternoon she arrived on my doorstep.

Ms Wills is in her mid-30s. She's also a grandmother. An energetic, vivacious lady whose single, 'If You Could Read My Mind' is currently climbing up the many UK charts. So, with her hatred of dance, I questioned why she chose to disco-ise another non-original song, bearing in mind her first hit was 'Gonna Get Along Without You Now'—a no 8 hit. "That single started out as the result of some session work I was doing. I suppose I consider both singles as sessions because they aren't really representative of me." She paused. "I'm doing what my producer wants me to do. If I'd waited longer and stuck to my guns perhaps I'd be doing something different; maybe not as successful though. That's the only thing that makes me say it's good that I did it."

How different? "I don't really know. Probably I'd write things that made me feel pretty good and I'd like to share that.... Session work isn't the worst thing in the world, you know. Hell, it pays the rent and you can keep yourself going on it. I'm paying my dues now; then perhaps I can do what I wanna do. I don't like it, but who wants to get up and go to work in the morning? They go to work each day and they really couldn't care a damn about who's making a C sharp or a D flat. All they want to listen to is something that's gonna soothe their minds.

"I don't think I'm deceiving anyone with this music because I happen to like the songs I'm singing. At the moment the trend tends to be to dance music, and there are certain standards that people set and policies that record companies set. Y'know, like the certain policy regarding records they want to put out; how they want to develop and push that sound—and I suppose this happens when you specialise in a certain type of music. I just happened to end up with a record company that likes this kind of music, and it's their theory to do oldies as they're successful,

VIOLA WILLS

because people like to hear them again. So I've fallen into this mould."

The Viola Wills story to date is quite remarkable. She hails from Watts. When I asked her if she was introduced to music via the church I was shot down. "God! I think that's so *average!*" she winced. "*Everyone* does that. I don't know anyone who didn't sing in church choirs while growing up. Everyone went to church, sang in the choir, all dressed up in their robes, unless they were little devils—and I really do mean devils. Hell, it's one thing that always comes up, especially with black artists, and it's all so stupid. That's not where singing starts. Singing is something you decide you wanna do. Like a lawyer, or doctor. That's what I wanted to be—a lawyer. But I wasn't in a position to do that. So singing was just the opt for me. I had a basic talent to do it, and it was available to me."

She worked with Barry White before he was a successful artist— "We had a nice time in Los Angeles, and he had a moderate hit. That was the first time I went into the studio. Barry and I split up after a few years, and that's when Joe Cocker came into town. Also here Gloria Jones comes into the story. She was a producer at Motown, as well as a singer and songwriter, and she'd had a really big hit with Gladys Knight. At that time she was organising some singers for Joe and I happened to be around. Joe liked us and we just started recording there and then. We became The Sanctified Sisters—Gloria, Beverley Gardner and myself. We were a gospelly sort of group, and we leaned on our roots. Because Joe was that sort of singer he gave us scope. He sang gospel and blues which is why the combination worked out so nicely."

The Sanctified Sisters lasted two years. Then Joe Cocker decided he was no longer happy with the setup. He instigated changes and Viola was one of them. This coincided with her being asked to record in London, a move that encouraged her to seriously write her own material, like 'Lost Without The Love Of My Guy' and 'You're Out Of My Mind'. Once settled in the city she said she was amazed at the way soul fans devoured American music. "I suppose because it was different. I don't think the States provides better music, but I've often wondered why the UK goes so mad on it. I think it's great to still hear R&B the way it was, and the way the kids are doing it now. It's also good to see they're writing their own stuff. As we grow older, we have a better ear for our music; we learn to discriminate between good and bad. When you're young, you don't care what's good or bad; you go for what you feel, and if that's what your thing is, then you do it. As you mature you find your own taste. The record companies take advantage of this naivety. The kids don't know where they want to be, and they're easy to manipulate; easy to push in any direction. Take me; I'm more set in my ways, and that's the same with most of my generation."

Living alone in London, Viola admitted she has no family with her, just a huge contingent of friends around. "I don't like living alone. I'd like to live with someone, but I'm not frustrated about not getting married. I've got a lot of men friends to whom I can relate. I rely on everybody because I've never been independent. Most of my friends put up with me, and I'd die if I couldn't depend on them."

With one silver disc for 'Gonna Get Along Without You Now' currently hanging on her bathroom wall (because it blends with the décor), what of future commitments? "When I got the disc I thought to myself it's an achievement and it shows me that a lot of people liked the record. It basically represents people. It seems I've got to learn to write songs like that if that's what the people want. I'll tell you something though, Sharon, I don't like to be recognised. It's pretty off-putting. 'Viola Wills' is a monster I created as a means to an end. Like, the wigs and the whole glamour trip. I thought that was what was needed to go out and get a silver disc, or whatever. Then I realised that was a load of bullshit and decided to hell with that plastic trip! People don't care about that stuff anyway; they can see right through it!"

Image or not, with seventeen years in the business behind her I accept that Vi Wills knows what she's about. Yet last year was the first time her talent secured her a place in the top ten singles chart, with—of all things—a session track! She laughed. "Well, the British do appreciate artists who have paid their dues. And, besides, maybe they thought I was ready for a hit.

VIOLA WILLS

My thanks to Paul Williams for first introducing me to Viola. The lady sure knows how to party, and it was great fun for us all. We all knew the disco bubble would burst, so we grabbed the good life and enjoyed it while we could. In 1986 Viola Wills' second UK hit was 'Both Sides Now'/'Dare To Dream' on Morgan Khan's Streetwave label. She continued to record throughout the nineties, notably singles including 'Think I'm Falling In Love' on Bite Records, 'I Can See Clearly Now' on MFS Records, and with ZYX Records' 'No News Is News' and 'A House Is Not A Home'. Returning to the States, Ms Wills settled in California where she reinvented herself as a jazz/pop singer.

LINDA WOMACK

Dateline: July 1984

Behind every successful man there's a woman. In the partnership of Cecil Womack and Linda Womack, she plays as much a part in her husband's business as in his personal life. And I had the pleasure of talking to her prior to their début British concerts.

Mrs Womack, in her mid-thirties, is a friendly type of lady; happy, talkative, enjoys a joke, but who never stops working. And now she's one half of what the press call 'the Ashford and Simpson of the Eighties'. "Yeah, I read that too. I think that's lovely. Ashford and Simpson are so talented and really it's quite an honour to have this comparison made."

With her voice getting louder to overcome her one month old baby's crying, Linda said they have seven children in all—three from Cecil's first marriage—and all but the baby were still in Los Angeles. "I miss them tremendously. They wanted to come with

LINDA WOMACK

us, but their schooling had to come first. They'd love London, there's so much for them to see and do. We probably wouldn't have had time to do any work though. They all seem to be musically inclined, which is great—except the youngest! Although, I don't know, judging by the way the vocal chords are being exercised! I'd be delighted if they followed in our footsteps, but they don't have to be in the entertainment side of our business as there's lots of jobs they could do in our organisation. Like secretarial work, lawyers, computer programmers...oh, there's lots to do. Mind you, we'd always encourage them into the music side if they were sincere about their intentions."

Linda is, of course, the daughter of the legendary Sam Cooke, who was tragically shot to death by a call-girl in a motel. However, Cooke knew Cecil Womack as he'd signed him and his brothers to his SAR label, first as a gospel group, then as The Valentinos, and introduced Cecil to his daughter, a mere eight year old. "My father would sing gospel with them and one day he told me he'd worked with these fantastic guys and had invited them over to our house. We talked and had a nice time, but my father was always strict about me going out with anyone. I was so young anyway. Still he always told Cecil, 'You're a nice guy. If I'd trust her to anyone I'd trust her with you.'"

Time passed and Linda was happy just staying at home while Cecil worked. "My father didn't want what he was doing to overwhelm us. But I said this was what I wanted to do. I'd practice the piano and sing behind closed doors and write. He was just my dad. When he passed away it was then I realised how much people really thought of him."

As Cecil's brothers went their separate ways to become involved in various projects, Cecil wrote and produced for other artists. Says Linda: "My dad taught us to use what we have and not depend on one thing like most artists, so we'd sing, write or play sessions for someone else. Whatever we're involved with is important to us. This is what we've always wanted to do and so long as we're playing, we're happy."

Writing songs from an early age is a talent not many possess. In Linda's case, her composing was a secret until she penned the gold selling title 'I'm In Love' recorded by Wilson Picket. "I wanted to come up slow and not jump out by putting out a record

CHINWAGGIN'

and thinking I'd be an overnight star. I grew up watching my father and both families—the Womacks and the Cookes—and had a pretty realistic approach, even though I knew you had to work hard to live."

James Taylor and Bobby Womack also enjoyed gold records with her 'A Woman's Gotta Have It', and the list of names she and Cecil have subsequently worked with is endless and awesome. Now, they're celebrating the success of their own 'Love Wars' project—the hit album and single bearing the same name. Linda was keen to chat about four of the tracks, starting with 'I Don't Believe In Magic'. "It's about a lady talking to a man who's jivin', and he's saying all these things about what he's going to do for her. However, she wants a real relationship. He gives her more jive, and she continues to retaliate by wanting something real.

"And in 'Catch And Don't Look Back', the lady is tired of dealing with relationships that aren't two way. She's had all these guys who do everything to catch you, but that's all. She wants more and she sees another guy like that and is hip to it. On 'You're The Kinda Woman', a woman has come into contact with a guy who's very good looking, and she's saying 'take my love as you're showing what you really are. If you got it, you got my love'. And 'Good Times'. This wraps up the whole story on the album about men and women in a relationship. It's a celebration song. It's sort of bittersweet too because the woman is telling the man that he's going to remember the good times even if they're apart, but it's really a happy song deep down."

As mentioned before, the couple have more than a handful of offspring to cope with. How does she juggle the domestic side with her career? She grinned. "Cecil helps me. He looks after the children, cleans up and cooks, especially fish and chicken, and his salads are something else. With his own dressings and all that. I think a lot of men are frustrated by little babies but Cecil is really into children. It makes our life a lot nicer because he's so different from a lot of other men. And of course, it's real fun having the man and the woman working together, because we'd have a lot of problems if we don't. We have a high regard for our family. When a husband does one thing and the wife another outside the business, it does in time cause immense problems.

LINDA WOMACK

With Cecil and myself being involved in the same thing we channelled our business together, halving the workload. We don't alter our way of life to cope with our music. Our family always comes first, no matter what, because they are the most important part of our lives. If our business interfered with it, then that would have to go.

"If there is a boss in the family, it's Cecil. I want him to take care of things for us and he does take the lead over the household, although he's not conscious of the fact. It's nice to have the man to do this. He's quite strict with the children, although they know he's really quite soft underneath...mushy inside."

The head of the household isn't, though, in control when it comes to business as Linda was quick to point out. "When it comes to writing I think you could say we're equal partners." Should there be an argument over lyrics or something Cecil invariably wins. However, her husband's timing for work is, she added, an arguable subject. "Oh yes. He'll think nothing of taking a guitar to bed with us! Or, he'll wake up in the early morning to write, then comes back to bed, wakes me up to help out. Or he'll sing to me what he's written at four o'clock in the morning. It gets a bit much sometimes, I can tell you, but I really don't mind."

In rare moments of relaxation, the Womacks like to read and talk, although going to the movies is a great treat. "Any film with a message we enjoy—light drama, comedy and some heavy action. Violent and scary movies are definitely out: there's no need for all this violence in films, there's enough going on in real life already. We'd never let the children watch these because they see enough unpleasantness in real life, or watching news programmes on the television. They have to encounter enough in their lives right now without watching added violence, or violence for violence's sake."

For some reason we started talking about Boy George; his life was one enjoyed by gays in San Francisco, and was a subject that required discussion with their children. "We have always been open with every subject with them. I told them Boy George was a very talented man who liked to wear a dress. And that there were a lot of men who liked to do that, and also there were men who liked men and not women. In fact, Los Angeles seems to be getting a lot like San Francisco now. So, instead of the kids seeing them and not understanding, I've told them the truth, made them face up to reality. Some people are victims of something, I said, and they shouldn't be shocked at what they see. Mind you, if one of my sons wanted to wear a dress, I'd have to do some serious thinking. I don't think there's a way I would allow that to happen."

Spoken like a true mother! Linda Womack is a delightful creature, and this new found success is well deserved, although how she's going to cope during the next few months I couldn't hazard a guess. However, I left with a lovely vision. Cecil, guitar in hand, changing baby's nappy, keeping one eye on the milk warming on the stove, and the other on the rest of his children. Life in the fast lane, Linda. She smiled.

At the close of the eighties, Womack and Womack released the album 'Conscience', and in 1991, 'Family Spirit'. When not recording their own material, the couple worked with other artists, and more recently, their own family. They proudly head up a band comprising their seven children. Called 'The House Of Zekkariyas', their most recent release 'Sub Conscience' follows their much acclaimed 1995 release 'The House Of Zekkariyas'.

VISUAL CREDITS

The author and publisher are extremely grateful to the following for kindly providing, and/or granting permission to reproduce, the visuals contained in this book. Every effort has been made to establish sources and to contact all copyright holders, but it is possible that an oversight has occurred, and for this we apologise. We will, of course, be pleased to correct any omission in future editions of this publication.

Blues & Soul (153 Praed Street, London W2 1RL); Ian Levine/ Motorcity Records; Brian Fooks; Jim Hegarty; Peter Scotney; Peter Vernon; Paul Howes (Dusty Springfield Bulletin, PO Box 203, Cobham, KT11 2UG); John Lester; Paul Nixon; Sharon Davis Collection, Ivan Constable, Paul Williams, Terry Thorp.